FRANCIS HOPKINSON
The First American Poet-Composer (1737-1791)

and

JAMES LYON
Patriot, Preacher, Psalmodist (1735-1794)

Da Capo Press Music Reprint Series

General Editor: FREDERICK FREEDMAN

University of California at Los Angeles

FRANCIS HOPKINSON
The First American Poet-Composer (1737-1791)

and

JAMES LYON
Patriot, Preacher, Psalmodist (1735-1794)

Oscar G. T. Sonneck

New Introduction by
Richard A. Crawford
University of Michigan

DA CAPO PRESS • NEW YORK • 1967

A Da Capo Press Reprint Edition

First Da Capo Printing — October 1967
Second Da Capo Printing — July 1969

*This Da Capo Press edition is an unabridged republication
of the first edition published in Washington, D.C., in 1905.*

Library of Congress Catalog Card No. 65-23393

INTRODUCTION

Scholarly books may be valuable for many different reasons including rarity, importance of subject, trustworthiness of scholarship, and clarity of presentation. Oscar George Theodore Sonneck's *Francis Hopkinson and James Lyon* qualifies as a valuable book on all four counts. Printed for the author in an edition of only two hundred copies in 1905, the work, actually two separate monographs bound under one cover, observes the highest standards of scholarship in examining the musical careers of the two most frequently mentioned candidates for the title of America's first composer.

In view of the well-known dependence of American musical life upon European antecedents, it seems appropriate that Sonneck, America's pioneer musicologist, received his schooling in Europe. Born in 1873 in Lafayette, a small community now incorporated into Jersey City, New Jersey, he went to Germany as a boy and was educated at Kiel, Frankfurt-on-the-Main, and the universities at Heidelberg and Munich.[1] The demanding German university curriculum gave him a rich background in humane letters—he published a small volume of German poems in 1895—and history, and while pursuing his work at the university, Sonneck also found time to study piano, music theory, and composition with private teachers. When he completed his university education in 1898, he remained in Germany for another year, studying instrumentation, composition, and conducting. A year of research in Italy followed. When Sonneck returned to his native country at the beginning of the

---

[1] Otto Kinkeldey, "Oscar George Theodore Sonneck (1873–1928)," *Music Library Association Notes*, XI (1953), 25–32, is the source of the biographical facts presented below.

v

present century, he was both a well-trained musician and a scholar of some experience. He possessed a magnificent background for the task he set himself: to compile materials about American musical life before 1800.

By 1902, when Sonneck was named the first Chief of the Music Division of the Library of Congress, his portfolio already contained two completed manuscripts: *Francis Hopkinson and James Lyon* and a *Bibliography of Early Secular American Music.* He had spent the two years since his return from Europe visiting libraries on the Atlantic coast, examining their holdings in music, and poring over eighteenth-century newspapers, which he found to be his best source of information. His diligence supplied him with material for *Early Concert Life in America* (1907) and *Early Opera in America* (1915), as well as for the two earlier volumes.

Among Sonneck's achievements at the Library of Congress, two stand out as especially noteworthy: his organization of the Library's holdings in music, and his decision to specialize in fields where the Library could acquire definitive collections. Sonneck carried out the former through development of a new classification system for music and books about music, a solution which other American libraries in increasing numbers have found practicable. As for the latter, Sonneck chose to concentrate on three fields: American music, British music, and opera. In none of the three were materials scarce or costly, and if the first two might be expected to hold little interest for scholars outside the Anglo-American community, opera represented a major genre of international interest. Under Sonneck's direction the Library acquired a collection of opera librettos and scores which has become the largest and most useful in the world.

In 1915 the New York publishing house G. Schirmer responded to a suggestion of Sonneck's by beginning publication of a new scholarly journal, *The Musical Quarterly.* Sonneck was named first editor of the *Quarterly,* a position he was to hold until his death. Two years later he resigned his post at the Library and took a full-time position with Schirmer's, adding the directorship of publications to his editorial duties; in 1921 he became vice-president of the firm. Sonneck also helped to found the Beethoven Association in New York (1918), and his later publications include three works on Beethoven which appeared in 1927, the centenary anniversary of the composer's death. Sonneck himself died in October, 1928.

Though he was followed by worthy successors in his roles as editor and librarian, not until the very recent past has Sonneck's example as an author been imitated. After he gave up his research, serious study in the field of early American music ceased until after World War II. Since that time, an increasing number of scholars have devoted attention to early Americana, finding Sonneck's pioneering works an indispensable foundation for their work.

As *Francis Hopkinson and James Lyon* demonstrates, Sonneck's method of historical writing prevents his books from becoming outdated. Quotations of original source material supply the evidence, and since the evidence is always kept in full view, the reader is always in a position to judge whether the author's interpretation is justified. Because Sonneck's works contain so rich a store of documented fact and because they reflect the relish with which their author undertook historical research, they remain as enlightening and fresh as when they were written.

It may have been coincidence that Sonneck devoted his first book to a study of America's first two known composers, but it is especially appropriate, and certainly a coincidence, that Francis Hopkinson and James Lyon, though almost exact contemporaries, represented different musical traditions. Hopkinson, to whom Sonneck refers as a "gentleman amateur," was chiefly interested in the songs and harpsichord pieces fashionable in eighteenth-century English and American salons and concert halls; Lyon composed and published religious choral music sung in rural and urban meeting houses and singing schools, to which eighteenth-century Americans referred, no matter what the source of its texts, as psalmody.

Many of the differences between psalmody and salon music are obvious. Psalmody, usually harmonized in four parts, was performed by a chorus; salon music was chamber music written for one or two performers. Psalmody was unaccompanied; salon music invariably needed a harpsichord for accompaniment. Psalmody was sacred; salon music, though apt to contain references to the Deity, was secular. Psalmody had as its primary purpose the praise of God, though an important attending value was that it provided recreation for the performers; salon music had no purpose other than to please and delight the performer and, perhaps, the audience.

The mention of an audience leads to the most profound distinction between psalmody and salon music. Only on rare occasions — most notably at singing lectures, held at the conclusion of a singing-school term, where the scholars demonstrated their newly gained musical literacy in public and a local minister delivered an oration in praise of sacred music — was psalmody performed for an audience. It was at other times music for the participants. Salon music, on the other hand, while it might be played or sung by a performer for his private gratification, was a soloist's music which lent itself, and indeed was usually intended, to be performed before an audience. And the existence of an audience, a group of people gathered expressly for the purpose of being entertained by the performance of music, presumes a certain degree of cultivation, a tendency to look upon music aesthetically, a concert site — whether private salon or concert hall — and a discriminating attitude toward both music and performer. In short, salon music, unlike psalmody, is art music.

Viewing psalmody on the one hand and art music on the other as separate, concurrent traditions provides a useful perspective for understanding the development of eighteenth-century American music. Psalm singing represented America's oldest musical tradition, extending unbroken from the arrival of the Pilgrims until well into the nineteenth century, and most early historians of American music confined their account of the eighteenth century to a description of New England psalmody. Sonneck's research revealed, however, that psalmody represented only a part of America's early musical life. *Francis Hopkinson and James Lyon* traces the beginnings of a tradition of art music in eighteenth-century Philadelphia; *Early Concert Life in America* demonstrates that performances of European instrumental and vocal works, as well as ballad operas, became increasingly common in America's larger cities as the century progressed, and that after the Revolutionary War, art music had won a large enough following to support professional European performers and composers on American shores. Though Sonneck avoided making sweeping generalizations, his works provide evidence that as American cities grew into centers of population, trade, and power, their inhabitants turned increasing attention to the cultivation of European art music, and the importance of psalmody as a medium for creative musical expression diminished.

The two subjects of Francis Hopkinson and James Lyon are difficult to compare because their careers were so dissimilar. Francis Hopkinson (1737–1791) was a remarkably versatile man. Well educated and resourceful, a jurist and sometime writer as well as a musician, a signer of the Declaration of Independence, Hopkinson was the only American musician of his time who can truly be called a public figure. Because he was a public figure, more is known about him than about his musical contemporaries, and what is known makes it clear that Hopkinson's artistic energies were channeled toward the encouragement and cultivation of art music.

Hopkinson's long association with the harpsichord may be taken as evidence of his devotion to art music. In 1754, when Hopkinson took up the instrument, the harpsichord, while by no means unknown in Philadelphia, was still something of a rarity. Hopkinson's harpsichord playing not only involved him in Philadelphia's concert life; it introduced him to a repertory of European vocal and chamber music, and this encounter with the fashionable Italianate music esteemed in English salons may be counted the crucial factor in shaping his musical taste. That Hopkinson responded enthusiastically to European art music is demonstrated by Sonneck's enumeration of the works by leading English and continental composers found in his library, and even more conclusively by his own compositions, especially the *Seven Songs* he published in 1788.

Hopkinson's contributions to sacred music must not be overlooked. He presided for some years at the organ of St. Peter's Anglican Church, wrote some anthems, and probably compiled a collection of psalm tunes to be sung in the Anglican worship. In fact, Hopkinson's reputation as a psalmodist was such that the Dutch Reformed Congregation of New York City requested him to translate their metrical psalter into English, a task which he accepted and completed in 1765. Despite his activity as a psalmodist, however, the few of Hopkinson's sacred works that survive resemble his secular songs in style, both in the Italianate curve of their melodies and in the common use of an obbligato instrumental accompaniment. Sonneck's comment on the rarity of the figured bass in early American music and Hopkinson's employment of that standard European device in his sacred music demonstrates his orientation perfectly. When one examines his entire musical career as a performer on harpsichord and organ, and as a composer of both sacred and secular music, it becomes clear that Francis Hopkinson's musical taste was substantially that of a cultivated Englishman, devoted to the practice of music as a fashionable art.

Far less is known about James Lyon (1735–1794) than about Hopkinson. A member of the Class of 1759 at Princeton, Lyon began his career as an active musician while a college student, and seems to have abandoned it some time before his ordination as a Presbyterian minister in 1764. An ode he composed for his college commencement proves that, like Hopkinson, Lyon did not restrict himself to the cultivation of one type of music, but his importance to the history of American music lies in the fact that he compiled *Urania,* the prototype of the eighteenth-century American tunebook.

Urania, published probably late in 1761 and modeled after English collections, was not the first book of tunes printed in America. It was preceded by two small instructional manuals which included some music – the first by the Rev. John Tufts, the second by the Rev. Thomas Walter, both initially published in Boston around 1720 and both going through a number of subsequent editions – and by a few tune supplements designed to be bound at the back of metrical psalters, providing music to which the psalms could be sung. *Urania* dwarfed these tiny collections in every way. Oblong in shape, a bulky 198 pages in length, Lyon's work began with a detailed set of instructions about note reading and singing, and continued with a voluminous collection of music, including seventy textless tunes to which metrical psalms were to be sung, twelve anthems – extended and relatively elaborate settings of prose Biblical texts – and fourteen hymns, settings of nonpsalmodic devotional poetry.

Though *Urania* might appear to be a self-instruction book, it enjoyed most of its sale as a textbook for use in singing schools. From the early eighteenth century until well into the nineteenth, the most important musical institution in America was the singing school, in which a singing master met with a group of aspiring singers, usually for two or three nights each week over a three-month period, to teach them to read music. The importance of the singing school cannot be exaggerated. The scholars benefitted from the instruction they received and became valuable members of their church choirs. But perhaps even more important was the benefit to the singing masters themselves. The typical American psalmodist was a tradesman who practiced music as a sideline. The singing school provided him with a living, albeit a meager and arduous one, as a professional musician. Moreover, the singing-school movement stimulated the publication of tune collections such as *Urania,* giving the psalmodist who was also a composer a means of presenting his compositions to the public.

As the singing-school movement waxed, the publication of tune-books increased, and by 1800 more than eighty different collections had been printed in America. Though there are some notable excep-tions, most tunebooks printed after the Revolutionary War contain at least a sampling of works by Americans, and by the mid-1780's a group of composers centered in New England were writing a style of sacred music differing substantially from anything produced by their European contemporaries. These Yankee musicians, including William Billings (1746–1800), Daniel Read (1757–1836), Justin Morgan (1747–1798), Supply Belcher (1751–1836), Lewis Edson (1748–1820), and Timothy Swan (1758–1842), among others, repre-sent the first school of indigenous American composers. Their com-positions, printed in tunebooks and carried southward from New England by itinerant music masters, were sung in churches, meet-ings, and singing schools throughout the young United States.

Urania stands at the beginning of this period of burgeoning musi-cal activity. Though few American tunebooks approached it in size, most retained its essential features: the oblong shape, the instruc-tions about singing, and the assortment of musical forms, from psalm tune to anthem. And it should not be forgotten that *Urania* established a healthy precedent by including, together with the com-positions taken from European sources, six of the compiler's own tunes.

Francis Hopkinson is remembered as one of America's founding fathers, a man of wide-ranging interests and considerable ability who claimed to have been America's first composer. James Lyon is remembered because he compiled *Urania.* Perhaps the point which most forcibly dramatizes the distance separating the musical tradi-tions represented by these two men, designated by Sonneck as America's first composers, is his investigation of their precedence. Hopkinson claimed the honor for himself in his dedication to the *Seven Songs* for voice and harpsichord published in 1788, writing, "I cannot, I believe, be refused the Credit of being the first Native of the United States who has produced a Musical Composition."

According to Sonneck's interpretation, Hopkinson's claim rests on the song, "My days have been so wondrous free," which he wrote in 1759. Since James Lyon composed a commencement ode in that year, and since Hopkinson was apparently acquainted with Lyon by 1761 and was living in Philadelphia when *Urania,* containing several of Lyon's own tunes, was published there, Sonneck contends that Hopkinson must have "been aware of the fact that James Lyon was a dangerous competitor for the title of first native of the United States who produced a musical composition." Then, attributing to Francis Hopkinson his own highly developed sense of historical scrupulousness, the author continues: "From all we know of Hopkinson's character I doubt not that he himself investigated the correctness of his claim and found his earliest compositions to antedate those of James Lyon."

Sonneck's explanation is not entirely satisfactory. To paraphrase him loosely: from all we know of eighteenth-century musicians, no matter how high their character, I doubt that it ever occurred to Francis Hopkinson to consider James Lyon a rival for the palm of precedence, and the suggestion that he claimed the honor on the basis of a song written nearly three decades earlier seems most unlikely. If "My days have been so wondrous free" loomed important in Hopkinson's mind as America's first composition, it is logical to assume that he would have published it as part of the collection of songs in which he advanced his claim. But the song was never published during the composer's lifetime.

An alternative interpretation is that Hopkinson's claim to being "the first Native of the United States who has produced a Musical Composition" rests on the *Seven Songs.* At first glance the claim appears to be false. By 1788 not only James Lyon but almost a dozen other American psalmodists had published collections containing tunes and anthems by native composers. Hopkinson was not unaware of these collections; he probably even produced a modest one of his own. The crucial point, however, is Hopkinson's definition of "musical composition." In his mind psalm tunes and anthems apparently did not qualify as compositions nor their creators as composers. The significance of Hopkinson's claim is that he considered himself America's first native composer of *art* music. An examination of Sonneck and Upton's *Bibliography of Early Secular American Music* supports him: Hopkinson's *Seven Songs* represents the first collection of solo secular songs composed and published by a native American.

That Francis Hopkinson, active in both art music and psalmody and by no means contemptuous of the latter, considered "composition" a term inapplicable to psalmody is an indication of the gulf which separated the traditions of art music and psalmody in eighteenth-century America.

Ann Arbor, Michigan   Richard A. Crawford
June, 1966

FRANCIS HOPKINSON
The First American Poet-Composer (1737-1791)

and

JAMES LYON
Patriot, Preacher, Psalmodist (1735-1794)

FRANCIS HOPKINSON

FRANCIS HOPKINSON

THE FIRST AMERICAN POET-COMPOSER

(1737-1791)

AND

JAMES LYON

PATRIOT, PREACHER, PSALMODIST

(1735-1794)

TWO STUDIES IN EARLY AMERICAN MUSIC

BY

O. G. SONNECK

WASHINGTON, D. C.
PRINTED FOR THE AUTHOR BY
H. L. McQUEEN
1905

TO
HORATIO PARKER

CONTENTS

THE MUSICAL CAREER OF JAMES LYON, Patriot,

PREFACE

A reliable and exhaustive history of music in the United States neither exists nor is to be expected until the various periods and sources of our musical life have been more critically investigated than heretofore.

Perkins and Dwight with their 'History of the Haendel and Haydn Society' of Boston; Henry Edward Krehbiel with his 'History of the Philharmonic Society' of New York City; W. G. Armstrong with his 'Records of the Opera in Philadelphia'; Louis C. Madeira with his 'Annals of Music in Philadelphia and History of the Musical Fund Society'; James Warrington with his 'Short Titles of Books relating to or illustrating the History and Practice of Psalmody in the United States, 1620–1820,' and a few other authors have opened to us younger historians the right path. We must follow them if we intend to be of any real service to the public or to the scholar destined, in a distant future, to collect the results of our special research for a reliable and exhaustive history of music in the United States.*

So far, our specialists have been interested mostly in the nineteenth century, and consequently the public is more familiar with this than with previous periods. I do not overlook writers like Allen, Burnham, Brooks, Champlin, Hood, Warrington, nor do I underestimate their efforts directed toward an accurate description of music as it was culti-

---

*Two years after this book was ready for a publisher, Mr. Louis C. Elson's 'History of American Music' appeared. Undoubtedly it supersedes both pioneer works on the subject, Ritter's 'Music in America' and Mathew's 'A Hundred Years of Music in America,' but, interesting though it is, comprehensive, sympathetic and brilliant, it can not be accepted as an authoritative history of our musical life. In particular, the work reads too much like a history of music in New England and the description of the formative periods is historically objectionable.

vated in the eighteenth century.   Nevertheless, a marked contrast is noticeable between our knowledge of musical life in the United States during the Presidency of George Washington and, for instance, of Abraham Lincoln.

Being convinced of this contrast I resolved to fill in some evident gaps.   Whether or not the monographs on Francis Hopkinson and James Lyon, whom we may consider the first two native American composers, contribute toward that end, I must leave to my critics. But this I know, the essays in their present form, whatever their historical value might be, would have been impossible without the access which Mr. and Mrs. Oliver Hopkinson of Philadelphia and Mrs. Florence Scovel Shinn of New York City gave me to their family papers and Mr. James Warrington of Philadelphia to his private library.   I am also under obligations to the Librarian of Congress and the Librarian of the Historical Society of Pennsylvania for the permission to photograph certain rarities.

O. G. SONNECK.

New York City, May, 1902.

LIST OF INSERTED ILLUSTRATIONS

FRANCIS HOPKINSON
THE
FIRST AMERICAN POET-COMPOSER
(1737-1791)

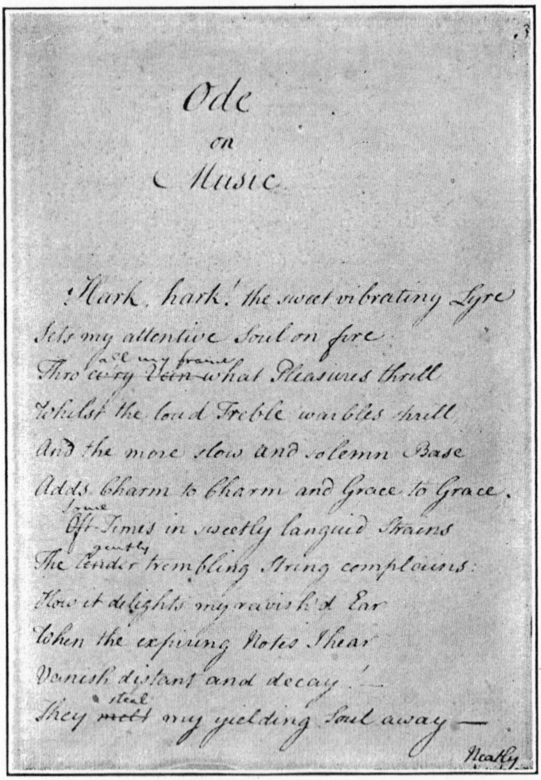

3

Ode
on
Music

Hark, hark! the sweet vibrating Lyre
Sets my attentive Soul on fire:
Thro' ~~every Vein~~ all my frame what Pleasures thrill
Whilst the loud Treble warbles shrill
And the more slow and solemn Base
Adds Charm to Charm and Grace to Grace.
Oft-Times some in sweetly languid Strains
The tender gently trembling String complains:
How it delights my ravish'd Ear
When the expiring Notes I hear
Vanish distant and decay!—
They ~~melt~~ steal my yielding Soul away—

Neatly

Hopkinson's 'Ode on Music,' 1754

PROLOGUE IN PRAISE OF MUSIC.

ODE ON MUSIC.

HARK! hark! the sweet vibrating lyre
Sets my attentive soul on fire;
Thro' all my frame what pleasures thrill,
Whilst the loud treble warbles shrill,
And the more slow and solemn bass,
Adds charms to charm and grace to grace.

Sometimes in sweetly languid strains,
The guilty trembling string complains,
How it delights my ravished ear,
When the expiring notes I hear
Vanish distant and decay!—
They steal my yielding soul away!

Neatly trip the merry dance,
And lightly touch, and swiftly glance;
Let boundless transport laugh aloud,
Sounds madly ramble mix and crowd,
'Till all in one loud rapture rise,
Spread thro' the air and reach the skies.

But when you touch the solemn air,
Oh! swell each note distinct and clear,
In ev'ry sound let sorrow sigh,
Languish soft, and sweetly die.

So shall th' admir'd celestial art
Raise and transport my ravish'd heart;
Exalt my soul and give my mind
Ideas of sublimer kind.
So great the bliss it seems to prove
There must be music too above.
That from the trumpet's silver sound,
Of wing'd arch-angels plac'd around
Thy burning throne—Oh! king of heav'n!
Most perfect harmony is giv'n!
Whilst happy saints in concert join
To make the music quite divine,
And with immortal voices sing
HOSANNAHS to their heav'nly KING.

From Francis Hopkinson's Miscellaneous Essays and Occasional Writings, Phila. 1792, v. III, p. 6 of Poems On Several Subjects.

A PROLOGUE

In Praise of Music—Spoken by Mr. Hallam,

At a play given for purchasing an organ for the college-hall in Philadelphia.

With grateful joy encircling crowds we view,
Well pleas'd the friends of music are not few;
Such worthy patrons may it ever find,
And rule with gentle sway the human mind.
When the loud organ fills the sacred choir,
The pious soul is wrapt in holy fire;
The trembling isles the solemn airs resound
And list'ning angels hang attentive round;
Harmonious strains with high devotion join,
And sacred themes make music more divine.
Another joy delights yon love sick swain,
Soft sounds alone can sooth his am'rous pain,
And ev'ry warble thrills through ev'ry vein.
Whilst the bold warrior hails the loud alarms,
When drums and trumpets call to arms! to arms!
His eager soul imbibes the martial strain,
And hastes to press the yielding foe again.
Such pow'r hath music o'er the human soul,
Music the fiercest passions can controul.
Touch the nice springs that sway a feeling heart,
Sooth ev'ry grief, and joy to joy impart.
Sure virtue's friends and music are the same,
And blest that person is that owns the sacred flame.

From Francis Hopkinson's Miscellaneous Essays and Occasional Writings, Phila. 1792, v. III, p. 54 of Poems On Several Subjects.

DESCRIPTION OF A CHURCH.

As late beneath the hallow'd roof I trod,
Where saints in holy rapture seek their God;
Where heart stung sinners suing Heav'n for grace,
With tears repentant consecrate the place.
Oh! how my soul was struck with what I saw
And shrunk within me in religious awe:

The massy walls, which seem'd to scorn the rage
Of battering tempest and of mouldering age;
In long perspective stretch'd, till breadth and height
Were almost lost in distance from the sight;
With monumental decorations hung,
They spoke mortality with silent tongue.
There, sorrowing seraphs heav'nward lift their eyes,
And little cherubs weep soft elegies.
I trod—and started at the mighty noise;
The hollow pavement lifted up its voice,
The swelling arch receiv'd the rising sound,
Responsive to the stroke the walls around,
And sent it murm'ring to the vaults around,
Thro' lengthen'd aisles prolong'd the solemn sound.

Far in the west, and noble to the sight,
The gilded *organ* rears its tow'ring height:
And hark! methinks I from its bosom hear,
Soft issuing sounds that steal upon the ear
And float serenely on the liquid air.
Now by degrees more bold and broad they grow,
And riot loosely thro' the isles below,
'Till the full organ lifts its utmost voice,
And my heart shudders at the powerful noise:
Like the last trump, one note is heard to sound
That all the massy pillars tremble around;
The firm flint building shivers on its base,
And vast vibration fill th' astonish'd place:
The marble pavements seem to feel their doom,
And the bones rattle in each hollow tomb.

But now the blast harmonious dies away,
And tapers gently in a firm decay :
The melting sounds on higher pinions fly,
And seem to fall soft oozing from on high ;
Like evening dew they gently spread around
And shed the sweetness of heart-thrilling sound ;
'Till grown too soft, too fine for mortal ear,
The dying strains dissolve in distant air.
Methought I heard a flight of angels rise,
Most sweetly chanting as they gain'd the skies ;
Methought I heard their less'ning sound decay
And fade and melt and vanish quite away.

Hail heav'n born music ! by thy pow'r we raise
Th' uplifted soul to arts of highest praise :
Oh ! I would die with music melting round,
And float to bliss upon a sea of sound.

From Francis Hopkinson's Miscellaneous Essays and Occasional Writings, Phila. 1792, v. III, pp. 59–60 of Poems On Several Subjects.

INTRODUCTION.

When Benjamin Franklin bequeathed his philosophical apparatus to Judge Hopkinson he hardly foresaw that his friend, by thirty years his junior, would survive him but a few months. Benjamin Franklin died on April 17, 1790, and Francis Hopkinson on May 9, 1791.

The newspapers and magazines which had showered eulogies upon the grave of Franklin were again under the sad obligation of paying their tribute to the memory of another of those patriots who had signed the Declaration of Independence.

. . . the various causes which contributed to the establishment of the independence and federal government of the United States, will not be *fully traced*, unless much is ascribed to the irresistible influence of the *ridicule* which he poured forth, from time to time, upon the enemies of those great political events.

Thus ends the 'Account of the late Francis Hopkinson' in the Columbian Magazine, Philadelphia, for May, 1791, and justly the anonymous eulogist dwells upon the

increasing activity and versatility of the powers of his mind

as the keynote of Francis Hopkinson's character.

" . . . be this truth upon his marble writ—
He shone in virtue, science, taste and wit,"

conclude some " lines sacred " to his memory, printed in the Columbian Parnassiad of the same number, and this poem is followed by an elegy with the " Leitmotif ": *A Sage expired.*

Naturally all these elegies, sacred lines, and biographical sketches dwell mostly upon Francis Hopkinson's merits as a patriot, politician, poet and inventor; but among his many talents the one for music is seldom forgotten.

In fact, Francis Hopkinson stood in the centre of musical life at Philadelphia. Quite in accord with his character in general, he was many sided even in the limited spheres of music. He stood forth not

7

alone as an enthusiastic lover of the art, but as psalmodist, teacher, organist, harpsichordist, essayist, composer, and improver of the harpsichord. We shall not find him very important in either direction if viewed from the standpoint of the art critic, but in his case the critic gladly bows to the verdict of the historian : FRANCIS HOPKINSON WAS THE FIRST NATIVE POET-COMPOSER OF THE UNITED STATES OF NORTH AMERICA.

It is a pity that a biography of Francis Hopkinson, worthy of this remarkable man, does not exist. Perhaps Mr. Hildeburn, who was a very intimate friend of his descendants, would have enlarged his biographical sketch, published by the Pennsylvania Historical Society, into a comprehensive work had he been spared us for a few more years. At any rate he assisted Mrs. Hopkinson, the wife of Francis' grandson, in arranging the voluminous Hopkinson correspondence and other documents of a highly interesting character; and to write a biography of Francis Hopkinson on the basis of these and others, equally important, now in possession of Mrs. Scovel Shinn, of New York City, the great-granddaughter of Francis, would be a most thankful task indeed. But it would be a difficult one, too, for Francis Hopkinson had this in common with so many of our colonial statesmen, with most of whom he was on intimate terms, that he was many sided and that nothing of human interest was alien to him.

He was one of our early bibliophiles, and a family tradition tells us that the Hessian officers admittedly were so impressed with the character and extent of his library in Bordentown that they did all in their power to save it from destruction. Then the transactions of the American Philosophical Society contain descriptions of several neat inventions of his, for instance of an improved candlestick and of an instrument to measure distances on the high sea. Hopkinson also tried his hand at painting, and maybe it was Benjamin West to whom he owed his skill in fine arts. However, he is best known as one of our Colonial poets and satirists. While not the irresistible efforts of a genius, the three volumes of his ' Miscellaneous Essays and Occasional Writings,' published at Philadelphia in 1792, contain much that is witty, talented, elegant, or impressive, and some ideas that are above mediocrity. I doubt not that, sooner or later, when our people, as a whole, shall sincerely and independently from commercial considerations appreciate the vital importance and stimulating influence of flourishing arts and sciences in the life of a nation, the services rendered by such men as Francis Hopkinson to their country will duly be recognized. To those among us who thus thirst for the Renaissance-spirit in our nation and who believe in other Gods besides politics and business, Francis Hopkinson is at least as interesting as the somewhat dry and pedantic John Adams, who thus described him in a letter to his wife:

> He is one of your pretty, little curious, ingenious men. His head is not bigger than a large apple. I have not met with anything in natural history more amusing and entertaining than his personal appearance, yet he is genteel and well bred, and is very social.

To save my readers the trouble of consulting the scattered chronological data of Francis Hopkinson's life I copied the following sketch from Edward Potts Cheney's 'History of the University of Pennsylvania' (Boston, 1901, pp. 288–289):

> Francis Hopkinson, LL. D., a graduate of the first class to receive degrees from the College of Philadelphia, and one of the most prominent patriots of the Revolutionary War, was born in Philadelphia, September 21, 1737, son of Hon. Thomas and Mary (Johnson) Hopkinson. He graduated from the College of Philadelphia in 1757, and took the degree of Master of Arts in 1760, and that of Doctor of Laws in 1790, also receiving the Master of Arts degree from the College of New Jersey, *gratiæ causa*, in 1763. He studied law under Hon. Benjamin Chew and was admitted to the Bar in 1761.
>
> His first public service was to act as secretary to a conference between the Governor and the Indians of the Lehigh region. In 1759 he became Secretary of the *Library Company;* as also of the Vestry of Christ Church and Saint Peter's, where he made use of his talents for music by instructing the children in psalmody. He visited England in 1766, and in 1768 he married Ann Borden of Bordentown.
>
> From this time on he took an active part in the politics of his country. In March, 1772, he was made Collector of the Port of Newcastle, and in 1774 he was appointed to a seat in the Provincial Council of New Jersey. In 1776 he resigned all offices which were incompatible with his allegiance to the colonial party and became a delegate to the Continental Congress. As a member of this body he signed the Declaration of Independence. In the same year he was appointed by Congress to " execute the business of the Navy under their direction."
>
> All through the war he was constantly writing prose and verse, mostly of a satirical character, in support of his political faith. The most famous of these articles was ' The Battle of Kegs,' written in 1778, and instantly achieving a widespread popularity. In 1779 he was appointed Judge of the Admiralty from Pennsylvania and he presided over this court until Admiralty Jurisdiction became vested in the United States. In 1778 he became a Trustee of the College of Philadelphia, serving in that capacity until his death. He was an active participator in the debates of the convention of 1787 which formed the Constitution of the United States, and he produced at this time a humorous work, entitled ' The History of a New Roof,' which seems to have had a great influence upon some of the most distinguished men of the time. He died of apoplexy May 9, 1791.

CHAPTER I.

The Dawn of Musical Life at Philadelphia.

When Francis Hopkinson was growing to manhood the Colonies could not as yet rival the Motherland in musical matters. Our early musicians lacked opportunities accumulated abroad during centuries of musical activity. Their own efforts were restricted to a feeble imitation of European conditions and to the development of our musical life out of a most primitive, toward a promising and noteworthy state of affairs.

However, it would be an error to suppose that our musical life in Colonial times was limited to psalmody and that secular music was scorned. To be sure, such persons were numerous, especially in New England, who, through a narrow-minded interpretation of religion, or through a lack of artistic instinct, had little sympathy with musical amusements; but such people existed and exist in all countries and at all times, not alone in Colonial America. How the erroneous opinion came to be impressed upon the public mind is easily explained. The first writers on early American music were interested mostly in the development of sacred music in New England. Later historians took their statements as if meant to cover all the phases and spheres of our musical life, directed their attention principally to the earliest musical publications in America which were of a sacred character, and strangely neglected the old newspapers, magazines, diaries, and the like, though these sources alone could throw clear light upon our early secular music. Naturally, investigations undertaken on such narrow lines would lead the historians into fallacies, the more so as they seem to have been prejudiced against positive results before they began their one-sided research.

In reality, sacred and secular music developed simultaneously throughout the Colonies. Sacred music dominated in the North (Boston),

10

secular in the South (Charleston), whereas in the Middle Colonies (New York and Philadelphia) both were of equal weight. That our musical life was very primitive during the first half of the eighteenth century and still later, especially outside of the principal cities, is but in keeping with the inner logic of general conditions. If we permit ourselves to express astonishment it should be because music progressed so rapidly after 1760.

Prior to this year Philadelphia, though in many other respects our foremost city, was not the most important of the four musical centres mentioned. In fact, it ranked last. But within a few years the Quaker city gained an equal footing with the three others and is found in the lead a generation later. Various circumstances and many an amateur or professional musician contributed to this result, but when the time will come that Philadelphians again have a right to feel proud of their musical life, and when they look back to its childhood, one man will eminently stand forth as a " Votary of the Goddess " of music: *Francis Hopkinson.*

In order to understand and appreciate the importance of his musical career, it becomes necessary to briefly trace the development of musical matters at Philadelphia before he entered upon the plane as a factor of further progress. The data which throw light upon the ground out of which Francis Hopkinson, the musician, grew are few insignificant, and seemingly incoherent, but nevertheless an upward-tendency will be noticeable.

It is surprising that this upward-tendency should have escaped the attention of Louis C. Madeira, who claims in his valuable 'Annals of Music in Philadelphia and History of the Musical Fund Society ' (Phila. 1896), on p. 17, that:

the only evidence of musical entertainments in Philadelphia before the middle of the eighteenth century is of a negative kind. In 1716, at the yearly Meeting of the Friends, members were advised against "going to or being in any way concerned in plays, games, lotteries, music and dancing."

Obviously Madeira commits a *contradictio in adjecto,* for his quotation implies that the friends polemized against existing temptations. But not until about a dozen years later do we gain data of a more than hypothetical nature, and these mostly from the old newspapers.

I submit my observations in form of a *calendarium.*

Like everywhere else in the Colonies, the dancing master seems to have preceded the musician at Philadelphia. But where there is dancing there is music, secular music, be it only some popular tunes played on the fiddle.

1728. Dancing is taught in boarding schools.*

In the same year, on September 2d,

> A committee having been appointed by the vestry [of Christ Church] " to treat with Mr. Lod. C. Sprogel about an organ lately arrived here, report that they had done the same, and that he insisted on £200, for said organ; and that they had procured men of the best skill this place could afford, to erect the said organ in a convenient house in town, to make trial thereof; which being done, it is said the organ proves good in its kind, and large enough for our church."
>
> It was thereupon resolved, that the said organ be purchased for the use of Christ Church in Philadelphia, and that Peter Boynton and others be a committee to procure subscriptions for that purpose, to " appoint a suitable place to erect it in, and that they order the moving it into the church forthwith, from the place where it now is." †

This seems to have been the first organ erected in a Philadelphia church—if it was erected at all.

1729. The first dancing-master mentioned by name appears: Samuel PERPOINT, who instructed both " the Art of Dancing " and the use of " the small sword," having " taught both Accomplishments in Jamaica." ‡

Presumably the first publication relating to music was issued at Philadelphia in this year. It was a reprint by Benjamin Franklin of the seventh edition of Watts' Psalms of David, the chief design of the work being, in the author's words, " to improve Psalmody or religious Singing."

The Pennsylvania Gazette in which the reprint was advertised on October 2, 1729, contains another interesting item.

The paper published for a while an alphabetical reprint of ' Chambers's great Dictionary ' instead of editorials. But when Franklin and H. Meredith issued the venerable Gazette on their own account, beginning with number L, they abandoned the idea as

> it will probably be fifty years before the whole can be gone thro' in this Manner of Publication.

---

* American Weekly Mercury, 172⅞, March 5-14.

† See ' A Historical Account of Christ Church, Philadelphia, from its Foundation, A. D. 1695 to A. D. 1841, and of St. Peter's and St. James's until the Separation of the Churches. By the Reverend Benjamin *Dorr*, New York and Philadelphia, 1841,' p. 61.

‡ American Weekly Mercury, 1729, July 31-August 7.

In the mean time musical souls in Philadelphia had the opportunity of pondering over the two musical items which had been printed under letter A, on January 20th and July 25th. They were informed that

> *Accent* in Musick, is a Modulation of the Voice to express Musical Composition

and that

> *Air* in Musick signifies the Mellody, or the Inflection of a Musical Composition.

1730. The Pennsylvania Gazette published an advertisement in Number LXIX (March 5–13) which will fill my lady-readers with justifiable pride and delight since it goes to show that *the first music teacher in Philadelphia on record was a woman :* Miss BALL. Mr. Thomas Ball, who taught

> Writing, Arithmetic with the true Grounds of the French Tongue at Twenty Shillings per Quarter,

added :

> His Wife teaches Writing and French. *Likewise Singing, Playing on the Spinet, Dancing, and all sorts of Needle Work are taught by his sister lately arrived from London.*

My respect for Miss Ball forbids me to pay more than passing attention to other data of this year : The ' Göttliche Liebes und Lobesgethöne' published by B. Franklin * and

> ' The Singing Master's Guide to his Scholars. With the Psalms according to the old and new Translations : The Old on one Side and the New on the other. By several Hands, viz. Sternhold and Hopkins, Barton, Patrick, Tate and Brady, Milbourn and Sandys Contrived for Common Use : With the Tunes in Two Parts. By Daniel WARNER, Singing Master.'
> For sale at B. Franklin's printing office.†

1732. We gain evidence, if such be needed, that music was deemed necessary when celebrating legal holidays. On March 1, St. David's Day, and the birthday of Her Majesty Queen Carolina,

> "The Society of Ancient Britons" met at "The Indian King," marched in procession to church, waited on the Governor after divine service who then partook with them of a sumptuous dinner, when "the Loyal Healths" were

---

* Sic in Mr. James Warrington's very important compilation of ' Short Titles of Books relating to or illustrating the History and Practice of Psalmody in the United States 1620–1820.' Phila. 1898. Printed privately.

† Pa. Gaz. July 9–16, 1730.

drunk under the discharge of cannon and the " Day concluded with Musick, Mirth and Friendship." *

In the same year Franklin published the ' Vorspiel der Neuen Welt.' (Warrington.)

1733. Brady & Tate's New Version of the Psalms was reprinted at Philadelphia. (Warrington.)

1735. A dancing-master by the name of Mr. Dering offered his services. †

1737. Franklin advertised a reprint of Watts' ' Divine Songs attempted in Easy Language for the Use of Children,' ‡ and on May 12–19 he presented his readers with the words of a ' New Year's Ode by Colley Cibber, Esq., Poet Laureate and set to Music by Dr. Green.'

As such reprints from the English papers became quite customary they must have instigated American poetic " geniuses " to burden Pegasus likewise with grandiloquent airs, recitatives, choruses of which such Odes generally consisted, and subsequently our early composers to ' set them to music.'

1738. The proverbial love of the Colonials for dancing induced a Mr. Bolton to settle at Philadelphia as master of this " polite " art. He soon found a dangerous competitor in Theobald Hackett, who taught " all sorts of Fashionable English and French Dances. §

1739. Christopher Saur of Germantown (a suburb of Philadelphia) published the ' Zionitischer Weyrauch Huegel ' and ' Ein abgenöthigter Bericht.' (Warrington.) Furthermore there was in the press of Andrew Bradford

' A Choice Collection out of the Psalms of David, the Book of Job, Hale, Contemplation, etc. By Magnus FALCONAR, of Bomess in Scotland, Mariner,'

who taught navigation in Philadelphia. ||

1740. For the benefit of the poor in Georgia were published at Philadelphia ' A Hundred and fifty-odd Hymns, composed by John and Charles Westly '(sic). ¶

1741. Franklin reprinted the 15th ed. of Watts' ' Hymns and Spiritual Songs ' (Warrington), and the 13th ed. of the Psalms of David ' by the same author. °

---

* Am. W. Merc. Feb. 27–March 7.   † Pa. Gaz. Jan. 2.   ‡ Pa. Gaz. March 17–24
  § Pa. Gaz. Aug. 3–10; 24–31. || Am. W. Merc. June 14–21; Oct. 11–18.
¶ Am. W. Merc. 1739, Dec. 6–13; 1740, July 17–24.   ° Pa. Gaz. Aug. 20.

1742. He again reprinted Watts' Hymns. (Warrington.) So did Isaiah Warner with the 14th ed. of the same book, * and C. Saur, Germantown, published the 'Hirtenlieder von Bethlehem.' (Warrenton.) But more important than these publications was the puppet show which Philadelphians had occasion to enjoy from December of this until February of the following year.

> At the Sign of the Coach and Horses against the State House, in Chestnut Street, Philadelphia,

> was acted every evening

> An agreeable Comedy or Tragedy by changeable figures of two feet high. A Sight of the Sea and Ships. A Merry Dialogue between Punch and Joan his Wife. With several other pleasing Entertainments. †

1743.   'A Choice Collection of Hymns with several new translations from the Hymn Book of the Moravian Brethren' ‡

was published at Philadelphia. " In the Moravian Church, at the corner of Race and Broad Streets, there were two organs in 1743 " (Madeira) and from this year, as far as our present knowledge goes, dates the History of the American Pianoforte, for *Gustavus Hessclius manufactured spinets in Philadelphia as early as 1743.*§

1744. William Black, Secretary of the Commissioners appointed by Governor Gooch, of Virginia, to unite with those from the Colonies of Pennsylvania and Maryland to treat with the Iroquois or Six Nations of Indians, resided during this year at Philadelphia. I do not believe that he was the only gentleman in the Quaker City who could have entered an entry in his Journal like the following :

---

* Pa. Gaz. Dec. 2.   † Pa. Gaz. Dec. 30, 1742 ; Feb. 10. 1743.   ‡ Am. W. Merc. July 21–28.

§ See editorial note in Pa. Mag. of History, XVI, 473 :

I here take occasion to call the attention to the highly developed musical life in the new Moravian settlement (1741) at Bethlehem, Pa. Their " Collegium Musium," founded, it seems, before 1750, was perhaps the first musical society in the Colonies deserving of such a name. Music was cultivated at Bethlehem with a taste, skill, and knowledge of the literature, both sacred and secular, undreamed of elsewhere in the Colonies until about 1765. The Moravians were famous for their musical abilities, as appears from entries in the diaries of Franklin, Samuel Adams and others. The direct influence of neither the Moravians nor of that true German " Original," Conrad Beissel and his brethren at Ephrata, Pa. (not to be confused with the Moravians) might not have been great but certainly hear-say and the reports of those who had heard their music indirectly benefited the lovers of music in Philadelphia and elsewhere.

For valuable information on Moravian music see ' Historical Notes on Music in Bethlehem, Pennsylvania, from 1741 to 1871. By Rufus A. Grider.' (Phila. 1873 ; out of print.)

Philadelphia, Friday June the 8th.
I rose from my Bed and pass'd two Hours in writing; the rest of the time
'till Breakfast I spent with my Fiddle and Flute . . .*

C. Saur, Germantown, published "Das Psalter . . . des
David" in this year (Warrington), and of amusements advertised
in the papers we notice:

among other Curiosities Eight Bells ringing truly, both round Ringing
and Changes, much in the Imitation of Ringing in England; with two young
Men and a Lady walking, and the Lady turning Head over Heels, like a
Mountebank, and the Clock drawing a Curtain. †

Though this curiosity might have pleased young Francis
Hopkinson immensely, his musical instincts received a by far
greater impetus if, as we might believe, his mother took him
to inspect

The Sola or Camera Obscura Microscope

exhibited together with

The Unparallelled [sic] Musical Clock, made by that great Master of
Machinery David Lockwood. It excels all others in the Beauty of its Structure
and plays the choicest Airs from the most celebrated Operas with the greatest
Nicety and Exactness. It performs with beautiful graces, ingeniously and
variously intermixed, the French Horn Pieces, perform'd upon the Organ,
German and Common Flute, Flageolet etc. Sonata's, Concerto's, Marches,
Minuets, Jiggs and Scots Airs, composed by Corelli, Alberoni, Mr. Handel and
other great and eminent Masters of Musick. ‡

A musical clock even if not playing music-hall songs, but
classic music as did the one by "that great Master of Machinery,"
would impress us moderns very little. § But in the childhood
both of nations and individuals the most insignificant occur-
rences help to form the character, and it is a fact that in those
early days the itinerant musical clocks did much toward
developing the love of good music in our people.

1747. Watts' 'Divine and Moral Songs' (Warrington) and 'The Scotch
Psalms, in a small neat pocket volume,' were reprinted by
B. Franklin. ‖

1748. The dancing assembly was founded and mention is made of
an organ having been in St. Joseph's, Willing's Alley, the
first Roman Catholic church in the United States, in 1748—

---

* Pa. Mag. of Hist. II, 40. (1878.)   † Pa. Gaz. May 24.   ‡ Pa. Gaz. July 12, Aug. 2.
§ On the other hand, a musical clock is said to have given Tschaikowsky's latent musical talents
an impetus.
‖ Pa. Gaz. May 28.

1750. The Rev. Robert Harding took charge of the church in 1750, and the music of the services was under the care of a cultivated musician, the choir was composed of the best voices obtainable, and new voices were sought for whenever there was an opportunity. (Madeira.)

1749. On March 21 appeared in the Pa. Gaz. the following advertisement:

> John BEALS, Musick Master from London at his House in Fourth Street, near Chestnut Street, joining to Mr. Linton's, collar maker, teaches the Violin, Hautboy, German Flute, Common Flute and Dulcimer by note.
>
> Said Beals will likewise attend young ladies, or others, that may desire it, at their houses. He likewise provides musick for balls or other entertainments.

The same year witnessed *the introduction of drama and opera in Philadelphia.* To be sure, the newspapers do not disclose the fact, but we have so much circumstantial contemporary evidence as to render the statement indisputable.

In the first place, we have an entry in John Smith's MS. Journal under date of "Sixth Month, 22d, 1749," which shows that on this day Addison's 'Cato' was performed at Philadelphia. Whether this was the first play-night we know not, but it is highly probable that it was not the last,

> since early in 1750 the Recorder, William Allen, afterwards Chief Justice of the Province, reported to the Common Council that certain persons had lately taken upon them to act plays in the city, and, as he was informed, they intended to make frequent practice thereof, he expressed the fear that their performances would be attended with mischievous effects. In consequence of this presentment, the board unanimously requested the Magistrates to take the most effectual measures for suppressing the "disorder," by sending for the actors, and binding them to their good behaviour. *

Moreover, the New York Gazette, under date of 26th of February, 1750, wrote that

> Last week arrived here a company of comedians from Philadelphia . . .

and the Pennsylvania Gazette, under date of March 6th, reprinted this notice in order to inform their readers, as we might suppose, of what had become of the comedians since their forced departure from Philadelphia.

The company was managed by Messrs. Kean and Murray

---

* Quoted from George O. Seilhamer's invaluable 'History of the American Theatre' (vol. 3, 1796, N. Y.) I, 2–3. Other important writers on the subject are Watson, Madeira, Durang, Armstrong.

and played at New York until July 8th, 1751. It consisted here of professional actors only, whereas

the probabilities in the case of the Philadelphia performers of 1749 are that the company was made up in part of actors who had had some experience in England and in part of amateurs who were desirous of adopting the stage as a profession. (Seilhamer.)

The performances took place in William Plumstead's warehouse in King street. As the Philadelphia papers paid no attention to them we are obliged to trace the plays possibly performed there by Kean and Murray from the New York repertoire. It contained about a dozen plays and an equal number of farces, usually performed as "after-pieces." Amongst the latter we notice as musical farces Cibber's 'Damon and Phillida'; Hill's 'Devil to Pay'; Cibber's 'Flora, or Hob in the Well'; Fielding's 'Virgin Unmasked'; the pastoral sketch of 'Colin and Phoebe,' and most successful of all Gay-Pepush's famous 'Beggar's Opera.' Between the acts or between the plays and after-pieces "Entertainments of Singing and Dancing" were given. From the advertisements of "benefit" performances we are able to glean the names of the principal performers: Mr. Thomas Kean, Mr. Murray, Mr. Tremain, Mr. Scott, Mr. Woodham, Mrs. Taylor, Miss Osborne and Miss Nancy George. The principal singers seem to have been Mr. Kean, Mr. Woodham and Mrs. Taylor. The "operas" were accompanied probably on the harpsichord, perhaps by John Beals, who, as we shall see, still resided at Philadelphia in 1758.

After this first frustrated attempt at opera and drama musical matters seem to have slumbered for a while at Philadelphia.

1752. C. Saur published 'Fuenff Schoene Geistliche Lieder.' (Warrington.)

1753. The 16th. ed. of Watts' 'Psalms of David' was reprinted and C. Saur published at Germantown 'Die Kleine geistliche Harfe' and 'Neu vermehrt und vollstaendiges Gesangbuch.' (Warrington.) In the Pa. Gaz. during January, a Robert COE, who

draws Bills, Bonds, Indentures, Leases, Releases and other Instruments of Writing . . . conceiving himself capable of teaching to play on that agreeable Instrument the German Flute, thinks proper to inform the Publick, that he will attend for that purpose, four Nights in the Week at his House . . . where any young gentleman may be taught, paying Fifteen Shillings Entrance and Fifteen Shillings per Month; or if required he will attend them at their Chambers, they paying the same Sum Entrance and Twenty Shillings per Month.

If Robert Coe was the exponent of secular music, Josiah Davenport taught

> Writing in all the different hands, arithmetick in a good and easy method and *psalmody in several necessary and useful parts.* *

1754. Robert Coe again offered to teach the German Flute by an easy method and

> as some Gentlemen are afraid to undertake it by Reason of its taking more wind than they think they can well spare . . [he] . . has invented a Mouth Piece, made either of Tin or Silver and does not in the least alter the Tone of the Flute but does the same as if blown by the nicest lip. †

Those whom neither their nice lips nor Coe's patent mouthpiece could induce to indulge in German flute music probably derived more pleasure out of David Chamber's publication of

> ' *The Youths' entertaining Amusement*, or a plain Guide to Psalmody; being a collection of the most usual and necessary Tunes sung in the English Protestant Congregation in Philadelphia, etc. in two Parts, viz. *Treble* and *Bass*, with all proper and necessary Rules, adapted to the meanest capacities. By W. Dawson, Writing Master and Accomptant, at the Hand and Pen, in Third Street, Philadelphia.' ‡

Perhaps Francis Hopkinson was one of the subscribers to this work, of which no copy seems to have come down to us.

But a by far more important musical event was the arrival of

> The Company of Comedians from London, which opened the New Theatre in Water Street, on April 15, 1754. §

The history of this company which, backed by William Hallam and managed by Lewis Hallam the elder, came to the Colonies in 1752 and played first in Williamsburg, Va., then in New York before proceeding to Philadelphia, is too well known to be repeated here. As a matter of fact, the company was of decided merit, plays by the best masters only were performed, and the American public profited by this company more than by the several previous companies combined.

---

* Pa. Gaz. Dec. 27.	‡ Pa. Gaz. July 11.
† Pa. Gaz. April 11.	§ Pa. Gaz. April 25.

Unfortunately the history of Lewis Hallam's activity in New York is clearer than his activity in Philadelphia, as the papers in this city printed but meagre theatrical notices.

At first Hallam's application to Governor Hamilton for permission to perform plays there with his company was stoutly resisted by the Governor himself and by the Friends. But the number of such influential persons who pleaded in favor of the theatre was so strong as to finally break the opposition and Hallam received leave to give twenty-four performances on condition that nothing indecent or immoral should be presented.

So it happened that Plumstead's warehouse again saw a short theatrical season. The first performance took place, as stated above, on April 15th, the last on June 27th. The advertisements in the Pa. Gaz. give us no adequate idea of the repertoire—it must be remembered that our early papers were issued once a week, but that the playing nights were on Mondays, Wednesdays, and Fridays. Only one performance is on record during which music played a prominent part, the one of June 17th. On this evening a 'Pantomime Entertainment, called HARLEQUIN COLLECTOR, or, the Miller Deceived,' was given. Necessarily this pantomime contained music, but nothing regarding it is to be gleaned from the papers. As Hallam had no orchestra during his Virginia and New York tour, but simply one solitary musician who accompanied the music on the harpsichord, we might imply that the same was the case at Philadelphia. Now a Mrs. Love was a prominent singing member of the company; a Mr. Charles Love, "musician from London," gave concerts and instructed on half a dozen instruments at New York during the company's sojourn there; and Mr. and Mrs. Love took a benefit at New York in 1754 with the 'Beggar's Opera.' We might therefore infer that it was Mr. Charles Love whose duty it was in this company to combine the functions of orchestra and conductor in his person by means of a harpsichord.

As in Kean and Murray's company the intermissions between the acts or plays were filled out with singing and dancing and occasionally with instrumental music. For instance, on Mr. and Mrs. Love's benefit Mr. Love played 'the Quaker Sermon' on the violin and a solo on the Hautboy.

Little difference appears between the operatic repertoire of this company and that of Kean and Murray. It consisted mainly of 'The Devil to Pay'; 'Flora, or, Hob in the Wall'; 'Damon and Phillida'; the pantomime of 'Harlequin Collector,' and the 'Beggar's Opera.'

The strength of the company will best be seen from the cast of this opera as it was performed at New York on November 19, 1753.

THE BEGGAR'S OPERA.

Peachum	by Mr. Hallam
Locket	Mr. Malone
Macheeth	Mr. Adcock
Filch	Mr. Miller
Mat o' th' Mint	Mr. Bell
Wat Dreary	Mr. Singleton
Nimming Ned	Mr. Hullet
Mrs. Peachum	Mrs. Adcock
Polly	Mrs. Beneley
Lucy	Mrs. Clarkson
Mrs. Coaxer	Miss Hallam
Diana Trapes	Mrs. Adcock
Mrs. Vixen	Mrs. Bigby
Jenny Diver	Mrs. Love
Molly Brazin	Mr. Clarkson.

After the season closed at Philadelphia the company went to Jamaica, in the West Indies, where Lewis Hallam died, and the organization disbanded. (Seilhamer.)

1755. For this year I have found but one item. However, it is interesting because it goes to show that Philadelphia now possessed a band of music. We read in 'Extracts from the Diary of Daniel FISHER 1755,' contributed by Mrs. Conway Robinson Howard, Richmond, Va., to the Pa. Mag. of Hist., v. XVII:

> . . . I should observe that on St. John the Baptist Day (June 24) there was the Greatest Procession of Free Masons to the Church and this Lodge, in Second Street that was ever seen in America. No less than 160 being in the Procession in Gloves, Aprons, etc. *attended by a band of music.*

If this procession filled Daniel Fisher with awe what were his emotions when in

1756 The Philadelphia Regiment consisting of upwards of 1000 able bodied effective men after being review'd and performing the Manual Exercise [marched]

thro' the Town in Three Grand Divisions . . with Hautboys and Fifes in Ranks . . [and] Drums between the third and fourth Ranks. ? *

But with due respect for this grand spectacle, for "the band of music" and "the Hautboys and Fifes in ranks," the year 1757 brought events which prove the upward-tendency in the musical life of Philadelphia better than the parade of 1756. With this remark I do not allude to the reprint of the 17th ed. of Watts' ' Psalms of David ' or the publication of ' Der Psalter David ' by B. Franklin and Armbruster (Warrington), or to the fact that Josiah Davenport kept a

Singing School, (for the Summer Season Evenings) . . where any Person may be instructed in Psalmody, that is capable to learn that agreeable Art,†

but to a bold venture by the college authorities. The college of Philadelphia had been founded in 1749 or 1753—there is a controversy on the subject—with a very progressive plan of studies. Amongst these was " Oratory," and, well aware of the fact that practical experiments would produce more beneficial results than mere theoretical explanations, the authorities selected as an " Oratorial Exercise " the ' Masque of Alfred,' written by Thompson-Mallet, and composed by Arne. With omissions and, on the other hand, with additions this masque was acted several times by

the young gentlemen of the college . . for their Improvement in Oratory

in the College Hall during January, 1757.

At present it is sufficient to have mentioned this truly remarkable enterprise. As Francis Hopkinson's musical career is linked with this performance, a full description must be reserved for the next chapter.

But the year 1757 is important for two other reasons. Though, presumably, concerts were given in Philadelphia at rare intervals before this year, the *first public concerts on record*, as far as I know, *took place in 1757*.

The first was thus advertised in the Pa. Gaz., Jan. 20.

By particular Desire.
On Tuesday next, the 25th instant, at the Assembly Room, in Lodge Alley will be performed a CONCERT OF MUSIC, under the direction of Mr. John Palma ; to begin exactly at Six o'clock. Tickets to be had at the London Coffee House, at one Dollar each ; and no Person to be admitted without a ticket.

---

*Pa. Journal, March 25.   †Pa. Journal, April 27.

The second concert was to be given on March 25th, this too at the Assembly Room, at one dollar a ticket, but no mention is made of the musician who arranged the entertainment.*

Passing by the year 1758, during which John Beals again advertised that he

> plays on the Violin at the Assembly Balls and all other Entertainments; and like wise teaches the Violin and other Instruments of Musick in a plain and easy Way by Book,

we are confronted in 1759 by a number of data which definitely prove the advance made at Philadelphia in musical matters since 1716.

Of publications we notice the ' Vollstaendiger Marburger Gesangbuch ' by C. Saur, Germantown, and the ' Liturgische Gesaenge der Bruder Gemeinen ' by H. Miller, Phila. (Warrington.) Furthermore appeared advertisements to the effect that

> Violin is taught in the best and neatest taste according to the new Italian Method by the Subscriber, an Italian born . . .
>
> 　　　　　　　　　　　Francis ALBERTI. †

and that

> Vocal Music [is] taught in its various Parts after the best Manner in the School House behind the Revd. Dr. Jenny's near the Church, where due attendance will be given every Monday, Wednesday and Friday Evenings from 5 to 8 o'clock. The second and fourth Wednesday of every Month will be public.‡

If this last advertisement leads us toward the age of well established music schools, one that appeared in the Pa. Gaz. on Dec. 27th clearly shows that business men now began to consider music a commercial factor.

Michael HILLEGAS, the " Wanamaker " of Philadelphia in those days, had for sale at his House in Second Street, opposite Samuel Morris, Esq. :

> an extraordinary good and neat Harpsichord with four stops; a good violoncello; an Assortment of English and Italian Violins, as well common ones, as double lined, of which some extraordinary; a Parcel of good German Flutes imported lately from Italy. Also imported in the last ships from London, a large Assortment of Music of the best Masters, viz: Solos, Overtures, Concertos, Sonatas and Duets, for Violins, German Flutes, Hautboys, French Horns, Violoncello's and Guitars, Voluntaries and Lessons for Organs and Harpsichords, ruled Paper of various Sorts for Musick, and Musick Books, Tutors or Books of Instruction to learn to play on the Violin, German Flute, Hautboy, or

---

Common Flute, without a Master, Song Books, Cantatas, Songs in Sheets and a choice Parcel of Violin Strings, etc.

moreover

as early as 1759 we hear of the *Orpheus Club* of the College,

apparently a musical society,* and the same year witnessed the third attempt at opera in Philadelphia.

The company, headed by Mr. Douglass, had arrived at New York in the autumn of 1758, and after performing there during the following winter it proceeded to Philadelphia in the spring of 1759.

As was to be expected, a host of hyper-religious people of several denominations vigorously opposed Douglass and a bill was passed forbidding the erection of play-houses or the acting of plays in Pennsylvania after Jan. 1, 1760. Fortunately for the development of the drama in America, this bill was set aside by the King in Council, September 2d, 1760. (Seilhamer.)

In the mean time, Douglass had erected a wooden theatre on " Society Hill," and gave a series of performances from June 25th to Dec. 28th. During this eventful season 'Hamlet' is said to have been performed for the first time in America. With respect to operas, or rather farces interspersed with music, no material difference appears between Douglass' repertoire and that of Kean and Murray or Lewis Hallam. The only important addition was Carey's ' A Wonder, or, an Honest Yorkshire man.' That the company was able to perform these now forgotten but once most popular works to the satisfaction of a critical audience will be seen from the cast (on Aug. 24th), in

THE BEGGAR'S OPERA.

Capt. M'Heath	Mr. Harman
Peachum	Mr. Tomlinson
Lockit	Mr. Scott
Mat of the Mint	Mr. Reed
Beggar	Mr. Morris
Player	Mr. Douglass
Jemmy Twitcher	Mr. Allyn
Harry Paddington	Mr. Horne
Filch	Mr. A. Hallam
Mrs. Peachum	Mrs. Harman
Polly	Mrs. Love
Lucy	Mrs. Harman
Mrs. Coaxer	Mrs. Douglass
Mrs. Slammekin	Mrs. Tomlinson.

---

*See 'A History of the University of Pennsylvania. By Edward Potts *Cheney*' (Boston, 1901), p. 227.

The last performance was given for the benefit of the Pennsylvania Hospital, the fore-last on Dec. 27th.

Towards the raising of a Fund for purchasing an *Organ* to the College Hall in this City and instructing the Charity Children in Psalmody. *

---

*Pa. Gaz. Dec. 27. The harpsichordist of the company might again have been Charles Love unless his career had ended behind the bars of a prison. I find the following characteristic advertisement in the Pa. Gaz. Oct. 6, 1757 :

" Williamsburg, Sept. 2, 1757.

" Run away from the Subscriber, at Stratford, in Westmoreland County, on Sunday the 28th of August, Charles *Love*, a tall thin Mann, about sixty of Age ; he professes Musick, Dancing, fencing and plays exceedingly well on the Violin and all Wind Instruments ; *he stole when he went away, a very good Bassoon, made by Schuchart,* which he carried with him, as also a Dutch or German Fiddle, with an old Hautboy and German flute which are his own ; he rode a small white Horse with a Virginia made Saddle, and coarse blue Cloak Housing. It is supposed he will make towards Charlestown in South Carolina.

" Whoever apprehends the said Love, and brings him to me in Stratford, shall have Eight Pounds Reward, if taken in Virginia, Nine Pounds, if taken in Maryland, or North Carolina, and Ten Pounds if taken anywhere else on the Continent.

" Philipp Ludwell LEE."

CHAPTER II.

FRANCIS HOPKINSON'S MUSICAL EDUCATION.

The musical data compiled in the foregoing chapter are few and primitive, surprisingly so if we remember the high grade of culture in Philadelphia about 1750. But it is not my object to trace the reasons for this contrast. It must be taken as a matter of fact. However, it must not be forgotten that such data resemble an excavated skeleton. Imagination has to add blood and life if a clear idea of the living body, be it ever so dwarfish, is to be gained. Without these primitive conditions not even an amateur-musician like Francis Hopkinson, who dwindles into insignificance if compared with a Palestrina, Bach, or Wagner, would have been possible.

The love of music is traditional in the Hopkinson family. We might therefore infer that young Francis was not guarded against the "evil" influences of this art, and we may well imagine his delight when hearing the musical clock with its choicest airs from the fashionable operas.

Such impressions certainly awakened his musical instincts and kept them alive until better opportunities allowed them to be developed systematically. But of his childhood hardly anything is known, and no anecdotes are current illustrating his early musical inclinations.

Not until 1754 does his name appear in connection with music.

The reader recalls the 'Ode on Music' as reproduced in the Prologue from Francis Hopkinson's manuscript. That the "sweet lyre" set his "attentive soul on fire" precisely in the year 1754 may easily be proved, for the American Magazine (Phila.) published the ode 1757 in its October number with this editorial remark:

Written at Philadelphia by a young Gentleman of 17, on his beginning to learn the Harpsichord.

Even if the MS. volume alluded to had been lost, the inquisitive

26

historian would be able to trace the author of the ode, since it is contained in another manuscript collection, now in possession of the Pennsylvania Historical Society, and furthermore, with slight alterations, in the third volume of Francis Hopkinson's ' Miscellaneous Essays and Occasional Writings,' Philadelphia, 1792.

To begin the study of a musical instrument at the age of seventeen is not favorable for the acquisition of a good mechanism and certainly Hopkinson saw many a day on which he despaired of ever mastering his favorite instrument. But enthusiasm and innate endurance helped to surmount the obstacles. Though he probably never became a virtuoso on the harpsichord, everything goes to show that his mechanism was that of an able amateur. At any rate, he gained quite a reputation among Philadelphians as performer, since many years after his death (in 1836) Longacre in the ' National Portrait Gallery ' remarks :

He was a musician of high grade in his performances on the harpsichord.

Whether or not Hopkinson began his studies as an autodidact, is a matter of conjecture. But we have traced for the years 1749–1758 a " John Beals, Musick Master from London," who taught among other instruments "the Dulcimer by note." Perhaps he or Charles Love, the musician in Lewis Hallam's company which came to Philadelphia in the year 1754, initiated him in the mysteries of the harpsichord and thorough-bass. Later on, in 1757, John Palma might have given him some lessons. A few years later a musician appeared in Philadelphia, whose name has puzzled European historians. I mean James BREMNER a relative, it seems, of Robert Bremner, the music publisher, editor, and composer. Concerning this James Bremner Fétis remarks in the ' Biographie Universelle des Musiciens '

Forkel and Lichtenthal citent un ouvrage d'un auteur nommé James Bremner sous ce titre :
' Instructions for the sticcado pastorale, with a collection of airs' (Londres in 4.° sans date.) Je n'ai trouvé ni ce nom, ni l'ouvrage dans les catalogues anglais.

Eitner, in his 'Quellen Lexikon,' mentions the same work, but he, too, without giving biographical information.

However, James Bremner existed. If his career in England seems to be unknown we can at least prove that he lived and died in America, respected as man of culture and esteemed as a musician.

It would appear from the newspapers that he arrived in Philadelphia in 1763. He opened in December of this year :

his Music School . . . at Mr. Glover Hunt's near the Coffee House in Market street where young Ladies may be taught the Harpsichord or Guitar, on Mondays, Wednesdays and Fridays from 10 o'clock in the Morning till 12, at Twenty Shillings Entrance Money. Likewise young Gentlemen may be taught the Violin, German Flute, Harpsichord, or Guitar, from 6 o'clock in the evening till 8, on Mondays, Wednesdays and Fridays, for the same Price and Entrance Money.*

Bremner's activity was not limited to teaching music, for he arranged and conducted concerts.   At least two are on record.

When the subscription for the Organ at St. Peter's Church had proved insufficient "for compleating the design" a concert was advertised for the same purpose under the direction of Mr. Bremner, to take place at the Assembly Room on Feb. 21, 1764. † In the following year on April 10 he arranged and conducted a truly remarkable

Performance of Solemn Music, vocal and instrumental, in the College Hall . . for the Benefit of the Boys and Girls Charity School. ‡

But Bremner was mainly an able organist.

An organ was erected in St. Peter's by Philip Teyring in 1763, the vestry providing

that neither the said organ, nor the organist shall be any charge to the churches, until the debt for building St. Peter's church is paid. §

Now, Bremner's name appears not in the vestry minutes of Christ Church and St. Peter's until 1767, and though the concert given under his direction in 1764 seems to indicate that he was engaged as organist for St. Peter's in 1763, this is by no means certain.   All we know is that he was organist at Christ Church in 1767.   (Dorr, p. 159.)

How long Bremner remained in this position is not recorded, but in December, 1770, he is spoken of in the vestry minutes as "the late organist."   He seems to have returned to Philadelphia after an absence of a few years for I find him mentioned as organist of Christ Church under date of Feb. 1, 1774, in the Diary of James Allen.‖   I am aware of no later allusion to his name or residence until his death, which occurred "on the banks of the Schuylkill, Sept., 1780."¶   This date is given in a footnote to the Ode 'In Memory of Mr. James Bremner' written by Francis Hopkinson, and of which more will be said in a subsequent chapter.

---

*Pa. Gaz. Dec. 1, 1763.   † Pa. Journal, Feb. 16, 1764.   ‡ Pa. Gaz. April 4 and 18, 1765.
§ See Dorr's 'Historical Account . . . ' p. 137.   ‖ Pa. Mag. of Hist. IX, 1885.
¶ As some of my readers may not be familiar with American topography, it will be of value to remark that part of Philadelphia lies on the banks of this beautiful stream.

I have dwelt with some length upon Bremner's career in America, for Hopkinson undoubtedly owed much of his musical education to him, as did Philadelphia in general. The sincere and impressive strains of the Ode in his memory prove the admiration and respect in which he was held by our first composer, and Hopkinson's cordial reception by Robert Bremner when in London certainly was the consequence of the friendship which had sprung up between him and James Bremner. But Hopkinson profited not alone by a friendly intercourse with the accomplished Scotch musician. We have evidence that he became a pupil of Bremner.

The venerable grandson of Francis, Mr. Oliver Hopkinson, himself an enthusiastic lover of music and skilful musician, possesses a book of ' Lessons ' in the handwriting of his ancestor, in which appear a ' Trumpet Air,' a ' Lesson,' a ' March,' an ' Overture by the Earl of Kelly adapted to the Harpsichord,' and ' Lady Coventry's Minuet with Variations,' all by James Bremner.

This fact and the title of the collection render it highly probable that Hopkinson took lessons from Bremner. We may add as further circumstantial evidence that the book contains numerous pieces for the organ. Now we know that Hopkinson became an accomplished organist as well as harpsichordist and that he succeeded Bremner as organist of Christ Church. We read in the vestry minutes under date of December 10, 1770 :

Mr. church-warden Hopkinson having been so obliging as to perform on the organ at Christ Church during the absence of Mr. Bremner, the late organist, the vestry unanimously requested of him a continuance of this kind office, until an organist should be appointed, or as long as it should be convenient and agreeable to himself. Mr. Hopkinson cheerfully granted this request.

It is not recorded how long Hopkinson volunteered his services as organist; perhaps until Bremner resumed the office in 1774, if he really did resume it. At any rate, the vestry minutes mention neither his nor Bremner's name again, and in 1782 a Mr. Curtz is spoken of as having acted as organist to the churches for several years *gratis*.

But it seems as if Hopkinson was proficient on the organ before Bremner's arrival at Philadelphia.

He is known to have been the first immatriculated student of the College of Philadelphia, to have graduated in 1757 and to have received his degree of A. M. in 1760. During the years 1757–1768 music played a part at the College more important than in the following years. Though not the only graduate to imbue his *alma mater* with a musical spirit, Francis Hopkinson was without doubt the most conspicuous figure in this respect, in fact the soul of this too-short-lived musical movement.*

The reader remembers that an organ was erected in the College-hall in 1760, the necessary funds having been raised by the theatrical performance on Dec. 27, 1759. The instrument was used, especially at Commencement, to accompany the usual Anthems and Odes. It is more than probable that the report of the Commencement Exercises of 1760, printed in the Pa. Gazette, May 15th, referred to Hopkinson when saying :

one of the Students, who received his Master's Degree on this occasion, conducted the organ with that bold and masterly Hand for which he is celebrated and several of the Pieces were also his own compositions.

Then we know that at Commencement of 1761 a patriotic Ode of his was sung and

accompanied by the organ, which made the music a very compleat and agreeable Entertainment to all present.

From all we know of the character of young composers we might rest assured that Hopkinson insisted on accompanying this Ode, which is said to have been

written and set to Music, in a very grand and masterly taste.

Even in later years Hopkinson would take a hand in the preparation and conduct of the Commencement Exercises for the glory of his *alma mater.*

The Pa. Gaz. wrote on Nov. 19, 1767 :

On Tuesday last was held the public Commencement . . An elegant DIALOGUE, written in Verse by Thomas Coombe, B. A. . . . . was also spoken on this occasion ; and an *Ode*, set to Music, was sung by Mr. John Bankson, with great sweetness and Propriety, *accompanied by the Organ, etc., under the Conduct of a worthy Son of the College, who has often shown his Regard to the Place of his Education, by honouring it on public occa-*

---

* I have not ventured to mention his name in the above narrative in connection with the Orpheus Club, said to have existed in 1759. If this musical society did exist at that time, Francis Hopkinson can not but have been a prominent member. Perhaps he was the founder of the club.

The Pſalmes of David, to fower
parts, for Viols and voyce,
The firſt booke Doricke Mottees,
The second, Divine Canzonets,
Compoſed by Giles Farnaby bachilar
of Muſicke
with a prelud, before the pſalmes, Cromaticke.

Title page of Giles Farnaby's 'Psalmes of David'

Hopkinson's Song, ' My days have been so wondrous free,' 1759

sions with his ready Service; the Band belonging to the 18th or Royal Regiment of Ireland, was kindly permitted by the Colonel to perform in the instrumental Part.

Who else could this " worthy Son of the College" have been to whom thus publicly a splendid compliment was paid except Francis Hopkinson?

To form a correct idea of Hopkinson's knowledge of musical literature is to-day, of course, impossible. But he certainly was conversant with the psalmodists of the day, either Europeans like Arnold, Williams, Tansur, or Americans like Tufts, Walther, Lyon; and probably C. Saur's and Franklin's German publications did not escape his attention. Not only did his duties as organist require a familiarity with psalmody but he himself was a composer of psalm-tunes and anthems, and it is recorded that he at one time instructed in psalmody. This fact appears from the vestry-minutes of St. Peter's and Christ Church as published by Rev. Dorr. We find under date of April 3, 1764, the following entry :

. . . the members of the vestry, who frequently attended while the children of the united congregations were improved in the art of psalmody, reported that they had observed Mr. William Young in connection with the secretary Mr. Hopkinson to take great and constant pains in teaching and instructing the children; it was therefore unanimously agreed that the thankful acknowledgments of this board be given Mr. Hopkinson and Mr. Young, for their kind services which they are requested still to continue.

But Francis Hopkinson's studies in the literature of music were not restricted to the relatively narrow field of psalmody. His descendants still possess parts of his musical library, and few as these volumes may be, they clearly demonstrate that he was a *connoisseur* of music.

He owned (in the author's manuscript)

'The Psalms of David, to fower | parts, for viols and voyce | the first book Doricke Mottoes, | the second, Divine Canzonets, | composed by Giles FARNABY, Bachelor | of Musicke | with a prelud | before the Psalmes, Cromaticke.' *

Next we notice :

'The Musical Miscellany ; being a collection of choice songs and lyrick Poems: with the basses to each tune, and transpos'd for the flute. By the most eminent masters.' (Six volumes. London. Printed by and for John Watts—1731.)

---

* *Farnaby* Giles, composer and spinnet player, born at Truro, Cornwall, about the middle of the sixteenth century, Mus. Bac. Onon. July, 1592. Date of death unknown. He lived mostly in London and Sevenoaks, Kent. This work of his is mentioned neither by Fetis nor Eitner nor by Brown and Stratton.

This musical miscellany contains mostly sentimental ballads and pastorals such as 'A Song in Praise of Polly' or 'Strephon and Flavie' (set by Dr. Pepush) or the 'Despairing Lover.'

Then the torso of a book with the memorandum "Francis Hopkinson, 1755," attracts our attention. It is in manuscript, possibly of the owner. Most pieces have a figured bass and are Italian, French, English trios, songs, and duets, arranged for the harpsichord, amongst them for instance 'A Song in the Triumph of Hibernia,' an 'Air in Atalanta' by Haendel, and a famous 'Water Piece' by the same author.

Not less curious is a manuscript music-book (obl. 4°) entitled 'Basso.' Three distinct hands may be traced in this volume but it certainly belonged to Francis Hopkinson, and the attempts at orchestration of 'the President March' and other pieces, to be dated about 1800, are easily separated from the earlier entries.

This volume contains the figured bass to several sonatas, one for instance by the famous Padre Martini,* to 'The Overture in Amorous Goddess,' a 'Basso Del Seignr. Jacomo Corfini,' followed by 'Violoncello and Cembalo 3. Sonata by Mr. Standell' and other bassi.

These volumes are in possession of Mr. Oliver Hopkinson, of Philadelphia. Mrs. Florence Scovel Shinn, of New York City, this lady too a descendant of Francis Hopkinson, cherishes among her inherited "Americana" as one of the most precious treasures an (obl. 4°) book of 'Songs,' in the original binding, which was "FRANCIS HOPKINSON HIS BOOK." Dated "PHILADELPHIA, DOMINI 1759." it is carefully and neatly written in the owner's hand. Originally it contained, according to the index, 109 pieces of music on 206 pages. Now two or three pages are missing. The 'songs' are arranged mostly for harpsichord accompaniment, many with a figured bass. The words seldom have a special staff, as the melody and the treble part of the accompaniment are identical in most songs. The collection was commenced in 1759 and can not have been finished much later than 1760, since the piece on p. 180 shows this year. The volume contains several compositions by Hopkinson but consists chiefly of pastoral songs from operas, cantatas, or of anthems, hymns, duets by other authors, most of them anonymous. The first forty pages are written in Italian, the rest with the exception of a French chanson in English (for instance, we notice on page 146 'Rule Britannia'). The authors mentioned by name are:

---

* Giambattista *Martini*, generally known as "Padre Martini," 1706-1784.

Haendel with ten pieces ('Samson' evidently being Hopkinson's favorite oratorio by the master), "Signr. Palma" and "Signr. Vinci," both with four; Arne with two; Pepush ('Alexis, a Cantata'), Dr. Boyce, Pergolesi, Giardini, and Purcell with one piece.*

Like the rest of Hopkinson's library this collection shows a strong inclination toward the Italians. If the enumeration of the composers represented in this volume must worst those who still claim that only ditties and psalm tunes were known in Colonial America, very much more so Hopkinson's book of ' Lessons,' already mentioned.

It is a quarto volume of 178 pages, mainly in Hopkinson's manuscript, and containing mostly pieces arranged for the harpsichord. But some were intended for the organ and several numbers require considerable technical ability. The book abounds in Airs, Dances, Lessons, Overtures, Concertos, Minuets, and Marches. The majority of the compositions is anonymous, but the authors mentioned are quite formidable:

Haendel (who predominates), Scarlatti, Abel, Stamitz, Vivaldi, Galuppi, Pugnani, Stanley, Smith, Pasquali, Valentini, Giardini, Corelli, Geminiani, Bremner, Lord Kelly. †

---

* *Vinci,* Leonardo, 1690-1732, celebrated opera composer of the Neapolitan school.

Arne, Thomas Augustine, generally known as Dr. Arne, 1710-1778, one of the most famous English composers, author of ' Rule Britannia.'

Pepush, John Christopher, 1667-1752, celebrated English composer and musical essayist, best known as composer of Gay's ' Beggar's Opera ' (1727).

Boyce, William, 1710-1779, English composer of standing.

Pergolesi, Giovanni Battista, 1710-1736, one of the stars of the Neapolitan school of composers; wrote his masterpiece, the comic opera ' La Serva Padrona,' at the age of twenty-three; his swan-song, the ' Stabat Mater,' is still occasionally performed.

Giardini, Felice de, 1716-1796, once celebrated as violin virtuoso and composer.

Purcell, Henry, (1658)-1695, without doubt the greatest English composer.

† *Scarlatti,* either Alessandro, 1659-1725, the socalled founder of the Neapolitan school of composers, a genius of enormous productivity, or Domenico, his son, (1683 or 1685)-1757, hardly less famous as composer for the harpsichord.

Vivaldi, Antonio, (ca. 1690)-1743, celebrated Italian composer of chamber-music; his influence upon Johann Sebastian Bach is well known.

Galuppi, Baldassare, 1706-1784, one of the most original Italian composers of comic opera.

Pugnani, Gaetano, 1731-1798, celebrated Italian violin virtuoso and gifted composer of instrumental music.

Pasquali, Nicolo, d. 1757, Italian composer of reputation, emigrated to Edinburgh.

Valentini, Giuseppe, ?, violin virtuoso and composer.

Corelli, Arcangelo, 1653-1713, classic composer for the violin.

Geminiani, Francesco, 1680-1762, important violin virtuoso, composer, pedagogue, and essayist.

Abel, Karl Friedrich, 1725-1787, famous German composer, favorite of the English public.

Stamitz, Johann Karl, 1717-1761, German composer of unusual talent, now underestimated.

Stanley, John, 1713-1786, gifted English composer, highly esteemed by Haendel.

Smith, John Christopher, 1712-1795, German composer of repute (*recte* Johann Christoph. Schmid) settled in England.

Lord *Kelly.* Kellie, Thomas Alexander Erskine, sixth Earl of, Scottish amateur musician, violinist, composer (1732-1781). He studied music in Germany under Stamitz.

Bremner, the already mentioned composer and organist.

(These notes taken mainly from Riemann and Brown and Stratton.)

In order not to arouse the suspicion as if I were exaggerating Hopkinson's familiarity with the famous masters of his time I copy from the ' General Index ' the group of

Overtures & Concerto's.

Corelli's 10th Concerto
Overture in Samson
    in Rodelinda
Concerto by Geminiani
    by Kelleri [sic]
    by Vivaldi, the 5th.
Overture in Otho
    in Alima
Stanley's 5th Concerto
    6th   "
Overture by Ld. Kelly
    by Abel
    by Stamitz
    in Atalanta. *

Passing from the manuscript collections to printed works, once owned by Francis Hopkinson and now in possession of his grandson, we notice :

Longman, Lucky & Co.'s collection of *Periodical Overtures* for the Harpsichord No. I–IX.
Six Divertiments for the Harpsichord and Violin composed by Pietro Guglielmi. †
Six Sonatas for the Piano Forte or Harpsichord. Composed by Frederick Theodor Schumann. Opera 5th London. ‡
Handel's Songs, selected from the Oratorios . . Printed by J. Walsh.
XII Concerti Grossi op. 6. by Arcangelo Corelli. Printed by J. Walsh. London.
    Vivaldi's most *celebrated Concertos* in all their parts for Violins and other Instruments with a Thorough Bass for the Harpsichord. Composed by Antonio Vivaldi. Opera Terza. London. Printed for J. Walsh.
    Giuseppe Matteo Alberti's Concerto's for three Violins, an Alto Viola and a Thorough Bass for the Harpsichord or Bass Violin. Opera Prima.§

Of course, Francis Hopkinson did not collect his entire musical library, of which the volumes mentioned are said to have formed a small part only, during his musical apprenticeship. Very likely he purchased a number of works from Robert Bremner when in England during the years 1766 and 1767. As his residence abroad certainly

---

* 'Rodelinda,' Italian opera, either by Perti (1710), Canuti (1724), Haendel (1725), Veracini (1744).
  ' Otho,' Italian operas of this name quite numerous, this overture probably from Haendel's work (1722).
  'Aleina, probably Haendel's opera by this name (1735).
  'Atalanta,' probably Haendel's opera (1736).
  † *Guglielmi*, Pietro, 1727–1804, best known as prolific opera composer.
  ‡ *Schumann*, Frederick Theodor.
  § *Alberti*, Giuseppe Matteo, b. 1685, about 1713 violinist at San Petronio in Bologna, 1721 president of the famous Philharmonic Academy there.

helped to refine his tastes and broaden his knowledge, the few musical data which are to be gleaned from his letters may find a place here. *

It will be seen in a later chapter that Hopkinson was engaged in 1764 to translate the ' Psalms of David ' from the Dutch into English for the use of the Reformed Protestant Dutch Church in New York City. He finished the work in 1765 and received £145 pounds New York currency, which he intended " to keep as a body reserve " in case he should go to England. This intention he carried out in the following year. He landed in London Derry and remained there a few days with a friend of his family, Mr. Conyngham, before continuing his voyage.

Under date of " Derry July 2, 1766," he wrote a charming letter to his mother, and among other things we read :

I am much pleased with the Church here, it is a large Gothic Building very venerable for its Age and solemn Appearance ; it has a very good Organ but so wretchedly out of order, that it is not fit to be used, having never been tuned since it was first erected which is 16 years ago—nevertheless it is made to squeal out most shocking Music, every time divine Service is performed . . .

He then describes with a good deal of humor the procession to Church and continues :

I dined the other Day at a Relation's of Mr. Conyngham's where among other good things we had a *Turbet* which is a Fish highly esteemed and very rare—it is indeed very delicate eating—whilst we sat at Table a blind Man was playing most melodiously on the Irish Harp, which diverted me much—I believe he played for two Hours without ceasing— . . .

In a letter to his mother dated " Dublin July 12th, 1766," he adopted a policy which before him and after him many a busy sight-seeing son has employed. He says :

It would be too tedious to give you a Description of all these Places, and of all the other things worth of notice which I am like to see before I get home, by Way of Letter. I must therefore defer that Pleasure till my Return.

Fortunately he did not consider it too tedious to add :

I happened yesterday in a Coffee House to meet with a Gentleman whom I knew at Phila. Glad was I to see anything I had seen before.—His Name is Mr. Flanagan ; *he used to come sometimes to my concerts—*

From Dublin he proceeded to London. Here, as a letter written to his mother on August 4th tells us, he was received by Benjamin

---

* All in possession of Mr. Oliver Hopkinson.

West, the famous artist, a friend of his family, " with the utmost cordiality," and he was invited by John Penn, but illness prevented him from calling. That his friend and master James Bremner had recommended him to his relatives in London would appear from the following passus :

> Mrs. Bremner has also treated me with great civility; but Mr. Bremner is gone to Scotland so that I have not seen him . . . *

They became acquainted later on and a friendship sprang up between them which lasted for many years. Bremner seems to have furnished Hopkinson with his publications and otherwise to have transacted business for him. But their correspondence was not limited to personal or commercial matters. The two men, both remarkable in their way, apparently exchanged their ideas on every topic of human interest, in particular, of course, on music. I infer this from two letters written by Bremner to Francis Hopkinson, now in possession of Mr. Oliver Hopkinson. Though they fall in a period very much later than the young Colonial's trip abroad, I submit them to the reader in this place for want of a more convenient opportunity.

Under date of " London 5 Feby., 1785," Robert Bremner wrote :

> My dear sir
>   Disappointments seldom ruffle my temper but I cannot help acknowledging of being much hurt when I found you had returned the cases of music. You certainly could find some worthy Bookseller or Stationer that would take them in on sale, or return which was the terms they were sent upon ; and as one third profit was allowed on what he sold he might gain but could not lose by the affair. You acknowledge that some of the favorite works you could have disposed of and perhaps they are wanted there, this might have prevailed on you to let the goods rest there 'till I wrote about them. The fact is that I hate to see any goods entering my shop that has once gone out of it, and had our unfeeling Custom House gentry allowed them to remain in the ship, they would have been your guests a second time; and as it is they shall remain unopened till I have the pleasure of hearing from you.

---

* *Bremner*, Robert, musician and publisher, was born in Scotland about 1720 [1713]. He was a pupil of Geminiani and taught music in Edinburgh. On December 13, 1753, he gave a concert in the High School, Leith. He commenced business as a music seller and publisher at the Golden Harp, opposite the Head of Blackfryars Wynd, Edinburgh, in 1754; in 1755 he changed his sign to the Harp and Hautboy ; and in 1759 he removed to another shop in the High Street. He removed to London and opened a shop with the Harp and Hautboy sign, in the Strand, opposite the Somerset House, in 1762. Both businesses were carried on till his death, the Edinburgh one being managed by John Bryson, who succeeded him. He died at Kensington Lore, London, on May 12, 1789.

Messrs. Brown and Stratton, from the valuable ' British Musical Biography ' of whom I have copied these lines, mention about a dozen works by Robert Bremner, mostly collections of Scotch songs and dances. Robert Eitner in his monumental 'Quellen Lexikon' enumerates works. To which of these Bremner alludes in his letter I am not able to say as most of them are undated. It might have been ' the Harpsichord or Spinnet Miscellany.' London, dated by Brown and Stratton [1760], by Eitner " c. 1763." Bremner's ' Some Thoughts on the performance of Concert Music' were prefixed to the undated Quartets op. 6, by Christoph Schetky (1740–1773).

In your letter you observe that there was too great a proportion of expensive Concert music and unknown authors. That my catalogue is the most substantial one in the world cannot be denied and for that very reason its contents ought to be seen in your new world. Therefore without making any plea of my being out of pocket by purchasing the works of other printers for your order, with freight and custom house expenses and I request your friendship in finding some worthy dealer there to whom I may consign them on the terms above mentioned for why should not my good works be seen there as well as the rubbish of others. Had this been done at first it would not have left our account unsettled as you apprehend, for I should have immediately transferred the charge from you to him who received them, but enough of this, only oblige me and find an open door for them for I cannot think of opening out and distributing them into their different appartments. Had they gone to the bottom in going out tho' not insured I believe I should not have been half so much shaggreen'd. I must here declare that the hint given about returning a part of the price for your invention was not from Broadwood but generated in my brain because I thought it hard for him to lose all seeing he could reap no advantage by it. I however saw him lately and read your sentiments on it to him when he expressed himself strongly in your favor as a man of great genius and said he would not receive a farthing back, for said he, it is my fault if I do not make use of it, and I prefer the friendship of so discerning a gentleman to triple the sum. Your observation is just in calling him the best Harpsichord maker in the world for so he is.

I hope Genl. Reed arrived safe and found all well, pray offer my best compts. to that gentleman.

It is three weeks since I heard of your Brother's family they were then well, the short days and cold weather prevent that intercourse between friends at a distance that could be wished for, however if their minds are in unity personal absence is of no great importance.

Having been ordered to sleep out of town this winter, I have stood it hitherto pretty well owing I suppose greatly to my walking in to dinner dayly and out again before dark. As I have only a lodging the long evenings lay heavy on my spirits 'till at last it came into my [?] to resume a pursuit of three years standing and of which I had dropt all thoughts long ago. It has made me exceedingly happy and I hope will you provided that the finest Harpsichord music that ever was can give you pleasure. There is none of it out yet but will be next ship when I shall send Mrs. Pen and yourself a specimen of it.

As I know your perse [verance?] is fond of investigating nature especially where music is concerned, I wish for your opinion about sound, not about its effects but what it really is in itself. I have discoursed many of our Philosophers about it and they lead me I think astray as may be seen in a note on page 2 of the thoughts on the performance of Concert-music by then calling it the agitations of the air which I now think must be nonsense, for air seems only a vehicle to every sound; and fish may as well be said to be only water and Birds air, because they float in those elements as suppose sound to be air because it floats in air.

Write me of this and believe me to be with my best wishes,

My Dear Sir,

Your unfeigned friend and sert.,

Robert Bremner.

London 5, Feb'y, 1785.

Inclosed I send the certificate requested and also the Bill of Lading discharged in case of need.

Bremner's second letter, though undated, apparently followed Hopkinson's reply to the one quoted above :

My much esteemed friend.

It is cruel in you to be so heavy on me. You write me from to time a parcel of undigested thoughts and want my opinion of them. You must suppose me a very clever fellow indeed if you think that my brain is capable of investigating and finding out the beauties and defects of all your musical speculations. Twenty years ago my head was as full of reveries as an egg is full of meat. I saw ten thousand defects that wanted remedying; sat up late and rose early writing to individuals and for newspapers, and wondered that all the world was not as much interested in those matters as I was. But experience has now taught me that the world has a way of its own which it will not be put out of, and therefore it shall take its own way for me. Perhaps experience will in time show you the fruitliness of your labours as it has done me. I am however very happy when I can be of any service to an individual, but nothing shall induce me to search for public praise.

You have a slap at me for my *universal love*, was your sound judgment and able pen to make that subject [?] ; (for I see they must be employed). You might in time have much more cause to rejoice than if you made leaves of trees to sing like Farinella [sic], and falls of water like Polyphemus. I am not nevertheless against your trying experiments for your own pleasure and to improve your instrument by them if possible but I wished you to take no further notice of them because it is not pleasant to have one's child vilified.

I have been from home four months and on my return saw Broadwood, who told me that your invention was offered to him but that it would not do, or it would be too expensive I forget which? Having now given all the answer I ever shall to the speculative parts of your letters hitherto received, except that I entirely agree with you about Swedenborg, whose works I have often tryed to read but cannot from their being so visionary. I shall now proceed to business.

And on this head I am at a loss what to say. That the expenses and damage was as represented you may be assured of. The Forte-piano strings were entirely spoiled. Fiddle strings damaged and as to the music I considered that only as the loss of paper and print it being of my own publishing. But I think it rather hard for me to sustain all this loss, yet when I consider that I myself gave the first hint that led to this disaster and that you did everything that you thought for the best. I know not what to do unless as follows. Inclosed you have a catalogue of my publications, pick eight or ten pounds worth out of it that you think you can dispose of amongst your friends there or to your music shopkeeper. If this can be done I will get something towards the loss and you will be nothing out of pocket for I shall make no further claim whatever on account of this unlucky affair and that you may still be the less liable to any loss by this transaction, if your order amounts to fifteen pounds at catalogue price, I shall charge you but ten pounds for it, the extra five pounds worth I allow as profit for the trouble of disposing of it. Should this plan meet with your approbation send your order as soon as possible because I have some thoughts of getting out of shopkeeping. Not that I mean to drop all business; My friends will not hear of that for fear I get hipped; I am now, on account of health, obliged to sleep from home every night which divides me from my children, therefore my intended plan is to drop the shop and take a house some where about the skirts of the town and to execute in the best manner I can such orders as my friends may choose to intrust me with, but all this to yourself, for the plan is not as yet digested.

I was very angry with your friends here for writing you about our affairs. All I said was that your returning all the goods without waiting for orders was a proof that your brain was as full of flights as ever. I told them they should not have meddled betwixt us, but have let us fight our own battles, however it is now over, therefore I think no more of it. With regard to my friendship, you know little of me if you think that such a trifle as this could alter it. I shall always esteem you do as you will, and as a proof of it should you not like to take the trouble of finding an open door for the music before mentioned I here renounce having any claim whatever on you on account of the goods returned.

To fill up my paper, let me in return to your abuse of my indolence, take you to task for taking no notice of my question about sound. I should like to put another which is this. How it comes to pass that man is the only creature that has a thirst of knowledge? but as you say, my speculations afford you no entertainment and therefore I despair of any answer.

I dined to-day with your country-man Parson Cooms, when expressing my fondness for two sermons by Dr. Cudworth, printed at the end of his Intellectual System and wishing to have them apart, he told me that Dr. Inglis rector of New York Churches had reprinted those sermons there. I wish you to read them. He points out every deviation from truth in the clearest manner, which he could not do but by seeing and knowing the truth. A scholar can only discover the ignorance of those who are not schooled. I wish you to send 2 or 3 of them. I am looking for a music master for you.
Yours affectionately,
R. Bremner.

The terminal point of Francis Hopkinson's voyage to England in 1766 was the magnificent Hartlebury Castle, where his uncle the Lord Bishop of Worcester resided with his sister Mrs. Johnson, whom Francis calls " our Couzin." Arriving there early in August the young Colonial was cordially received by the Bishop. Of this reception, of his delight of the surroundings, then again of his home-sickness and of his anxiety concerning the future, the letters which he wrote to his mother give a vivid description but they seldom relate to music. Some of his letters might have been lost, but in those extant I find one musical item only. However this is of some importance. It stands in a letter forwarded home from London, where he had gone " shopping," under date of Sept. 23, 1766 :

From thence [London] I went to Glocester, where I had the Pleasure of hearing the *Messiah* and other solemn Pieces of Musick performed by the best Hands.

CHAPTER III.

FRANCIS HOPKINSON'S CONCERTS.

The most interesting item in the extracts from Francis Hopkinson's letters to his mother is the allusion to his concerts. These, of course, must have taken place before his departure to England. The passus quoted unfortunately is the only direct information we have concerning his career as concert-manager or performer. But by combining with it other *quasi* anonymous data we might be able to trace his concerts.

Hopkinson might have appeared for the first time before a public larger than the circle of his relatives and personal friends when the altered 'Masque of Alfred the Great' was performed at the College Hall of Philadelphia as an 'Oratorial Exercise.'

This happened in January, 1757. The "instrumental parts" of Arne's music were played by some "gentlemen," the vocal parts were sung by several young ladies. It is reasonable to suppose that Francis Hopkinson, still an undergraduate, was chosen to accompany the chorusses and songs on the harpsichord.*

---

* Compare Pa. Gaz. Jan. 20, 27. Feb. 3, 10, 1757. Two of the young ladies were addressed by admirers of their performance with poetical effusions. The one was Francis' sister, Miss Hopkinson, to whom " on her excellent performance of the vocal parts " Jacob Duché, jun., afterwards her husband, dedicated a poem beginning :

> " To thee sweet Harmonist ! in grateful lays
> A Kindred muse the softest tribute pays
> Bids every art with every grace combine
> For thy fair brow the laureate wreathe to twine."

The other young lady was a Miss Lawrence. Francis Hopkinson evidently was so charmed by her voice and beauty that he could not but immediately mount good-hearted Pegasus and deliver in her praise the following lines which, at least, have the merit of being better than those of Jacob Duché, the future brother-in-law.

> "TO MISS LAWRENCE, ON THE SAME.

> The pleasing task, sweet maid ! be mine,
> To spread thy growing fame ;
> For early virtue such as thine,
> An early honour claims.

The same duty might have fallen on him in the performance at the theatre on Society Hill, Dec. 27, 1759.

We read in the Pa. Gaz., for the same day :

By Permission and by particular Desire Towards the raising a Fund for purchasing an Organ to the College Hall in this City and instructing the Charity Children in Psalmody. At the theatre on Society Hill, this evening will be presented the interesting History of George *Barnwell* . . .

Before the Play and between the Acts several celebrated Pieces of Concert Music will be performed by some Gentlemen of this city, who have kindly consented to promote the Design of this Entertainment ; for which Purpose a neat Harpsichord will be provided.

Also a Prologue in praise of MUSIC will be spoken by Mr. Hallam and an occasional Epilogue by Mr. Douglass.

To which will be added a Farce called *Lethe*, or Aesop in the Shade—

N. B.—As this Benefit is wholly intended for improving our Youth in the divine Art of PSALMODY and CHURCH MUSIC in order to render the Entertainment of the Town more compleat at Commencements and other public occasions in our College, it is not doubted but it will meet with all due encouragement from the inhabitants of this Place.

To begin exactly at Six o'clock.

Tickets to be had at Mr. Dunlap, Mr. Henry and of several gentlemen.

That Francis Hopkinson was one of the gentlemen to promote the design, there can be no doubt, since we know that he was the author of the ' Prologue in Praise of Music,' spoken by Mr. Hallam on this occasion. Nor do we doubt that he, too, figured among the gentlemen who performed celebrated pieces of concert music, and the provision of a neat harpsichord would indicate his functions.

But neither his appearance on this occasion nor at commencement during the following years would have been styled by him " my concerts." Unless these were musical at-homes, we must depend

---

'Twas nobly done to lend thy voice,
And soft harmonious song ;
When the great theme was freedom's choice
That warbled from thy tongue.
Yet, not the tuneful voice you lent,
Or song we most admire ;
Good nature, and the good intent
A nobler praise require.
Tho' just the fair musician's boast,
Of yet unrivalled skill ;
'Tis not the *deed* obliges most,
The virtue's in the *will*.
Thus still proceed in virtue's sphere,
Above all pride to shine ;
So to the good thou'lt still be dear
Still favor'd by the mind.

Yours, etc.,

Phil. Feb. 1, 1757.   F. Hopkinson.''

These two poems were printed in the Columbian Magazine, Phila., March, 1792.

upon the newspapers in order to discover the entertainments to which
he was alluding.

After the two concerts given at Philadelphia in 1757 we do not
find any recorded until 1764.

In this year, on January 12th, the Pa. Gaz. printed the following
advertisement :

> Philadelphia, January 12, 1764.
>
> On Thursday, the 19th instant, at the Assembly Room in Lodge Alley, will be performed a *Concert of Musick*, to be continued every other Thursday, till the 24th of May, following.
>
> No more than 70 Subscribers will be admitted, and each, on paying Three Pounds for the Season, to have one Lady's Ticket, to be disposed of every Concert Night, as he thinks proper. Subscriptions are taken in at Messieurs Rivington and Brown's Store, and by Mr. Bremner, at Mr. Glover Hunt's, in Market street, near the London Coffee House.
>
> N. B. The Concert to begin precisely at 6 o'clock.

Unless James Bremner arranged these fortnightly subscription
concerts we might argue, on the basis of Francis Hopkinson's letter to
his mother, that he was the moving spirit of the enterprise.

It seems to have met with the favor of the subscribers, for a second
season was thus advertised in the Pa. Journal on Nov. 1, 1764 :

> SUBSCRIPTION CONCERT, at the Assembly Room in Lodge Alley, begins on Thursday the 8th day of November next and to continue every other Thursday 'till the 14th of March following.
>
> Each subscriber on paying Three Pounds to be intituled to two Ladies tickets for the season. Subscriptions are taken in at Messrs. Rivington and Brown's bookstore . . .
>
> The Concert to begin precisely at Six o'Clock in the Evening.

The subscription concerts seem not to have been continued during
the winter of 1765, at least I have found no information to that effect.

Unfortunately it became customary to advertise the date only of
regular subscription concerts and not their programs, a habit which is
easily explained. They were not public entertainments but accessible
only, as a rule, to the subscribers, and therefore it was hardly necessary
to publish the programs in the newspapers. Programs, in the majority
of instances, are traceable only in the papers if a public concert was
arranged for the benefit of individual professional musicians.

For these reasons we shall never know exactly—unless the programs
are extant in some collection of early play bills and the like—
what works were performed and who performed them at these concerts.
If the programs were arranged by Francis Hopkinson, his library

would furnish a clue to the character of the compositions played and we might argue that the subscribers had ample opportunity for becoming familiar with

a Variety of the most celebrated Pieces now in Taste,

as Stephen Forrage expressed himself when advertising "A Concert of Music," to take place on Dec. 31st, 1764,

for the benefit of Mr. Forrage and others, Assistant Performers at the Subscription Concert in this city.

In this concert, by the way, Forrage introduced

the famous ARMONICA, or Musical Glasses, so much admired for their great Sweetness and Delicacy of its Tone.*

Naturally all these concerts, either public or private, resemble one another. Now the reader will recollect the concert given at the College Hall in April, 1765, under the direction of Mr. Bremner for the benefit of the Boys and Girls Charity School. Of this entertainment not alone the very characteristic advertisement is on record but also the printed " Plan," or program is extant. By submitting the two items a clear idea of the character of Hopkinson's subscription concerts may be gained and I am sure of the reader's surprise on seeing such remarkable concert programs performed in Colonial Philadelphia.

The tenor of the advertisement is so interesting as to deserve to be copied in full. It appeared thus in the Pa. Gaz. on April 4, 1765:

College of Philadelphia, April 4, 1765.
For the Benefit of the Boys and Girls Charity School.
On Wednesday Evening next there will be a Performance of Solemn Music, vocal and instrumental, in the College Hall, under the Direction of Mr. BREMNER. The vocal Parts, chiefly by young Gentlemen educated in this Seminary, and the Words suited to the Place and Occasion, being paraphrased from the Prophets, and other Places of Scripture, upon the Plan of the musical performances in Cathedral's, etc. for public charities in England.

The *Chorus* and other sublime Passages of the *Music* will be accompanied by the *Organ*, and the Intervals filled up with a few Orations by some of the Students.

It is hoped that the Merit of the Performance as well as the Nature of the Charity, by which several Hundreds of destitute Youths for more than 15 years past, have at a great Expense received the Benefits of Education, and been rendered useful to the Community, will entitle this Design to a general Countenance.

The Hall will be properly illuminated and the Music so disposed, that the Galleries and the Body of the House will be equally advantageous for hearing. The Performance will begin precisely at Six o'Clock, and there will be no Admittance but by Ticket, and

---

*Pa. Gaz. Dec. 27, 1764. The invention of the "Armonica" is generally attributed to Benjamin Franklin. As a matter of fact, Franklin only improved the instrument.

through the great South Door, which will be opened at Five. Any Persons desiring a printed Copy of the Words to be sung, may have the same gratis, on Delivery of their Tickets at the Door, and Care will be taken that the greatest Order be preserved.

Tickets, at one Dollar each, to be had of Mr. Kinnersly, Mr. Bremner, and Mr. Bradford, or by sending to any of the Trustees or Masters.

On April 18 the Pa. Gaz. reported that:

The whole was conducted with great Order and Decorum, to the Satisfaction of a polite and numerous Audience. Thirty Pounds was raised for the Benefit of the Charity Schools belonging to the said College.

The Persons who so desired received a printed copy of

The Plan of a Performance of Solemn Musick;

to be in the Hall of the College of Philadelphia, on Wednesday Evening April 10th, 1765, for the Benefit of the Charity School.

Oration.

Act I.

Overture, *Stamitz*

Air. Prov. iii. from ver. 13 to 17, and iv, 8

Richer far is Wisdom's Store,
Than from Mines of *Gold* can flow ;
Brighter is her heavenly Lore,
Than the Ruby's proudest Glow.
Thrice happy he, whose youthful Mind
Seeks in her Courts his joyful find !

II

Her right Hand gives *length* of Days,
Honour in her Left she bears ;
Pleasure waits on all her Ways
Peace in all her paths appears.
Around their Brows, who her embrace,
Her Hand a Wreathe divine shall place.

Sixth Concerto, *Geminiani.*

Oration.

Act II.

Solo, on the Violin

Overture, Earl of *Kelly*

Air. Isaiah lv. 1. 2. John vii. 12

Parted from celestial Truth,
Science is but empty show ;
Come to God in early youth ;
Where the living Fountains flow !

Come and drink the waters *free ;*
Why in fruitless Searches toil?
Wisdom's ever-blooming Tree
Loves to Spread in Virtue's Soil.

Second Overture, *Martini*

Oration.

Act III.

Overture in Artaxerxes; *Arne.*

Sonata on the Harpsichord.

Chorus Ps. XLVI. from ver. 1 to 5.

God is King ! from Day to Day,
Let each Tongue his Praise resound ;
To each Land his Fame convey,
Tell it to the Heathen round.

II

Tell them, from those Gods to fly,
By their erring Lips ador'd ;
He who made yon radiant Sky,
Thron'd in Glory, is the Lord.
Hallelujah ! Let us Sing ;
God made the Skies, is King ! *

The " Subscription Concerts " of which Francis Hopkinson seems to have been the manager probably were not interspersed with choral music, but would best be classified, to use a modern term, as soirées of chamber-music. The works which called for the largest number of performers certainly were the Concerti Grossi, concertos for several solo-instruments with orchestra-accompaniment. To play these not more than a dozen musicians were required, and this number could easily have been recruited among the gentlemen-amateurs and professional musicians of Philadelphia. Extracting the names and their specialty from the newspaper advertisements we might form the following idea of the orchestra :

Francis Hopkinson would preside at the harpsichord. The strings would be represented by James Bremner, Stephen Forrage, John Schneider, Governor John Penn † and two or three other amateurs. When occasion called for it, John Schneider would play the French horn, Ernst Barnard, George D'Eissenburg or, if he still resided at Philadelphia, John Stadler the German flute ; and that oboists were to be had in the Quaker City we know from the first chapter.

Amusingly primitive as all this may seem to readers not historically trained, it was a beginning, and the seventy subscribers certainly enjoyed the music as much if not more than hundreds and thousands of those who fill a modern concert-hall and listen attentively to music much of which, though now considered immortal, will be forgotten as have been forgotten the compositions by such gifted men as Valentini, Corelli, Pugnani, Stanley, Geminiani, etc., played by Hopkinson, his friends and the "Assistant Performers." ‡

---

* Copied from a copy at the Library Co. of Phila. (t. p. v. bl ; p. 3–4.)

† John *Penn*, Lieutenant-Governor of Pennsylvania, friend of Francis Hopkinson, and amateur musician, was born in London 1729 and died in Bucks County, Pa., in 1795.

‡ I doubt very much whether Hopkinson, in anticipation of modern methods, permitted the "brand" of his harpsichord to be pointed in huge letters toward the audience like guns of a battleship. At any rate he seems not to have been very well satisfied with his instrument. I infer this from the fact that

After his return from England Francis Hopkinson again seems to have taken up the idea of arranging concerts. Two letters exchanged between him and his friend John Penn are extant giving information to this effect.

Penn embarked for England on May 4, 1771, and returned in August, 1773. Francis Hopkinson addressed a very interesting letter " To the Hon'ble John Penn, Esq., Cavendish Square, London, pr. Capt. Sparks," under date of " Philad'a Oct. 17th 1771." It contains the following passus which is of importance for my narrative :

> When I was in London I was surprised and pleas'd at the objects which daily attracted my Notice ; but that Surprise would have been without any Mixture of Pleasure had not the Thought being ever before me of shortly returning to my native Land—then more amiable and dear to me than ever—All partiality aside I do sincerely believe that every *real* Comfort in Life may be enjoyed here in great Perfection.
>
> I had two Lines and an half from Mr. Bremner. I hope he sells a great deal of Music—he is always so very *busy* when he writes to me that one would think all London had crowded about his Doors to buy Ballads—He is a very good Friend ; but a wretched Correspondent.—
>
> *Music* is at present in a very deplorable Condition here—Sigr. *Gualdo* lies in Chains in one of the Cells of the Pennsylva. Hospital; and poor *Butho* [?] was kill'd a few Weeks ago by a Fall from his House—Except *Forage* and myself I don't know a single Votary the Goddess hath in this large City.—I w[ish] you would send some poor Devil ov[er here to] take the Church Organ, and teach the [young] Misses to play Foot's Minuet and the Re[gimental?] March on the Spinnet—I think a tolera[ble good] Master would find Encouragement.*

In his reply, dated " Cavendish Square, June 26th 1772," John Penn remarked :

> . . . I propose to be in Philadelphia next Summer; I cannot precisely fix the time, as that must depend a good deal upon the sailing of the Ships. I wish to was there now, for I do not see what good I am likely to do by staying here, when my Inclination leads me so strongly to return to America. The best proof I can give you of the

---

he ordered a Kirkman harpsichord in 1765. Mr. Oliver Hopkinson possesses a letter which is interesting not alone in this respect but for the manner in which commercial transactions were made in Colonial days. It is a letter by Benjamin West, the artist, who wrote to Francis Hopkinson under date of " London, Aug'st 1765 " as follows :

". . . Doubtless you will have been frightened when Capt. Friend arrived in Philadelphia without bringing along with him your Harpsichord. but the Truth is Mr. Kirkman's great Hurry of Busyness preventing his getting it quite ready at that Time the Ship sailed but as I was determined to take no exchise and have it sent over by Budden it was got ready and put on Board and hope it will get safe the other side Seas. The Bill you have sent to my care will not be accepted as Mr. Hulston tell me he can do nothing with it and the money comeing to you in that office must be received by a Power of Attorney which you must send over to me or him but till then he knows nothing what sum of money is coming to you. but as I was determined this should be no denial to the Harpsichord's going I have settled that Point with Mr. Kirkman so you'll be so good as to forward the Bills or the Power as my word is given to Mr. Kirkman . . ."

*The letter (in Hopkinson's autograph) is to be found in the New York Public Library in Dr. Thos. Addis Emmet's costly ' History of the Inception and Drafting of the Declaration of Independence,' which is more or less a collection of autographs and portraits of all the " Signers."

preference I give to your part of the world will appear by my fixing my Standard at or somewhere near Philadelphia, when I hope your harpsichord and my Fiddle will again join in Concert.

I sympathize with you upon the deplorable state of Music in Phila.: I even think poor Gualdo a great loss. I wish I could relieve you but I have no acquaintance with any poor fellow that would venture to go to America upon an uncertainty. It is scandalous the Church people will not enter on to a Subscription for a number of years to support a good organist or at least to make it worth his while to go over. If a thing of this kind could be set on foot and the Subscribers would be honest enough [. . ?] no doubt Mr. Bremner could be induced to return among you, which must be more agreeable at any rate, than having a stranger you know nothing about, and who may be a low-lived fellow, we cannot be upon the same footing with that we can with him. I am very sorry for the fate of poor Butho [?] I believe he was an honest fellow though he often occasioned much discord in our small Concerts . . .*

These two letters will seem rather mysterious to readers not familiar with the musical life at Philadelphia about the year 1770. A few points however stand forth: The "very deplorable condition" of music in the Quaker City in 1771; the "small concerts" during Penn's residence there; and the misfortunes of "Sigr. Gualdo."

In his 'Record of the Opera in Philadelphia' (1884. Phila. p. 6) W. G. Armstrong writes:

Even in the last century it was usual for families to have meetings at their houses for their improvement in music. Governor Penn, who played the violin, had musical *soirées* every Sunday evening at his house in South Third Street during a portion of the year. Dr. Adam Kuhn, himself an amateur, attended them . . .

Mr. Penn's fiddle and Francis Hopkinson's harpsichord joined in concert at these *soirées*, I presume. But were these the "small concerts" in which poor honest Butho often occasioned so much discord, or were they of a more public character and when did they take place? Queries which I am not able to answer positively, except that the assistance of Gualdo, the dates of the correspondence and the fact of Hopkinson's call on Governor Penn 1766 in London prove that they were performed after his and Penn's return from England, between 1767 and 1770.

Moreover, orchestral chamber-music would have been quite impossible in those days without the assistance of "gentlemen-performers," not alone in Philadelphia, but in many a provincial town of Europe. Even to-day provincial orchestras both in Europe and America frequently have to rely upon the assistance of amateurs. To play the German flute, harpsichord, or violin in subscription-concerts could not have been considered unbecoming to a "gentleman," as the entertain-

---

* This letter is in possession of Mr. Oliver Hopkinson. Though unsigned there can be no doubt that it was Penn's answer to Hopkinson.

ments were of a more or less private nature arranged principally by
the amateurs for their own amusement and improvement and resemb-
ling to a certain extent the concerts of the many philharmonic
academies in Italy, for instance, or of many a "collegium musicum"
in Germany.

The same applies to the really public concerts, given by professional musicians for their own benefit. However unwilling the aristo-
cratic Colonials were to put themselves on an equal social footing with
a poor devil of musician, they hesitated not to lend a helping hand for
his "Benefit" if he were "an honest fellow."

But to resume the narrative, was the condition of music at Philadelphia really so deplorable, notwithstanding the fact that the Goddess
had such enthusiastic votaries like Penn and Hopkinson?

It would be preposterous to contradict these two gentlemen, who
certainly knew more of the true state of affairs than a historian will
ever know from reconstruction and combination of recorded data.
But they were familiar with conditions in England. Being sincere
lovers of music they would naturally deplore the contrast between
things abroad and at home, would exaggerate matters in their correspondence, as we all are inclined to do in similar cases; would expect
more of Philadelphia than the city possibly could give, and would see
night instead of dawn.

To begin with, Philadelphians had ample opportunity to enjoy
operatic music during the theatrical seasons from Nov. 21st, 1766,
to July 6, 1767; Sept. 24 to Nov. 23, 1767; Oct. 21, 1768, to Jan. 6,
1769; Nov. 8, 1769, to May 24, 1770; Oct. 28, 1772, to March 31,
1773.

The performances took place at Mr. Douglass' newly built "South-
wark Theatre," and the company, known later on under the name of
the "Old American Company," was in every respect remarkable.

Needless to say, the opponents of the theatre tried their best to
undermine the performances, but it was John Penn himself who, in his
capacity as Governor, frustrated the attacks by never interfering with
the players. The repertoire of musical farces and ballad operas consisted mainly of Gay-Pepush's 'Beggar's Opera'; Coffey's 'Devil to
Pay, or, the Wives Metamorphosed'; Cibber's 'Damon and Phillida';
Mendez-Boyce's 'The Chaplet'; Bickerstaff-Arne's 'Love in a Village'
and 'Thomas and Sally'; Bickerstaff-Arnold's 'Maid of the Mill";
Bickerstaff-Dibdin's 'Lionel and Clarissa' and 'The Padlock'; Cibber-

Bate's 'Flora, or Hob in the Well'; Carey's 'Contrivances' and 'A Wonder, or an Honest Yorkshireman'; O'Hara's burletta of 'Midas'; Arne's masque of 'Neptun and Amphithrite'; Milton's masque of 'Comus,' Shakespeare's 'Macbeth,' both interspersed with music; and the pantomimes of 'Harlequin Collector' and Love's 'The Witches, or Harlequin Restored.'

"Singing and dancing between the acts," of course, was not missing. At times these secondary entertainments would become quite conspicuous. On June 4, 1767, for instance, was performed for the first time in Philadelphia the "musical entertainment" of 'The Chaplet,' an afterpiece to the comedy of 'The Country Lasses,' the latter being interspersed

With Entertainments, viz.

In Act I.   The Sheep-shearing Song, by Mr. Woolls.
    An occasional country-dance.
End of Act I.   God save the King, by Mr. Woolls and Miss Wainwright.
End of Act II.   The Spinning Wheel, by Miss Wainwright.
End of Act III.   A Duet, written on the Marriage of the Princess Augusta and the Prince of Brunswick, composed by Dr. Arne, and sung before their Majesties.
End of Act IV.   Lovely Nancy, by Miss Wainwright.
After the Play, dancing by Mr. Mathews.

That Arne's duet was sung properly we may rely upon, since both Miss Wainwright and Mr. Woolls were known as pupils of the composer.

How lively the intercourse was between the Motherland and the Colonies, also in musical matters, will readily be seen if it is remembered that the opera of 'Love in a Village' had its first performance in England during the year 1763, at Philadelphia on March 19, 1767; 'The Maid of the Mill' in 1765, resp. Jan. 5, 1770; 'The Padlock,' 1768, resp. Nov. 6, 1769; 'Lionel and Clarissa,' 1768, resp. Dec. 14, 1772.

Not even an English public would have been dissatisfied if hearing 'Love in the Village' with the following cast, as on the "first night" in Philadelphia:

Justice Woodcock	Mr. Douglass
Hodge	Mr. Hallam
Hawthorn	Mr. Woolls
Sir William Meadows	Mr. Morris
Young Meadows	Mr. Wall
Eustace	Mr. Allyn
Rosetta	Miss Wainwright
Lucinda	Miss Hallam
Margery	Mrs. Harman
Mrs. Deborah Woodcock	Mrs. Douglass.

A critic remarked in the Pa. Gaz. that the opera was " done here beyond expectation " and that

Miss Wainwright is a very good singer and her action exceeds the famous Miss Brent; Mr. Hallam exceeds every thing in the character of *Hodge*, and Mr. Woolls almost equals Beard in *Hawthorn.*

Had previous theatrical seasons at Philadelphia been hampered from want of an orchestra, an improvement in this respect came with the year 1767, for we know from an advertisement in the Pa. Gaz. (Sept. 24) that the music was

accompanied by a Band of Music.

At any rate, the orchestra seems to have been an established institution during the season of 1769–1770. We read the following characteristic notice in the Pa. Gaz., Nov. 30, 1769 :

. . . The Orchestra, on Opera Nights, will be assisted by some musical Persons, who as they have no View but to contribute to the Entertainment of the Public, certainly claim a Protection from any Manner of Insult.

For the good name of Philadelphia we hope that the " Olympian Gods " agreed with Mr. Douglass as to the proper treatment of these " musical Persons." Still, those who witness all things human from this exalted position under the roof have their own codes of Do and Don't, and if, for instance, the frequenters of the " family circle " in modern Italy consider it necessary for the maintenance of an artistic spirit to insult, at times " substantially," orchestra, singers, and audience, we should not be too severe in judging the behavior of the Colonials, especially not, as manners were not more refined in the public theatres of Europe.

We may reasonably suppose that the same musical persons who lent a hand in the subscription concerts assisted on opera nights, occasionally under Mr. Hallam as conductor,* and if some buried diary were excavated in which Francis Hopkinson is named among these art-loving gentlemen the fact would cause us no surprise.

These remarks would be less than cursory if I left unmentioned Andrew Barton's

'new American Comic Opera of two Acts called THE DISAPPOINTMENT; OR THE FORCE OF CREDULITY.'

---

* He conducted the orchestra, when 'Comus' was performed for the first time at Philadelphia by the Old American Company on March 9, 1770. See Pa. Journal, March 8.

Under this title the libretto was published at Philadelphia in the year 1767. Leaving aside the question whether or not Andrew Barton was a pseudonym for Col. Thomas Forest of Germantown, it will be sufficient to lay stress upon the fact that 'The Disappointment' was the first opera libretto written by a native American and printed in the Colonies. It is a low-comedy, coarse in its language and obscene in some of the scenes, but throughout irresistibly comical with its brilliant persiflage of the many innocent souls who believed in the famous pirate Blackbeard's hidden treasures and who spared neither fatigue nor expense to recover them.

The work is entitled a comic opera for being interspersed with songs. Like in numerous other ballad operas, these songs are lyric, not dramatic. In fact we would not miss them at all if the opera were given as a comedy pure and simple. They were not sung to original music but, like in other ballad-operas, to popular tunes, indicated in the libretto, among them 'Yankee Doodle.'

'The Disappointment' is full of situations remarkably well calculated for stage-effect. Mr. Douglass, the manager, evidently saw this, for he accepted the play, rehearsed it and announced it for performance on April 20, 1767. But he had overlooked one important drawback. The author had given his opera so much local color that a performance would have hurt the feelings of the persons caricatured and made them victims of public derision. Warned probably by gentlemen who knew their fellow-citizens better than he, and not willing to force the wrath of influential treasure-seekers upon his company, Douglass preferred not to produce the play. He thus announced the withdrawal on April 22d.

'The Disappointment' (that was advertised for Monday), as it contains personal reflections, is unfit for the stage.

Under these circumstances we can easily imagine that Barton, from a pecuniary point of view, had not to regret the publication of his libretto!

Many years later, in 1796, a second edition of 'The Disappointment' was issued, revised and altered. It had now become an opera in three acts, the obscenities were fewer, and the language was more in keeping with polite society. On the other hand, these alterations totally robbed the play of its freshness, boldness and dramatic force.

These cursory remarks on the operatic seasons at Philadelphia from 1766 to 1773 show a distinct advance of one side of the musical life in the city, a progress which can not have been without beneficial influence upon Francis Hopkinson and which he can not have over-looked.*

Consequently he had in view concert-life only, when deploring its condition about 1771. Indeed, improvements in this respect are less perceptible than the progress in opera during the years 1767 to 1771.

Music as a trade was spreading and the art was still cultivated with success at the College of Philadelphia, but the concert-life was at a very low ebb from 1767 until late in 1769. Then we again notice an upward-tendency, and this tendency was due mostly to the efforts of "poor Gualdo."

> John Gualdo, Wine Merchant from Italy, but late from London . . . opened a Store in Walnut-street, between Second and Front Streets . . . in August 1767.†

But not until February 13–20, 1769, does Gualdo appear as a musician.

Then we read in the Pa. Chronicle the following highly charac-teristic advertisement :

> John *Gualdo* (In Front street, next door but one to the Bank Meeting House) has for Sale, a few Violins ; German Flutes; guittars; mandolins ; spinnets; clavichords ; late invented music stands; together with a variety of music strings for the violino, guittar, etc. etc. He has also engaged some able people, who under his direction, improve and repair every kind of musical instrument in neat manner and on very reasonable terms. Likewise he has a servant boy who copies music; therefore if any Gentleman or Lady should want a particular song, sonata, trio, duet, solo, minuet or country dance, they may be supplied with them, without buying the whole book, in which such song, sonata etc. might be printed.
>
> He adapts and composes music for every kind of instrument as usual. Next October at furthest, Mr. Gualdo intends to set off for Europe, where he is going to transact some particular and advantageous business for himself and other gentlemen of this town, therefore begs the favour of every person indebted to him, to make a speedy payment, and in so doing they will enable him to discharge his own debts before he leaves America, for which part of the world every free man in his right senses, should have an everlasting regard, for reasons before now quoted by gentlemen more learned than the subscriber.
>
> John GUALDO.
>
> P. S. To be sold, the time of a smart Dutch Boy, who has got four years and six months to serve, for further particulars inquire as above.

Equally interesting and of importance for an insight into Francis Hopkinson's musical surroundings is a notice which Gualdo inserted in the Pa. Journal, Sept. 21, 1769 :

---

* These notes on opera at Philadelphia have mostly been extracted from my own material. Other sources were the books by Seilhamer, Durang, Armstrong.

† Pa. Chronicle, Aug. 24–31, 1767.

John GUALDO begs to acquaint his friends and the public that he proposes to teach a few Gentlemen to play on the Violin and German flute, and a few Ladies on the Guittar or Mandolin, either at his house, in Front street near the Bank meeting, or at their places of abode.   His terms are a Guinea entrance and a Guinea a month, teaching every other day; but if any Gentleman or Lady should live at a great distance from his dwelling house, or out of town, they cannot expect to be attended, on the above terms.   He continues also to sell music, musical instruments, strings, etc. etc.

John GUALDO.

Evidently our merchant-musician had abandoned his intention " to set off to Europe." Judging from his future experiences he probably did not possess the necessary means. This is not to be regretted as it thus came to pass that Hopkinson, Penn and others improved under his leadership as orchestral-performers and promoted the cause of good music in Philadelphia.

The first concert given by John, or more correctly, as he was an Italian, Giovanni Gualdo, was announced in the Pa. Journal Nov. 9, 1769, in the following manner:

At the Assembly Room, on next Thursday, (being the sixteenth of November) will be performed a *Grand Concert of Vocal and Instrumental Musick;* with Solos played on different instruments: the concert to be directed by Mr. Gualdo, after the Italian method.

Tickets at a Dollar a piece to be had of the Waiter at the London Coffee House, and at Mr. Gualdo's in Front-street, near the Bank-meeting.   To begin exactly at half an hour after Six o'clock.

N. B. Hand Bills will be printed mentioning what pieces shall be performed in the two acts.   The evening to be ended with a ball (if agreeable to the Company) without further Expense.

As the Pa. Journal printed the program on the day of performance we are not at a great loss if none of the printed hand-bills are extant:

Act I.
Overture composed by the Earl of Kelly.
' Vain is beauty, gaudy flower,' by Miss Hallam.
Trio composed by Mr. Gualdo, first violin by Master Billy Crumpto.
' The Spinning Wheel,' by Miss Storer.
A German flute Concert, with Solos, composed by Mr. Gualdo.
A new Symphony after the present taste, composed by Mr. Gualdo.
Act II.
A new Violin Concerto with Solos, composed by Mr. Gualdo.
A Song by Mr. Wools.
A Sonata upon the Harpsichord, by Mr. Curtz.
Solo upon the Clarinet, by Mr. Hoffman, junior.
A Song by Miss Hallam.
Solo upon the Mandolino, by Mr. Gualdo.
Overture, composed by the Earl of Kelly.

Truly a program worth noticing, especially as it shows Gualdo in his capacity as composer. His works not being extant, we have no right to express an opinion concerning their merits. At any rate, Gualdo himself seems to have been very much in favor of his music if he ventured to devote an entire evening more or less to his own works; and I doubt not that this concert of November 16, 1769, was the first " composer's-concert " given in our country.

The affair was clearly for Gualdo's own benefit, since the Subscription Concerts did not begin until November 30. On this day we read in the Pa. Gaz. :

To the Philo Musical Ladies and Gentlemen.

This evening will be performed the first Concert by Subscription, at Mr. Davenport's in Third Street. The Vocal Music by Messieurs Handel, Arne, Giardini, Jackson, Stanley and others. The Instrumental Music by Messieurs Geminiani, Barbella, Campioni, Zanetti, Pellegrino, Abel, Bach, Gualdo, the Earl of Kelly and others.

Tickets for one Night, at five shillings a Piece to be had of the Waiter of the London Coffee House, and at Mr. Davenport's. No admittance will be given without the Tickets, nor Money received at the Concert room. To begin at Six o'Clock.

N. B. In the best Part of the Room Chairs will be placed for the Ladies and Benches for the Gentlemen.

Gualdo is moving here in exceptionably good company. If all the Subscription Concerts were of the same standard then we moderns are not justified in haughtily smiling down on Gualdo and his assistant performers, for a glimpse into musical dictionaries will show that most of the composers named were by no means mediocrities. But what counts more than this, they were contemporaries of Gualdo, Hopkinson, and Penn, and just as modern in those days as are now Brahms, Wagner, Tschaikowsky, Richard Strauss, Debussy. Consequently, the ready appreciation of foreign novelties by the American public is an inheritance of Colonial times and not the result of German immigration during the nineteenth century.[*]

The next concert under Gualdo's direction which I was able to trace is instructive, as its program discloses the fact that none of the orchestra-instruments employed in Europe for concert purposes were missing at Philadelphia, not even the Clarinet, at that time by far less common than to-day.

We read in the Pa. Chronicle, Oct. 1–8, 1770 :

---

[*] The *Bach* mentioned was not Johann Sebastian but his son Johann Christian, 1735–1783, who settled in England, which fact procured him the name of the " London " or " English Bach." Once celebrated, his works are now underrated.

To the Public.

By particular desire, on Friday, (being the 12th of October) a concert of music will be directed by Mr. Gualdo, in which the following pieces will be performed in two acts.

Act I.

Overture with Violins, German Flutes, French Horns, etc.— Concerto with Solos for two German Flutes—Quartetto— Trio—Solo upon the Clarinet—Symphony— Solo upon the Violin.

Act II.

Overture—Concerto upon the German Flute—Solo upon the Harpsichord—Quartetto— Solo upon the Mandolin—Symphony.

N. B. Tickets at a Dollar a Piece, to be had at Mr. Gualdo's in Norris Alley, and at the Waiter of the London Coffee House.—To begin at half an Hour after six in the Evening.

In the Pa. Journal November 8, 1770, a similar concert was advertised " two days after Christmas," with the remark that

at the request of several Gentlemen and Ladies, Mr. Gualdo, after the Concert, will have the room put in order for a Ball, likewise there will be a genteel Refreshment laid out in the upper room for those Ladies and Gentlemen who shall chuse to Dance, or remain to see the Ball. For the Ball he has composed six new minuets, with proper cadence for dancing, and he flatters himself will be favourably received.

Tickets at Ten Shillings a piece . . .

N. B. If any Gentleman or Lady should chuse to go away after the concert, the Porter will return Half a Crown to each Person.

I doubt very much whether many persons took advantage of this *N. B.*, for from all we know of the Colonial dames and cavaliers they would rather have missed the German flute concertos and symphonies than Gualdo's " six new minuets with proper cadence for dancing."

One month later, on Jan. 24, 1771, Gualdo advertised another concert, to take place on Feb. 8. This was probably the last concert which he conducted for his benefit. He announced on Aug. 22d his intention to direct a " Concert of Music at the Assembly Room," on the eighteenth of October, but cruel Nemesis interfered. By the seventeenth of this month

Sigr. Gualdo lies in Chains in one of the Cells of the Pennsylva. Hospital.

Melancholically Francis Hopkinson added in his letter to John Penn

and poor Butho was kill'd a few Weeks ago by a Fall from his House.—Except Forage and myself I don't know a single Votary the Goddess hath in this large city.

Grief must have dimmed his eyes. Could poor Gualdo have

announced a concert for the eighteenth of October, unless there were
sufficient votaries of the Goddess to play and sing at her altar? At any
rate, hardly had John Penn received his friend's lines when the Pa.
Gaz. on Nov. 28th, 1771, printed the following advertisement:

> By Permission and Particular Desire.
>
> For the benefit of Mr. John M'Lean (Instructor of the German Flute) will be per-
> formed at the Assembly Room in Lodge Alley, CONCERT OF MUSIC (Vocal and Instru-
> mental) to begin precisely at Six o'Clock in the Evening on Thursday the fifth of
> December.
>
> The Concert will consist of two Acts, commencing and ending with favourite Over-
> tures, performed by a full Band of Music, with Trumpets, Kettle Drums, and every
> Instrument that can be introduced with Propriety. The Performance will be inter-
> spersed with the most pleasing and select Pieces, composed by approved Authors; a
> Solo will be played on the German Flute by John M'Lean; and the whole will con-
> clude with an Overture composed (for the Occasion) by Philip Roth, Master of the Band
> belonging to his Majesty's Royal Regiment of North British Fusileers.
>
> Several Gentlemen, who wish to encourage and reward Merit, have suggested this
> public Amusement, and have designed to honour with their Protection the Person for
> whose Benefit it is intended; one Instance of their condescending goodness, he will
> ever gratefully acknowledge, in consenting, it should be Known, they have been pleased
> to offer their Assistance in the Performance, which every possible Means will be used
> to render agreeable and entertaining to the Company, for whose further Satisfaction, it
> is also proposed, that after the Concert there shall be a Ball; on this account the Music
> will begin early, and as soon as the 2d. Act is finished the usual Arrangement will be
> made for dancing.
>
> N. B. The Tickets for the Concert may be had at the different Printing Offices in
> this city, at the Bar of the Coffee House and at Messieurs Duff and Jacob's Taverns, in
> Second and Third Streets. Price 7s 6.

A few years later the War for Independence broke out. Everywhere fiddle and harpsichord gave way to fife and drum. Our musical
life, which not alone at Philadelphia but at Boston, Charleston, New
York and in cities of minor importance had steadily been developing,
was crushed and remained crippled for years after the war. Then
indeed conditions were deplorable, and we need not wonder if English,
French and German officers and travelers, with a few exceptions,
invariably entered in their diaries notes to the effect that very little
music was to be found in the United States. These gentlemen were
good observers, but poor historians, and to apply their observations to
the ten or fifteen years preceding the Revolution would show absolute
ignorance of the real conditions.

After peace had been signed, the element of the people which,
previous to the war, had opposed all theatrical or musical amusements
for the sake of a narrow, though well-meant, principle and for the

salvation of their philistine souls, now gained the upper-hand for a while. This was but natural. A degenerated, frivolous nation may sing and dance merrily over the fresh graves of thousands of brave patriots, but not so a young, God-fearing nation. Gradually, however, as the wounds inflicted upon the population by this glorious but fearful war began to heal, arts, sciences and entertainments returned, and they are not less essential to the welfare, vitality and progress of a nation than politics or commerce.

It lies not within the plan of this monograph to describe the musical surroundings in which Francis Hopkinson lived after the war. A simple reason forbids this. His activity had been necessary, previous to the great struggle for Independence, to awaken and keep awake the musical life at Philadelphia. *But now the days of the amateur-musician had passed, the professional took his place.*

Andrew Adgate laid the foundations of his " Uranian Academy " in 1785 and gave splendid choral concerts during the following years— on one occasion (May 4th, 1786) the chorus numbering 230 singers and the orchestra 50 performers. Alexander Reinagle, pianist, conductor, composer, theatrical manager, settled at Philadelphia in 1786, and simultaneously with him, as the centre of musical progress till Benjamin Carr arrived in 1793, labored able musicians like William Brown, Henry Capron, J. G. C. Schetky, John Bentley, Philip Phile, Philip Roth, James and Alexander Juhan and many others. Good Symphony concerts, both by subscription under the name of "City Concerts" and "Amateurs Concerts," or for the benefit of individual musicians, were numerous and the number of music-loving families increased steadily. Organ builders, manufacturers of other instruments and dealers in music also became quite numerous. There was a constantly increasing demand for opera librettos, for operatic concert-music, for instruction books, for any kind of compositions, either in collection or in sheets, and the publishers in Philadelphia failed not to see their opportunity. Even theatrical amusements were not missing, though at first prohibited by law and ostracised by large numbers of citizens. Under the disguise of " Lectures, Moral and Entertaining," " Spectaculum Vitae " and other headings the " Old American Company " evaded the law, but Francis Hopkinson lived to see the players drop their mask, lift their performances out of a sphere dangerously near to Music-Hall entertainments, and again devote their energies and talents to pure drama and English opera.

In short, the golden age of music in Philadelphia, the period from 1790–1850, was fast approaching. Without doubt Francis Hopkinson's love of music was as deep after as we know it to have been previous to the war. For this statement we have more than one argument in store, but his position had somewhat changed. It was less the musician Hopkinson than the music-lover, the " Macænas " who now influenced matters, if we except his activity as composer and improver of the harpsichord. We may rest assured that Reinagle and the others were welcome at his house, received from him all due protection, respected him as their most important forerunner, and well knew that without the foundations laid by him, Bremner, Penn, and Gualdo their own position would have been precarious and difficult to hold. One of these musicians, at least, has left an eloquent tribute of gratitude : *William Brown*, in 1787, composed and published ' Three Rondos, for the Pianoforte,' which he

Humbly dedicated to the Honorable Francis Hopkinson, Esqr.

CHAPTER IV.

Francis Hopkinson's Letter on the Conduct of a Church Organ.

After James Bremner resigned, Francis Hopkinson consented to take his place at the organ until the appointment of a new organist. During these years he had ample opportunity to form ideas concerning the proper conduct of organs in church. They are embodied in the second volume (pp. 119–126) of his 'Miscellaneous Essays and Occasional Writings' in form of a letter to the Rev. Dr. White, Rector of Christ Church and St. Peter's.*

It is a pity that musical reviews did not exist in the United States of the eighteenth century. If this had been the case Hopkinson's ideas would have attracted wide-spread attention and borne fruit among our early organists. Some oddities excepted, the letter shows so much common sense and artistic spirit as to be of educational value even to-day. I hesitate not to declare that little has been written on the subject in so few lines with superior lucidity and correctness.

Our organists have made wonderful progress as virtuosi during the last hundred years but the development of their esthetic faculties has not kept pace with their technical skill. In this respect they have not advanced a single step beyond the standpoint of the Colonial amateur-organist. On the contrary, he surpasses them with his ideas of a true organ-style in church. Never would Francis Hopkinson have profaned the instrument of a Frescobaldi or a Bach by turning it, as many a modern organist does, into a concert-instrument, into a kind of orchestrion for which anything will do from a fugue to operatic pot-pourris.

A Letter to the Rev. Doctor White, Rector of Christ Church and St. Peter's on the Conduct of Church Organs.†

I am one of those who take great delight in sacred music, and think, with royal David, that heart, voice, and instrument should unite in adoration of the great Supreme.

---

* The letter was reprinted in the Columbian Magazine (Phila.) Sept., 1792.
† The Right Rev. William White, D. D., held this position from 1779 to 1836.

A soul truly touched with love and gratitude, or under the influence of penitential sorrow, will unavoidably break forth in expressions suitable to its feelings. In order that these emanations of the mind may be conducted with uniformity and a becoming propriety our church hath adopted into her liturgy, the book of psalms, commonly called *David's Psalms*, which contain a great variety of addresses to the Deity, adapted to almost every state and temperature of a devote heart, and expressed in terms always proper, and often sublime.

To give wings, as it were to this holy zeal, and heighten the harmony of the soul, *organs* have been introduced into the churches. The application of instrumental music to the purposes of piety is well known to be of very ancient date. Indeed, originally, it was thought that music ought not to be applied to any other purpose. Modern improvements, however, have discovered that it may be made expressive of every passion of the mind, and become an incitement to levity as well as sanctity.

Unless the real design for which an organ is placed in a church be constantly kept in view, nothing is more likely to happen than an abuse of this noble instrument, so as to render it rather an obstruction to, than an assistant in, the good purpose for which the hearers have assembled.

Give me leave, sir, to suggest a few rules for the conduct of an organ in a place of worship according to my ideas of propriety.

1st. The organist should always keep in mind, that neither the time or place is suitable for exhibiting all his powers of execution; and that the congregation have not assembled to be entertained with his performance. The excellence of an organist consists in his making the instrument subservient and conducive to the purposes of devotion. None but a master can do this. An ordinary performer may play surprising tricks, and show great dexterity in running through difficult passages, which he hath subdued by dint of previous labour and practice. But *he* must have judgment and taste who can call forth the powers of the instrument and apply them with propriety and effect to the seriousness of the occasion.

2nd. The voluntary, previous to reading the lesson, was probably designed to fill up a solemn pause in the service; during which the clergyman takes a few minutes respite, in a duty too lengthy, perhaps, to be continued without fatigue, unless some intermission be allowed: then, the organ hath its part alone, and the organist an opportunity of showing his power over the instrument. This, however, should be done with great discretion and dignity, avoiding everything light and trivial, but rather endeavoring to compose the minds of the audience, and strengthen the tendency of the heart in those devout exercises, in which, it should be presumed, the congregation are now engaged. All sudden jirks, strong contrasts of *piano* and *forte*, rapid execution, and expressions of tumult should be avoided. The voluntary should proceed with great chastity and decorum; the organist keeping in mind, that his hearers are now in the midst of divine service. The full organ should seldom be used on this occasion, nor should the voluntary last more than *five minutes* of time. Some relaxation, however, of this rule may be allowed on festivals and grand occasions.

3d. The *chants* form a pleasing and animating part of the service; but it should be considered that they are not songs or tunes, but a species of *recitative*, which is no more than speaking musically. Therefore, as melody or song, is out of the question, it is necessary that the harmony should be complete, otherwise *chanting*, with all the voices in unison, is too light and thin for the solemnity of the occasion. There should at least be half a dozen voices in the organ gallery to fill the harmony with bass and treble parts, and give a dignity to the performance. Melody may be frivolous; harmony never.

4th. The prelude which the organ plays immediately after the psalm is given out, was intended to advertise the congregation of the psalm tune which is going to be sung ; but some famous organist, in order to show how much he could make of little, has introduced the custom of running so many divisions upon the simple melody of a psalm tune, that the original purpose of this prelude is now totally defeated, and the tune so disguised by the fantastic flourishes of the dexterous performer, that not an individual in the congregation can possibly guess the tune intended, until the clerk has sung through the first line of the psalm. And it is constantly observable that the full congregation never join in the psalm before the second or third line, for want of that information which the organ should have given. The tune should be distinctly given out by the instrument, with only a few chaste and expressive decorations, such as none but a master can give.

5th. The interludes between the verses of the psalm were designed to give the singers a little pause, not only to take breath, but also an opportunity for a short retrospect of the words they have sung, in which the organ ought to assist their reflections. For this purpose the organist should be previous informed by the clerk of the verses to be sung, that he may modulate his interludes according to the subject.

To place this in a strong point of view, no stronger, however, than what I have too frequently observed to happen ; suppose the congregation to have sung the first verse of the 33d psalm.

> " Let all the just to God with joy
> Their cheerful voices raise ;
> For well the righteous it becomes
> To sing glad songs of praise."

How dissonant would it be for the organist to play a pathetic interlude in a flat third ; with the slender and distant tones of the echo organ, or the deep and smothered sounds of a single diapason stop?

Or suppose again, that the words sung have been the 6th verse of the VIth psalm.

> " Quite tired with pain, with groaning faint,
> No hope of ease I see
> The night, that quiets common grief
> Is spent in tears by me—."

How monstrously absurd would it be to hear these words of distress succeeded by an interlude selected from the tag end of some thundering figure on a full organ, and spun out to a most unreasonable length ? Or, what is still worse, by some trivial melody with a rhythum so strongly marked, as to set all the congregation to beating time with their feet or heads? Even those who may be impressed with the feelings such words should occasion, or in the least disposed for melancholy, must be shocked at so gross an impropriety.

The interludes should not be continued above 16 bars in *triple,* or ten or twelve bars in *common* time, and should always be adapted to the verse sung ; and herein the organist hath a fine opportunity of showing his sensibility, and displaying his taste and skill.

6th. The voluntary after service was never intended to eradicate every serious idea which the sermon may have inculcated. It should rather be expressive of that cheerful satisfaction which a good heart feels under the sense of a duty performed. It should bear if possible, some analogy with the discourse delivered from the pulpit ; at least, it should not be totally dissonant from it. If the preacher has had for his subject, penitance or sin, the frailty and uncertainty of human life, or the evils incident to mortality, the voluntary may be somewhat more cheerful than the tenor of such a sermon might in strictness suggest; but by no means so full and free as a discourse on praise, thanksgiving, and joy, would authorize.

In general, the organ should ever preserve its dignity; and upon no account issue light and pointed movements which may draw the attention of the congregation and induce them to carry home not the serious sentiments which the service should impress, but some very petty air with which the organist hath been so good as to ascertain them. It is as offensive to hear lilts and jigs from a church organ, as it would be to see a venerable matron frisking through the public streets with all the fantastic airs of a *columbine.*

CHAPTER V.

Francis Hopkinson's Improved Method of Quilling a Harpsichord.—His Harmonica with Keyboard.—His Bellharmonic.

Francis Hopkinson's favorite instrument, the harpsichord, was invented about 1400.* It is first mentioned under the name of clavicymbalon in the rules of the Minnesingers, by Eberhard Cersne, in 1404. The name of harpsichord is the English variant of the original harpsichordo, which like clavicembalo, clavicordo, spinetto, and pianoforte betrays an Italian origin. Built on the plectrum principle, it was incapable of dynamic modification of tone by difference of touch ; the strings were set in vibration by points of quill or hard leather, elevated on wooden uprights known as jacks, and twitching or plucking them as the depression of the keys caused the point to pass upwards.

Leather points were probably used first, but about 1500 the Canon Paul Belisonius of Pavia is said to have introduced quills. With the crow-quill as plectrum the harpsichord gained a popularity during the 16th, 17th and 18th centuries, similar to that now accorded the pianoforte. With its uniform but penetrating tone it was employed as the backbone of the orchestral body, as a matter of principle, even in concertos, and during the time of Haendel and Bach and still later it was the constant support to the *recitativo secco* (Hopkinson's " speaking musically "), its weak notes being reinforced by violoncellos and double basses. Toward the end of the eighteenth century the instrument was withdrawn, and the big fiddles were left by themselves to accompany the ordinary recitative in a fashion more peculiar than satisfactory.

---

* The following cursory remarks on the history of the harpsichord, without which a clear understanding of this chapter would be difficult to readers not familiar with the subject, have been borrowed, partly verbatim, from Grove's ' Dictionary of music and musicians ' ; Rimbault's work on ' the Pianoforte, its origin, progress and construction ' (London, 1860) ; Weitzmann's ' History of Pianoforte Playing ' (From the 2d German ed., translated by Dr. Th. Baker, 1894), and Riemann's ' Musik Lexikon.' I considered these sources sufficiently accurate for my purposes.

Good harpsichord-makers were numerous, but the Ruckers family of Antwerp (ca. 1579–1651), in particular Hans and Andreas Ruckers, held a position with respect to the harpsichord as Amati, Stradivari or Guaneri do for the violin.

It was the school of Ruckers transferred to England by a Fleming named Tabel, that was the real basis of harpsichord making as a distinct business in this country, separating it from organ building, with which it had been, as in Flanders, often combined. Tabel's pupils, Burkhard Tschudi (anglicised *Shudi*) and Jacob Kirchmann (anglicised *Kirkman*) became famous in the eighteenth century for having developed the harpsichord in the direction of power and majesty of tone to the farthest limit. In fact, the harpsichords built in England during the 18th century are conceded to have been superior to those made on the continent.

The innate defect of the instrument, it not permitting a shading of the tones, caused—about 1700—the invention of the Pianoforte, as it was called for obvious reasons by the inventor, Bartholommeo Christofori (b. 1655 in Padua, d. 1731 in Florence).*

However, neither he, nor the Frenchman Marius, nor the Germans Ch. G. Schroeter and Gottfried Silbermann, nor the pianoforte makers following these pioneers were able to destroy the popularity of the harpsichord. It took almost a century before this instrument gave way to the pianoforte. Most amateurs and professionals clung to the harpsichord, fully convinced of its superiority over the pianoforte, though not blind to its shortcomings. This admitted, innumerable attempts were made to *improve the harpsichord as a harpsichord.*

The principal result of these various experiments led to the invention of the socalled stops, of which there were three kinds: the *forte* stop, which raised the dampers; the *soft* stop, which partly stopped the vibration of the strings; and the *buff* stop, which interposed a layer of cloth or soft buff leather between the jacks and the strings. These stops seem to have been the origin of the pedals.

The need of improvement in the quality of tone, which had always been harsh and disagreeable to delicate ears, led artists to attempt a disguise, at least, of a defect like this by artificial means. Instruments were accordingly constructed with more than twenty different modifications; to imitate the tones of the harp, the lute, the mandolin, the bassoon, the flageolet, oboe, violin and other instruments.

---

* It is not generally known that one of the first pianofortes on record forms part of Mrs. Crosby Brown's collection of instruments in the Metropolitan Art Museum of New York City.

Says the famous historian Charles Burney (1726–1814) in Rees' Cyclopædia :

> Besides arming the tongues of the jacks with crow and raven quills, several other means were tried by which to produce a softer tone, and to be more durable. As the quilling a harpsichord with three stops was nearly a day's work, leather, ivory, and other elastic substances were tried; but what they gained in sweetness, they lost in spirit.

Richard, a French artist, about 1620, was the first who conceived the idea of substituting small slips of cloth in the place of the quill, for producing the sound; by this means he succeeded in obtaining tones more agreeable and yet without diminution of power.

One William Barton, an Englishman, took out a patent in 1730 for his

> new invention of pins of silver, brass, steel and all other sorts of metals, to improve the use of harpsichords and spinnets.

Pascal Taskin, a native of Theux in Liège, is credited with the introduction of leather as an alternative to quills and his Clavecin " en peau de buffle," made in 1768, was pronounced superior to the pianoforte.

> Wiegleb, an organ and musical instrument maker of Berlin, made harpsichords and spinets in 1724, in which the strings were sounded by brass or metal tongues instead of the bristles or crow quills. This idea was revived some few years later, in 1788, by a maker named *Hopkinson*, (an Englishman), resident at Paris . . .

Rimbault (p. 82) probably took this item from Joseph Fishhof's 'Versuch einer Geschichte des Clavierbaues' (Wien. 1853) where we find, on p. 10, the same name, the same date, the same residence. So we do in Mendel-Reissmann's 'Musikalishes Conversations Lexikon' (1875) and in Welcker von Gontershausen's work entitled 'Der Klavierbau in seiner Theorie, Technik, und Geschichte' (Frankfurt a M. 1870) this author adds (on p. 160):

> Oesterlein in Berlin and Schmal and Spaet in Regensburg imitated this process with slight alterations, calling their harpsichords 'Tangentenfluegel' . . . Hopkinson's improvement, on the whole unimportant . . . was the last glory of the harpsichord.*

However unimportant the improvement might have been, it is clear that this Hopkinson must have attracted more or less attention in Europe. But if he was an Englishman and a resident at Paris, why should he be mentioned in a monograph on the musical career of Francis Hopkinson, the American?

---

* Kielfluegel, or simply Fluegel, was the German name for the Harpsichord, probably because the form of the instrument resembled the wing of a bird.

The reason will become clear if certain passages in Robert Bremner's letters to Hopkinson are recalled and if a glance is cast at the voluminous correspondence of Thomas Jefferson as preserved at the Library of Congress. The versatility which Jefferson displays in this correspondence is truly astonishing and reminds one of Leonardo da Vinci or Goethe. While in Paris he exchanged quite a few letters with his friend Francis Hopkinson. They deal in particular with Hopkinson's musical activity, and, if we except for instance a criticism of Burney's doctrines, mostly with his efforts to improve certain musical instruments. The following extracts will tell, I believe, an interesting and unknown story:

Hopkinson to Jefferson, Philadelphia, March 31, 1784.

. . . Mr. Morris' Harpsichord, which I wrote for last fall, is arrived, & is indeed a very charming Instrument.—Mr. Bremner agrees with me in Opinion respecting Forte Pianos, he says there is one Merlin who has contrived to unite the F. P. & Harpd. but he adds the one Instrument injures the other so that neither of them is good — & that they are frequently to be had at Second hand for half Price.

I shall look for my Harpd. in about four or five weeks.

Hopkinson to Jefferson, Philadelphia, May 12, 1784.

. . . By Letters from London, I find that my improved Method of *Quilling* did not get to Mr. Bremner's House before the last of February — that he was at that Time very ill & incapable of Business & that from the Tenor of my Letters it was thought not advisable to open the Box till he should be able to take the Business in Hand — so that I am uninformed of the Event of my Discovery & disappointed in my Expectations of receiving a Harpd. so soon as I had promised myself. . . .

Hopkinson to Jefferson, Philadelphia, November 18, 1784.

. . . I have received my Harpsichord from London & a very excellent one it is, with Shudi & Broadwood's Patent Swell & quilled according to my Method, for which Invention they have struck off 30 Guineas from their Bill. They have suggested however an Inconvenience attending it, which I have also fully obviated I have not time to explain this, otherwise than by enclosing the rough Draft of the account I gave of it to the Philosophical Society. This altho' very rough, will I hope be intelligible, & to make it the more so I will enclose a Model of a Tongue quilled in a complete manner, as I think they ought always to be, & answer fully the Purpose intended—I wish you may be able to turn this Improvement to my advantage — but if it should not be profitable, I at least deserve the Credit of the Discovery.

Jefferson to Hopkinson, Paris, July 6, 1785.

. . . I received yours of Nov. 18 and about three weeks ago that of Mar. 20th came to hand, soon after the receipt of the first I published your proposition for improving the quilling of the harpsichord. I enclose you a copy of the advertisement. one application only was made, and that was unsuccessful. I do not despair yet of availing you of it as soon as I can get acquainted with some of the principal musicians, but that probably will not be till the beginning of winter as all the beau monde leave Paris in the summer, during which the musical entertainments of a private nature are suspended. I communicated to Doctr. Franklin your idea of Mesmerising the Harpsichord. he has not tried it, probably because his affairs have been long packed & packing, as I do not play on that instrument I cannot try it myself. the Doctr. carries with him a pretty little instrument. it is the sticcado, with glass bars instead of wooden ones, and with keys applied to it. it's principal defect is the want of extent, having but three octaves. I wish you would exercise your ingenuity to give it an upper and lower octave, by finding out other substances which will yield tones in those parts of the scale, bearing a proper affinity to those of glass bars. the middle octave of this is very sweet. . . .

Hopkinson to Jefferson, Philadelphia, April 20, 1785.

. . . I have written two or three Letters to you. . . . In one of them I enclosed a Model of my further Improvement in the Manner of quilling a Harpd. which I believe, effectually completes that Business.—It answers to Admiration in my Harpd. which has been freely used since last Fall & not one Quill has failed—the Instrument remaining in perfect Touch—which is certainly a very great Acquisition.

Jefferson to Hopkinson, Paris, September 25, 1785.

My last to you was of the 6th of July. Since that, I have received yours of July the 23d. I do not altogether despair of making something of your method of quilling, though, as yet, the prospect is not favorable. I applaud much your perseverance in improving this instrument and benefiting mankind almost in spite of their teeth. I mentioned to Piccini the improvement with which I am entrusted. he plays on the pianoforte and therefore did not feel himself personally interested. I hope some better opportunity will yet fall in my way of doing it justice. I had almost decided, on his advice, to get a pianoforte for my daughter; but your last letter may pause me, till I see its effect.

Hopkinson to Jefferson, Philadelphia, September 28, 1785.

. . . I am sorry my Improvement in Quilling Harpd. has cost you so much Trouble. I resign any Expectations from that source. I have since made a further & more important Improvement. I have long suspected that the Quill did not draw the full Power of Tone from Strings so long & so advantageously stretched, & on experiment found my Conjecture was right. My Harpd. has not now got a single Quill in it & for Richness of Tone & the Body or Quantity of Sound it yields, exceeds any Instrument of the kind I ever heard. The enclosed model will give you a full Idea of the Contrivance & save the Trouble of Description. My Harpd. is at present furnished thus.

The First Unison with sole-Leather well rubb'd with black Lead, the Second Unison, a kind of soft Morocco Leather, for the Piano of the Instrument, & the Octave with wooden Tongues polish'd with black Lead, for giving Vivacity to the whole—all mounted on Springs according to the Model. I say nothing as to the admirable Result. Let Experiment determine.

Hopkinson to Jefferson, Philadelphia, October 25, 1785.

It is not long since I wrote to you & . . . sent you a Model of my last Improvement in the Harpsichord. The Effect produced by furnishing an Instrument in that Way is truly astonishing. I have discovered the Reason. It causes the Instrument to sound the Octave below the Tones produced by the Quill. The full Tone of the

Harpd. has never yet been drawn forth. The Quill on Account of it's Substance & the smallness of it's contact with the String, being only in a Point (because the Back of a Quill is a Portion of a Circle) has not been sufficient to put the String in a uniform Vibration thro'out it's whole length. It vibrates in two halves, & those halves vibrate in contrary Directions — so that the Tone produced will be only the Octave above that of the whole String. My Method draws forth the full clear & genuine tone.

This will be delivered to you by Mr. Hudon. . . . As he had given me so much Pleasure I endeavored to please him also in my Way — I played for him on my Harpd. as well as I could. He was surprised at the Effect of the Instrument. I wish you would ask him what he thought of it.

Jefferson to Hopkinson, Paris, January 3, 1786.

I wrote you last, on the 25th of Sept. Since that I have received yours of Oct. the 25th, inclosing a duplicate of the last invented tongue for the harpsichord. the letter enclosing another of them . . . has never come to hand . . . you have not authorized me to try to avail you of the new tongue. indeed the ill success of my endeavors with the last does not promise much with this. however, I shall try. Houdon only stopped a moment, to deliver me your letter, so that I have not yet had an opportunity of asking his opinion of the improvement. I am glad you are pleased with his work. he is among the foremost, or, perhaps the foremost artist in the world.

Hopkinson to Jefferson, Philadelphia, December 31, 1785.

. . . I wrote you some time ago an account of my Discovery of a new Method of drawing the Tone from a Harpsd.—I believe I sent you a Model. I am much pleased with this Invention — it answers to admiration. I have instructed an ingenious Workman here & he is engaged in altering the Harpds. of this City according to my Plan— if you should ever have the Opportunity of having a Harpd. so furnished you will be surprised at the Effect. All the Jingle, so much complained of in that Instrument is removed. The Tone is full, round & mellow, & in the Bass, very like the Diapason Stop of an Organ. I am confident that the Power of the Instrument was never before drawn forth. Crow Quills will hereafter be totally thrown aside. I sent this Discovery to a friend in England.— he was to offer it for 50 gs. but writes in answer that my Invention has been anticipated. I see I am to be defrauded both of the Money & Credit — but I will have the matter investigated.

Jefferson to Hopkinson, Paris, May 9, 1786.

I am just returned from a trip to England. I was in the shop of Mr. Broadwood, the maker of your Harpsichord, and conversed with him about your newest jack. he shewed me instruments in his shop with precisely the same substitute for the quill, but I omitted to examine whether it had the same kind of spring on the back. he told me they had been made some time before your model came over; & I now recollect that when I advertised your improvement of the quill here a workman sent me a jack with buff leather as a substitute for the quill. . . . [A minute and enthusiastic description of Walker's "divine" celestine stop for the harpsichord.]

I wait till I hear more particularly from you as to your last improvement before I order a harpsichord for my daughter.

Jefferson to Hopkinson, May 8, 1788.

Will you be so good as to tell me how your method of quilling the harpsichord, and also your 2d invention for substituting leather for the quill stand the test of experience?

Jefferson to Hopkinson, New York, June 13, 1790.

I wanted to enquire of you whether by sending the jack of a Spinet to Philadelphia by way of model there is any workman there who could make me a set of jacks on your plan ; but I will wait for this till you are able to attend to it.

Jefferson to Hopkinson, New York, August 14, 1790.

I wrote to you a good while ago on the subject of the quilling of the harpsichord & you were so kind as to answer me with an account & model of your cork tongue instead of quill . . .

With this letter the musical correspondence between Jefferson and Hopkinson ends, and I now turn to the following entry in Fétis' monumental 'Biographie Universelle des Musiciens,' which will furnish the missing link in this chain of evidence.

HOPKINSON (François), mécanicien anglais, a proposé in 1783 divers perfectionnements pour le clavecin, qui consistaient à substituer le cuir à la plume dans les sautieraux, et à se servir de ressorts métalliques pour leur languette au lieu d' employer la soie de porc. La première de ces inventions n'était pas nouvelle, l' autre n'eut point de succès, parceque les ressorts métalliques ont trop de rigidité pour agir avec la rapidité nécessaire : les lames de baleine avaient sur ces ressorts un avantage in contestable. Hopkinson proposa aussi quelques moyens mécaniques pour faciliter l'opération de l'accord du clavecin.

Le mémoire de Hopkinson a été publié dans le deuxième volume des Transactions de la Société américaine (p. 185) sous ce titre : *An improved method of quilling a harpsichord.*

We are under obligations to Fétis for having referred to the underscored title. It proves beyond a shadow of doubt that *Francis Hopkinson, improver of the harpsichord, was not an English mechanic, resident at Paris, but Francis Hopkinson, American lawyer, poet, musician, inventor, painter, signer of the Declaration of Independence, a resident at Philadelphia.*

The second volume (1786) of the ' Transactions of the American Philosophical Society Held at Philadelphia for Promoting Useful Knowledge,' contains as No XIX on pp. 185–194 an essay entitled :

'An Improved Method of Quilling a Harpsichord, by *F. Hopkinson,* Esquire.'

The individual papers were read on Dec. 5, 1783 ; in (Nov.) 1784, and on Jan. 28, 1786. It is unnecessary to copy them in detail as their contents appeared in condensed form in

' The Description of an improved Method of tongueing a Harpsichord or Spinnet, by F. H. Esq.'

which was published in the Columbian Magazine, Philadelphia, for May, 1787 (reprinted with some slight alterations in the 'Miscellaneous

Essays and Occasional Writings' of Francis Hopkinson in Vol. I,* pp. 421–423).

DESCRIPTION OF AN IMPROVED METHOD OF TONGUEING A HARPSICHORD OR SPINNET, BY F. H. ESQ,

The strings of a harpsichord are made to vibrate by the impulse of small pieces of a crow quill; these, from the manner in which they are applied, are compelled to perform their office to such disadvantage that many become weak, and fail with a little use, and what is called the *touch* of the instrument becomes thereby unequal and disagreeable, both to the performer and hearer. I attempted two or three years ago to remedy this imperfection. My first idea was to increase the length of the quill, so as to make it act more like a spring, but the horizontal length of the quill, cannot by the construction of the instrument, be more than about one-quarter of an inch ; I effected my purpose, however, by mounting the quill in the manner represented in the plate, B [fig. 3] † by this means the spring of the quill was advantageously encreased, without increasing its horizontal length.

But it was objected, that the quill being thus forcibly bent, was apt to spring back in some instances, so that not only the point of the quill became too short to reach the string it should strike, but the curved part would interfere with the string next behind it. And though this convenience was rather a fault in the execution than in the design, yet the project was not adopted, because of the uncertainty.

My next device was, to throw aside the quills altogether, and taking hard and well seasoned sole-leather, I cut therefrom the intended tongues which I mounted on springs, as at C. and D. This contrivance seemed to answer very well, the tone produced was full and noble, the touch not disagreeable, and promised permanency, because the elasticity required is not in the tongue, which gives the stroke, but the zig-zag wire-spring, which, if properly annealed, will not be likely to fail.

The objections to this design were, that the touch was not so lively and agreeable as that of the common quill; but principally that the machinery was too complex and delicate for general use.

Both these contrivances are fully described in the second volume of the 'Transactions of the American Philosophical Society of Philadelphia.'

I interrupted Hopkinson's narrative here in order to quote from the paper read in November, 1784, remarks which show that his ideas were approved of abroad by "proper judges," and in what consisted his devices for tuning a harpsichord, mentioned by Fétis.

In the beginning of last winter, I had the honour to lay before the society an improved method of quilling a *Harpsichord*. Wishing to bring my discovery to the test of full experiment and to the judgment of abler critics, I forwarded a description and a model of my improvement to a friend in London, requesting that it might be submitted to the examination of proper judges, and directing, in case it should be approved of, that an instrument made by one of the first artists and quilled according to my proposed method, should be sent to me. I have accordingly received an excellent double harpsichord made by Messrs. *Shudi* and *Broadwood* of London, and quilled according to my method, with this difference, I had rounded off the top of the tongue and bending the

---

* 'A Description of a Candle Case, invented by F. H., Esq.' precedes it.
† Cp. p. 73.

quill over it, kept it in a horizontal position by means of a small wire staple; as will be more fully understood by referring to my former description. But Mr. *Broadwood* has left the tongue of its full length and usual form: But made the hole, in which the quill is commonly fixed tight, so large that the quill has free room to play therein; and then fixing the quill below, has bent it round and brought it through this hole; which renders a staple unnecessary; the top of the tongue answering the same purpose. The principle on which the improvement depends is the same in both; but his is the best method of executing it.

He informs, however, that one inconvenience occurs, viz the quills being forcibly bent in the curved part, are liable in some instances, to spring back, and so become not only too short to reach the string it should strike, but the projection of the curve will be apt to touch the string behind it, when the stop is pushed back.* . . .

. . . I have need to apologize to the society for directing so much of their attention, to an object which may appear to some to be of little importance. To the musical tribe, however, this improvement will present itself in a different light. Many persons who play very well on the harpsichord, are not able to keep the instrument in order: And to send for a person to repair the quills and tune the instrument as often as it shall be necessary, is not only troublesome and expensive, but such assistance is not always to be had, especially in the country. And for these reasons many a good harpsichord or spinnet lies neglected, and the scholar loses the opportunity of practice. To such persons a method of quilling that shall seldom want repair is a *desideratum* of no small importance. And this, I flatter myself, I have accomplished.

The difficulty of *quilling* being thus removed, I considered in what manner *tuning* might be made easy to the practioner in music. Harpsichords are tuned by means of *fifths* and *thirds;* but such is the musical division of the monochord as to make it necessary, that none of these *fifths* or *thirds* should be perfect; an allowance must be made; and to do this with judgment, so that the chords may be good and the instrument be in tune, requires much attention and practice. Of the numbers that play, there will not be found one in an hundred that can tune a harpsichord. To render this task easy, I have procured *twelve tuning forks* for the *twelve semitones* of the octave; these I had perfectly tuned; and as they will not be sensibly affected by any change of weather, they remain as standards. I take it for granted that any person at all accustomed to musical sounds can tell when one tone is *in unison* with another; and that a very little practice will enable him to tune one sound *an octave* to another, these conchords are so manifest that they cannot easily be mistaken. There is then nothing to be done but to tune the twelve strings in unison with the twelve forks; this will fix the scale, or temperature for one octave, which is the whole difficulty; the rest of the instrument is easily tuned by unisons and octaves to the scale as ascertained . . .

My set of forks are tuned, from the middle C sharp to the C above inclusive.

"Notwithstanding the long-established prejudice in favor of the crow quill, and the prevailing opinion that no substance can supply its place to advantage," Francis Hopkinson continued his experiments with the result, as we have seen, that he threw aside the quills and introduced in their place tongues of sole leather mounted on springs.

We know the objections raised against this device. Still, Hopkinson's mind was bent upon solving the problem, at least to his own

---

* Neither Hopkinson's models nor the "double harpsichord" seem to be extant.

satisfaction. *The device which he finally adopted is not mentioned by the European historians,* as becomes evident from the article in the Columbian Magazine, where it was interrupted above.

Not discouraged by these disappointments, I have again endeavored to attain the object I had in view, and flatter myself that I have now fully succeeded.

The desideratum is a substance to supply the place of the crow quill, sufficiently elastic for the purpose to afford a brilliant and easy touch to draw from the strings a full and agreeable tone, and to be permanent in itself, and applied with as much ease and simplicity as the quill.

After many fruitless experiments I have found the following construction to answer all purposes required.

I took what is called *velvet cork* of the very best kind, perfectly free from dolts, cracks, or blemishes, I cut this cork into plates about one-quarter of an inch thick, and glued upon them thin and well polished leather, from this I cut the tongues, and fixed them tight into mortices cut in the palates, in the same manner and with the same ease that the common quill is fixed in the little hole punched for its reception. The tongue thus fixed must be slanted off underneath, from the point where it must be very thin to the root, where it will be thickest, and then nibbed like a pen, to the proper length, and the touch may be easily and nicely adjusted by shaving away more of the cork from underneath, with a sharp pen-knife or fine file.

REMARKS.

1. The *Cork* (as was before observed) must be of the kind called *velvet cork*, of an elastic substance, and perfectly free from imperfections of any kind.

2. The *Leather* should be thin, well stretched, and of a polished surface—that which I used was from the cover of a bound book, which answered very well, after I had well scraped and washed its under surface.

3. The *Paste or Glue.* In my first experiment I made common glue, pretty thin and with this glued the leather to the cork — but found afterwards, when the weather became very dry and frosty, that the touch was harsh and disagreeable — because glue, in dry and frosty weather, becomes as hard as horn. I have obviated this inconvenience by dissolving a little isinglass, or fish glue in hot water, and with this and some flour made a moderately thin paste, in the common way, and with this I pasted the leather on the cork, putting the plates under a press 'till the paste was dry.

4. In cutting the tongue from these plates of cork, faced with leather — care must be taken that the grain of the cork shall run lengthways, from end to end, and not across the tongue — the reason is obvious.

I have found these tongues to answer every requisite. The cork is sufficiently elastic for the service it is to perform, and afterwards a lively and pleasant touch. The polished leather forms a most agreeable surface of contact with the metal string, and shields the cork, which would otherwise soon be cut thro' by the string. The tone produced is full and very pure — being perfectly free from that clicking, jingling noise which the strokes of a common quill unavoidably produces, and which has been justly complained of in the best harpsichords.

And lastly, the tongue thus prepared will be durable if I may judge from the experience of seven or eight months almost daily use — very few having failed in that time, except in instances where either there was some imperfection in the cork, or the grain lay a-cross and not the lengthway of the tongue — and where this happens nothing is easier than to cut and shape a new tongue from your plate of cork and leather, which may be fitted in the mortise, and adjusted in as little time as a common quill, and with as little trouble.

Harpsichords or spinnets quilled in the usual way, may be furnished in the manner now recommended with great facility, and at a trifling expense—nothing more is necessary than to dismount the palates (commonly called the tongues) from the jacks—take away the quills and cut mortises of a suitable size—the little hole in which the quill had been fixed, serving for the upper limit of the mortise—and then furnish the palate with the tongue of cork, faced with leather as above directed.

Explanation of the Figures.

[Fig. 2].   *A*. A profile of the palate, (commonly called the tongue) furnished with a piece of crow quill in the usual way.

B. The palate with the quill, fixed according to my first design.

C. A profile and *D* a back view of the palate, with a tongue of sole leather movable on a pin and governed by a zig-zag spring of life wire, fastened by one end to the root of the tongue, and by the other to a small staple, drove into the palate at (*a*)

E. A front view of the palate, with a mortise cut thro' for the reception of the tongue *F*. in the manner now recommended.*

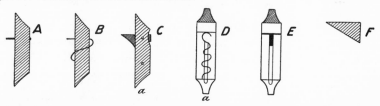

This chapter was in the hands of the printer and it was therefore too late to investigate the matter thoroughly, when I came across an item which connects Francis Hopkinson with Benjamin Franklin's Armonica, invented about 1760. This instrument was a very ingenious improvement of the Musical Glasses. The improvement consisted in this, that Franklin arranged the glasses in taper form on a spindle connected with a wheel. This wheel served as a fly to make the motion equable, when the spindle, with the glasses, was turned by the foot like a spinning-wheel. The instrument was played upon by sitting before the middle set of glasses as before the keys of a harpsichord, turning with the foot, and rubbing the moving glasses that represented the desired tones with a wet finger.

Franklin's Armonica, thus called, as he informed Padre Beccaria, in honor of the musical Italian language, created a sensation both in America and Europe and rapidly became known under its original name and also as Harmonica, Glassychord, Glass-Harmonica, etc. Quite a few musicians made a specialty of the Armonica, as for instance,

---

* The figures copied from the separate, interleaved plate.

Marianne Davies, Stephen Forage, Dussek, Röllig, Frick, Pohl, and even Beethoven wrote compositions for the instrument.

Owing to the fact that Franklin's Armonica had its defects, Abbé Mazucchi and especially the virtuosos interested in the instrument soon tried to improve it in various ways. The most striking idea was to apply a keyboard to the instrument.* With whom this idea origi- nated is, I believe, rather difficult to ascertain. At any rate, it seems to have remained unknown that Francis Hopkinson was among those who conceived the key-board idea. The proof for this is again found in Jefferson's correspondence. In a letter written to Francis Hopkin- son under date of " Paris, December 23, 1786," we read :

> I am very much pleased with your project on the Harmonica, & the prospect of your succeeding in the application of Keys to it. it will be the greatest present which has been made to the musical world this century, not excepting the Piano-forte. if its tone approaches that given by the finger as nearly only as the harpsichord does that of the harp, it will be very valuable. . . . [Continues with a minute description of Krump- holtz " Footbass."]

Evidently Hopkinson had informed Jefferson of his experiments with Franklin's instrument, but I did not find the letter. However, under date of " Philada. April 14th, 1787," Hopkinson has this to say :

> . . . I shall now begin again upon the Harmonica. From the experiments I have made, I have no Doubt of the Success. I have already applied Keys to the Glasses, fur- nished with artificial Fingers which answered perfectly & most delightfully in a great Part of the Scale. Where they did not succeed so well was owing to the Glass not being truly mounted, so that I must, I find, take off the Glasses from the Spindel & mount them anew.

That Hopkinson succeeded to a certain degree with his experi- ments, appears from a hastily written letter to Jefferson under date of " Philada. July 8th, 1787," in which he also describes his " contriv- ance for the perfect measurement of time " by means of a peculiarly constructed syphon—and his Bellharmonic.

> . . . I succeeded in making the Harmonica to be played with Kees [sic] as far as I believe the instrument is capable : — but it required too much Address in the Manner of wetting the Cushions for Common Use. In the Course of my Experiments I discover'd a Method of drawing the Tone from metal Bells by Friction — to an amazing Perfection —without the necessity of Water or any Fluid. I am getting a Set of Bells cast, & expect to introduce a new musical Instrument — to be called the *Bellarmonic.*

Surely an interesting letter, but I have been unable to ascertain

---

*Those interested in Benjamin Franklin's Relation to Music I refer to my article in ' Music,' 1900, Nov. pp. 1-14. A very much enlarged article on the subject I intend to publish in course of time.

what became of this new musical instrument, and the only further reference to it I again found in Jefferson's letters. Says the future President under date of " Paris, May 8, 1788 " : *

> I am anxious to know what progress you make with the Bellarmonica, which I think, if it can be made perfect will be a great present to the Musical world.

---

* In the same letter Jefferson describes " a very simple improvement of the Harmonica " ... " lately seen." It consisted in this that the glasses were wetted by a piece of woolen cloth pasted on the edge of the case in front and touching the glasses. " it spares the trouble of perpetually wetting the fingers and produces a more agreeable tone. I think the artist mixed a little vinegar with the water for wetting it. his object in this was the preservation of the cloth."

CHAPTER IV.

FRANCIS HOPKINSON AS POET-COMPOSER.

In January, 1757, was acted in the College Hall at Philadelphia by "the young gentlemen of the College . . . for their Improvement in Oratory " an " Oratorial Exercise " entitled :

'THE REDEMPTION OF THE DANISH INVASION BY ALFRED THE GREAT,' originally written by the pious and philosophic Mr. Thompson in Connection with Mr. Mallet, and in the year 1751 altered and greatly improved by the latter.

. . . alterations, together with the Introduction of some new Hymns and Pieces of Music, instead of some necessarily left out, the extending of the Hermit's Prophecy of the future Greatness of England, so far as to include the Colonies . . . occasioned near 200 new Lines, besides a new Prologue and Epilogue . . .

As the scene in which Alfred and the Hermit retire

to the sacred Cell there to employ themselves in the sublime Exercise of Devotion before the Throne of their God . . . conveys one of the noblest Lessons to Youth it was thought proper to enlarge the Plan of it, to add several new Lines and represent the Singing of a Hymn over the Cave by some aerial Spirits, joining with Alfred and the Hermit in their divine Strains. The Hymn is grand and awful, and the Introduction of it in this Place has a happy Effect. The Words are Milton's, and the Music Handels . . .*

This performance of the 'Masque of Alfred the Great' (music by Dr. Arne), at which, we remember, several gentlemen played the instrumental parts and several young ladies condescended to sing the vocal, remained for many years the most remarkable "Oratorial Exercise" in American colleges.

To dwell at length upon 'The Redemption of the Danish Invasion by Alfred the Great' lies not within the plan of this monograph. But if such efforts were possible in Colonial America, the musical culture can not have been so primitive, at least not in academic circles, as it generally is supposed to have been. If Francis Hopkinson almost certainly rendered services as harpsichordist on these occasions (the masque was performed repeatedly) his contribution of a musical com-

---

*Quoted from the detailed account in the Pa. Gaz. Jan. 20, 27 ; Feb. 3, 10, 1757.

position becomes at least probable. I infer this from a passus in the
newspaper report :

. . . Alfred is . . . confirmed in his noble Purposes, by the following Song, sung by
two invisible Spirits in the Character of his Guardian Angels ; which was altered from
the Original, retaining only two Lines ; and fitted to an excellent Piece of new Music by
one of the Performers—

First Spirit.

Alfred Father of the State !
Hark ! thy Guardian Gods declare :
Dangers prove the Hero great
Banish from thee dark Despair.
Rise in all thy native Fires ;
Britain calls, and Heaven inspires.

Both Spirits.

Let the World thy Virtue know ;
Wake thy Hope, thy Heart expand :
Joy how great to lighten Woe !
Rise and save a sinking Land.
Rise in all thy native Fires ;
Britain calls, and Heaven inspires !

Unfortunately the editor of the Pennsylvania Gazette did not
foresee that a future historian might become interested in the composer of this duet. Had he mentioned Francis Hopkinson in this
connection, he would have aided toward the solution of the interesting problem of who *the first native American composer* was.

As our knowledge stands to-day, it was not the tanner and psalmodist William Billings of Boston (1747–1800). Though public and
historians have worshipped this eccentric but remarkable man, whose
crude utterances contain a spark of genius, as the Father of American
Composers for well nigh a century, the title belongs to either James
Lyon of Newark, N. J. (1735–1794), or Francis Hopkinson. As if to
baffle the pardonable ambition of deciding in favor of one or the other,
the two earliest recorded compositions of the two competitors were
written in the same year, the one with certainty, the other with great
probability, in *1759.*

The New York Mercury informs us on October 1, 1759, that an ode,
set to music by James Lyon, one of the students, was performed at
Nassau Hall (College of New Jersey, or Princeton) Commencement,
September, 1759. The music to this ode is not extant. On the other
hand, the collection of 'Songs' dated 1759 in Francis Hopkinson's own
hand, now in possession of Mrs. Florence Scovel Shinn, and described
in the second chapter of this monograph, contains on page 63 a song
beginning with the words —

My Days have been so wondrous free.*

This harmless but pretty little piece bears, like several others in the same volume, Francis Hopkinson's initials: *F. H.* It is undated, but as the collection was evidently begun in 1759 and as toward the end of the book, on page 180, appears an anthem dated " F. H. 1760," it is highly probable that the song on page 63 was written in 1759.

So far, of course, James Lyon seems to be in the lead. But Hopkinson positively claimed in the dedication of his 'Seven Songs' (1788) to George Washington to have been our first native composer.

He says:

However small the Reputation may be that I shall derive from this Work *I cannot, I believe, be refused the Credit of being the first Native of the United States who has produced a Musical Composition.*

This reads as if Hopkinson possessed evidence for the correctness of his claim. Now he certainly knew James Lyon's psalm-tune collection ' Urania,' published in 1761 or 1762, and which contains several compositions by Lyon. In the second place, Lyon resided at Philadelphia in 1760, and being college-bred and a musical amateur, he might have met Hopkinson. Furthermore, if Lyon was still in Philadelphia when on May 23, 1761, an anthem of his and an ode by Hopkinson made part of the Commencement exercises, both composers must have formed an acquaintance. At any rate, Francis Hopkinson must have been aware of the fact that James Lyon was a dangerous competitor for the title of first native of the United States who produced a musical composition. James Lyon was still living and he still had admirers at Philadelphia, among them principally Andrew Adgate, when Hopkinson filed his claim. Under such circumstances it would have been unwise to do this without the support of indisputable facts. From all we know of Hopkinson's character I doubt not that he himself investigated the correctness of his claim and found his earliest compositions to antedate those of James Lyon.

Nevertheless he might have been mistaken, and may be others will succeed in proving that neither he nor James Lyon is to be considered as the " Father of American composers." However, on the basis of our present knowledge we might declare with safety:

FRANCIS HOPKINSON WAS THE FIRST NATIVE AMERICAN COMPOSER OF SONGS OF WHOM WE KNOW, AND HIS SONG 'MY DAYS HAVE BEEN

---

* The poem was written by Dr. Parnell and was known under the title of ' Love and Innocence. Compare, for instance, ' The Musical Miscellany,' v. 4, London, 1730.

SO WONDROUS FREE' IS THE EARLIEST SECULAR AMERICAN COMPOSITION EXTANT, DATING BACK TO 1759.

I have stated in a previous chapter that the volume of 'Songs' contains quite a number of anonymous pieces. Several of these seem to have been written by Francis Hopkinson, for instance on —

Page 157, an Anthem, 'Sing we praises to the Lord.'
172, 'A solemn dirge in Romeo and Juliet.'
175, The 4th Psalm (3-part setting with figured bass).
176, Anthem (2-part setting with figured bass).
187, Hymn.

If these are somewhat doubtful, the following compositions, besides the song mentioned and reproduced, certainly must be attributed to Hopkinson, since they all bear his initials, *F. H.*

Page 111, a song entitled

THE GARLAND.

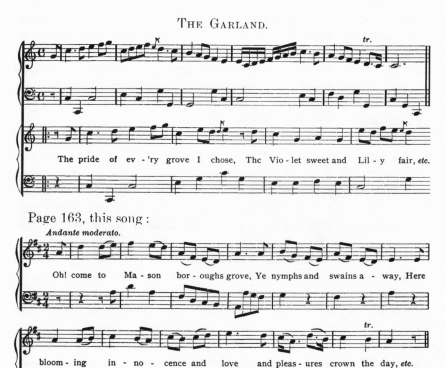

The pride of ev - 'ry grove I chose, The Vio - let sweet and Lil - y fair, *etc.*

Page 163, this song:

Andante moderato.

Oh! come to Ma - son bor - oughs grove, Ye nymphs and swains a - way, Here

bloom - ing in - no - cence and love and pleas - ures crown the day, *etc.*

Page 169, this song:

With pleas - ure have I past my days, And ev - 'ry min - ute

blest, no se - cret sigh con - troll'd my ease, No wish dis - turb'd my rest, *etc.*

Page 179 : The Twenty-third Psalm (See page 92).

Pages 180, 181, 'An Anthem from the 114th Psalm,' dated "*F. H.* 1760." (See Appendix.)

It will readily be noticed that the songs betray the period in which they were written. Hundreds and hundreds of similar simple, grace-ful songs for the voice with harpsichord accompaniment were composed by Hopkinson's contemporaries. It would be erroneous to suppose that his settings for " treble " and bass reveal uncommonly primitive efforts. This was the style adopted by high and low in the kingdom of music about 1750, and it should always be kept in mind when per-forming such songs that it was left to the discretion of the harp-sichordist to make the accompaniment sound fuller by adding proper chords, even when the bass was not figured. As a rule, the song com-poser gave, so to speak, the frame only, and the knowledge of thorough bass, with which in those days every amateur was familiar, added the color. Where our American composer falls short is in his basses, which are rather amateurish and stiff though real grammatical blunders are but few.

The same remark applies to the two sacred compositions. Of these the anthem is by far the most interesting to the historian. A figured bass is a *rara avis* in early American music. For instance, none will be found in Lyon's ' Urania.' It would seem as if most of our first composers abhorred the thorough bass as a black art, and preferred ignorance of its mysteries to the vain attempt of mastering its occult wisdom. Francis Hopkinson, however, hesitated not to take upon himself the troublesome burden of this *crux in musica*. But the fig-ures marked with *sic* will show how badly he fared at times.

In the second place, the Anthems will prove that he was fully convinced of "the Lawfulness, Excellency, and Advantage of Instrumental Musick in the Public Worship of God" years before an anonymous "Presbyterian," perhaps James Lyon, endeavored to "urge and force" this doctrine "from the Scripture and Examples of the far greater Part of Christians in all Ages" by publishing a pamphlet under the above title at Philadelphia in 1763.* Not only was Hopkinson's 'Anthem from the 114th Psalm' to be accompanied by the organ, and possibly the venerable "bass viol," but he introduced violins, a proceeding which certainly would have called forth the indignation of the conservative element in the congregation had the anthem been performed in Christ Church. But I am inclined to believe that it was sung and played — at least for the first time — on May 1st, 1760, in the College Hall, the day appointed for Commencement. We read in the Pa. Journal on April 24, 1760, that

> Besides the Youth that are to receive their Bachelors Degree as usual, the Class that obtained their first Degree of the Institution in May, 1757, being now of standing for their Master's Degree, will receive the same.
>   . . . Besides the Orations and Disputes by the Candidates, there will be occasionally some Pieces of Music and Psalmody by the Charity Boys.

and in the Pa. Gazette, May 15, 1760:

> one of the Students who received his Master's Degree on this occasion, conducted the organ with that bold and masterly Hand for which he is celebrated and several of the Pieces were also his composition.

Francis Hopkinson — to whom this report certainly alludes — was among the candidates for the master's degree; as his anthem is dated 1760, as the exercises were interspersed with "some Pieces of Music and Psalmody," and as it became customary to perform works written and composed by students or graduates, we may agree that the 'Anthem from the 114th Psalm' was sung on said occasion by the Charity Boys, with proper accompaniment, the young composer himself presiding at the organ.

In the following year, on May 28, 1761, the Pa. Gazette printed an account of the Commencement exercises which fortunately does not oblige us to take refuge to conjectures:

> On Saturday last the public Commencement was held in the College of this City, before a vast Concourse of People of all Ranks. Besides the usual exercises (which gave

---

* More on this pamphlet will be found in the monograph on James Lyon's musical career.

great satisfaction to the Audience) there was performed in the Forenoon an elegant *Anthem*, composed by James Lyon, A. M. of New Jersey College; and in the Afternoon an *Ode*, sacred to the Memory of our late gracious Sovereign George II, written and set to Music, in a very grand and masterly Taste by Francis Hopkinson, Esq. A. M. of the College of this City. A Sett of Ladies and Gentlemen, in order to do Honour to the Entertainment of the Day, were kindly pleased to perform a Part both of the *Anthem* and *Ode*, accompanied by the Organ, which made the Music a very compleat and agreeable Entertainment to all present.

This Ode as "written and set to music by Francis Hopkinson, Esq." was printed together with a Dialogue by W. Dunlap of Philadelpia under the title of —

'An Exercise containing a Dialogue and Ode Sacred to the Memory of His late gracious Majesty, George II. . . .

A foot-note in the Miscellaneous Essays and Occasional Writings of Hopkinson, where the Ode stands on pages 77–82 of Volume II, informs us that the Dialogue was written by the Rev. Dr. Smith. Hopkinson's music seems not to be extant, but from the "libretto" we gain an idea concerning the form of the Ode, which is typical for the majority of early Commencement-Odes:

Recitative

Why looks the visionary Maid so sad?
Ah! why Britannia thus in Sable clad?
Oh speak the Cause from whence thy Sorrows flow,
That by partaking we may ease thy Woe!

Air. Britannia

Lend, lend your Tears, ye Virgin Train,
Whilst Music swells her softest strain;
Oh! let the solemn Dirge resound
And spread religious Sorrow round;
With me the deepest Loss deplore
My Son, My Son is now no more!

Symphony *
Chorus

Then let the solemn Dirge begin
Whilst our Voices join,
Thro' Earth's Extent to spread his Name,
Our Woe shall equal Thine.

---

* This term is not to be interpreted here in our modern manner, but in accord with the parlance of that period, merely as a symphonic or orchestral interlude of a few bars.

Symphony *

Air

The glorious Sun, Britannia's King,
Withdraws his golden Light;
His setting Ray
Glides swift away
And yields to conqu'ring Night.

II

See in the deep and dreary Tomb
His mortal Past must lie;
And ev'ry Bell
Now tolls his Knell,
Tears flow from ev'ry Eye.

III

: S: †   Far o'er the wild and watry Waste
Hear the loud Cannons roar
Whilst Winds convey
The Sounds away,
And die along the Shore.

IV

But lo! his Sainted Soul ascends.
High thro' th' etherial Road;
And Britain's Sighs
Like Incense rise
To waft him to his God.   *: S:*

In 1762 was printed by W. Dunlap:

'An *Exercise* containing a Dialogue and Ode on the Accession of His present gracious Majesty, George III, Performed at the public Commencement in the College of Philadelphia, May 18th, 1762.'

Though the publication is anonymous, the authors of the Exercise are easily traced. The Ode is contained in Francis Hopkinson's Miscellaneous Essays (in the same volume as the ode of 1761), and we read —

The Ode set to music by F- H-   . . .   The Dialogue by the rev. Mr. Duché.

The form of this ode differs somewhat from that of the other. It begins:

Bright ascending in the Skies
See Britannia's Glory rise!
Cease your Sorrows, cease your Fears!
Night recedes and Day appears!
Another George majestic fills the Throne
And glad Britannia calls him all her own.

---

* In the ' Miscellaneous Essays ' stands "A slow symphony."
† This sign stands for symphony.

Chorus.

Let the tuneful Chorus join
And high their Voices raise,
To celebrate in Notes divine,
The youthful Monarch's Praise.

The second stanza sings of "Rejoicing Science," of the "Sweets of
Liberty," of "Justice and Religion," the third sees "resplendent at his
Side . . . his modest blooming Bride." The fourth and last runs:

Rough War shall humbly at his Feet
Her bloody Laurels lay;
Him gentle Peace shall kindly greet
And smile beneath his Sway.
Then Britain! hail these golden Days!
Illustrious shalt thou shine:
For George shall gain immortal Praise,
And Britain! George is thine.
To distant Times he shall extend thy Name
And give thy Glories to a deathless Fame!

The chorus follows every stanza with the same four lines, only the
epitheton in the last line being changed. In the first stanza it is the
"youthful," in the second the "pious," in the third the "happy," and
in the last the "British" Monarch. Consequently the music of the
chorus remained throughout the same. Otherwise the musical form
is not so clearly indicated as in the Ode of 1761. The only distin-
guishing heading in Dunlap's publication of 1762 is "Chorus." But
in Hopkinson's 'Miscellaneous Essays' the second to fourth stanzas
are called Airs, and I doubt not that this Ode, too, began with a
Recitative.

The 'Miscellaneous Writings' contain a third Ode, which shows
exactly the same form as the second. The Recitative begins,
"when heav'n spreads blessings with unsparing hand." The Ode
was "designed for a public Commencement in the college of
Philadelphia," but a performance of it is not recorded. Perhaps
Hopkinson wrote it for the Commencement of 1763, when, to quote
from a letter written by Rev. Richard Peters to Rev. William Smith,
D. D., First Provost of the College of Philadelphia, under date of
Philadelphia, 28th May, 1763:

a foolish but tart difference [arose] between the Faculty and our good Friend Francis
Hopkinson on account of a grammatical squabble, wherein Mr. Hopkinson was the
Aggressor . . . The Faculty applied to Sam. Evans to write the Dialogue and to Mr.

Jackson to write the Ode for them, Mr. Duché and Mr. Hopkinson declining to have anything to do with it by means of this squabble about the grammar.*

Likewise intended for a musical setting was Hopkinson's poem 'Disappointed Love.' It stands in his 'Miscellaneous Essays' (Vol. III) and was reprinted from these in the Columbian Magazine, Philadelphia, in August, 1792. The poem consists of a Recitative and Air. I copy the first lines of both.

Recitative

High raised in aether, from her silver throne,
The moon in melancholy mildness shone.

Air

Farewell to all that promised joy ;
No flattering hopes my thoughts employ ;
A wounded heart bleeds in my breast !
And death alone can give me rest.

Whether our poet-composer set these melancholical lines to music I am unable to say. Of Hopkinson's musical manuscripts but very few are extant, and among the few appear neither the three Odes, nor the ' Disappointed Love,' nor a song to which he thus alludes in an undated letter—

Philada. Saturday Evening
My dear Nancy.

This morning I wrote the enclosed Song which I shall set to Music & play for you on the Guitar when I visit you next . . .

nor an Ode which he wrote and composed when in England. The poem makes part of the ' Miscellaneous Essays,' where it stands in Vol. III, pp. 137–138, under the title of :

AN ODE

Set to Music on Mrs. B—'s Birthday.†

Recitative

When *Cæsar's* birth-day glads Britannia's isle,
The earth exults and nature seems to smile :
Th' uplifted trumpet's awful sound
United acclamation's round,
And thund'ring cannons' awful roar
Shake with rude transport *Albion's* shore.

Air

But in more soft and pleasing lays
Let us our joy display,
Oh ! swell the tend'rest note of praise
To hail Eliza's day.

---

* Compare Pa. Mag. of Hist. X, 350.   † Mrs. Bremner?

For with fair truth and love divine,
Her peaceful soul is blest;
And all the winning virtues shine
Serenely in her breast.
Like some pure placid stream that flows
Gently and free from stain,
Dispensing blessings as it goes,
Along the flow'ry plain:

So she thro' life her equal way
Glides on with spotless name:
Oh! may this oft returning day
Encrease her modest fame!
                 Hartlebury Castle, 1766.

In the year which saw the squabble over the grammar between the college authorities and their good friend Francis Hopkinson a now excessively rare booklet was published at Philadelphia entitled:

This collection—I have examined the copy in possession of the Pennsylvania Historical Society—is beautifully engraved on excellent paper in obl. 8vo. and contains t. p. (v. bl.); on p. [iii–iv] a dedication; [v]–ix 'A Short introduction to the Art of Psalmody'; on pl. i a few Examples illustrating the introduction; on pls. ii–xxii thirty-six tunes, etc., mostly in 3 parts and with a figured bass for organ accompaniment; on pl. xxii a ' General Index.'

The introduction is indeed short and well calculated for the needs of children, but otherwise not remarkable or original enough to call for a detailed description. It treats:

> First, of the Notes, and their Lengths . . . Of the Cliffs . . . Of the Characters denoting the Time or Movement . . . Of the Pauses or Rests in Music . . . Of the Sharps, Flats and Naturals . . . Of other Characters used in Music . . . Of Bars . . . Of Keeping Time . . . Of Intonation . . .

A few quotations will be sufficient to illustrate the width and depth of these rules. We read on p. ix:

Of Keeping Time.

> In slow Common Time the *Bar* must be divided into equal Parts, telling One, Two, Three, Four, distinctly.
>
> In a quick Sort of Common Time each *Bar* may be divided into four equal Parts; and in Triple Time into three. The Hand or Foot being always struck down to the first Note of every *Bar*, be the *Time* what it will.

Of Intonation

> Intonation is the exact Conformity of the Voice, in singing any Note, to the Tone or Sound that Note would have if struck on a well-tuned Instrument. In order to be able to sound the Notes justly, it will be proper to practice the two or three Lessons I have adjoined in Plate 1st, till the younger student can sing them with Ease and Truth; after which the singing of the Psalms will become quite familiar; and after them the Hymns and Anthems. There are several other Rules and Characters in Music; but it is hoped if these few are well understood, they will serve at least as a good Introduction to the Study of Music.

The " short introduction " is not of sufficient historical importance to call for a minute investigation of its sources. They are essentially the same as those of James Lyon's ' Urania,' this latter work, however, included. I refer the reader to the monograph on Lyon's musical career, if he cares for fuller information on the subject.

The individual tunes in this collection of 1763 are entitled as follows:

Pl. II. St. James Tunes. Canterbury Tune. York Tune.
 III. Coleshill Tune. Mear Tune. St. David's Tune.
 IV. St. Mary's Tune. Southwell Tune. Westminster Tune.
 V. London Old Tune. London New Tune. Martyr's Tune.
 VI. St. Ann's Tune. Brunswick Tune. St. Humphrey's Tune.
 VII. Proper Tune to the 81st Psalm. Proper Tune to the 100th Psalm.
 VIII. Standish Tune. Bedford Tune. Portsmouth Tune.
 IX. The New 100th Psalm Tune. Proper Tune to the 113th Psalm.
 X. Proper Tune to the 119th Psalm.
 XI. Proper Tuneto [sic] the 148th Psalm.

                 } for three parts.

 XII. Hymn ('Sing we Praises to the Lord')
 XIII. Hymn ('When all thy Mercies')
 XIV. Hymn ('The Spacious Firmament on high')
 XV. Hymn ('Thro' all the changing Scenes of Life')
 XVI. Hymn from the 137th Psalm. ('When we our wearied Limbs')

                 } for two parts.

 XVII. Hymn ('My Soul thy great Creator praise') [Air] for two parts,
      Chorus for three.

 XVIII. Chiddingstone.
 XIX. The 4th Psalm.
 XX. The 23d Psalm.
 XXI. Hallelujah. ('Praise ye the Lord ye immortal Choir')
 XXII. The 98th Psalm.

                 } for three parts.

None of the pieces bears an author's name, not even the "entirely new." That these were productions of the compiler goes without saying. But unfortunately the booklet is anonymous. Consequently if authorities in psalmody, like Mr. James Warrington of Philadelphia, were able to separate the old from the entirely new "tunes," the difficulty would still remain of ascertaining the composer of the latter and thereby the compiler of the collection or *vice versa*.*

However, we are aided in this direction by the dedication, which reads in part:

To the Reverend Mr. Richard *Peters*, Rector of the United Churches of Christ Church and St. Peter's Church in Philadelphia.

. . . permit me to hope this Attempt To the Improvement of our Psalmody or Church Music will meet with your favorable Acceptance and Encouragement. Something of this kind was thought the more necessary, as it is highly probable there will be Organs erected in both our Churches before it be long; which would be but a needless Expense if the Congregations could not join their Voices with them in the singing of Psalms. For this Purpose, I have made this Collection of Psalms, Hymns and An-

---

*In the Brinley Catalogue (pt. IV) James Lyon is pointed out as the possible author of this collection. I have not entered upon a discussion of this hypothesis, as it lacks all necessary foundation, for instance, James Lyon was a Presbyterian and Christ Church is Episcopalian!

thems, and prefixed a few Rules for Singing in as clear and easy a Manner as possible;
so that children, with very little Attention, may understand them. . . .

The Editor.

Now we know from Rev. Dorr's ' Historical Account ' that Francis
Hopkinson was a prominent member of the congregation and that in
1764 the thankful acknowledgments were given Mr. Hopkinson and
Mr. Young for their "great and constant pains in teaching and instructing the children " in psalmody.

On these grounds the great bibliographer Hildeburn attributed in
his ' Issues of the Press in Pennsylvania ' (I, 387) the collection to the
pen of Francis Hopkinson.   Indeed, the argument is reasonable that
one of the two gentlemen mentioned in the vestry minutes edited the
booklet.   Hildeburn pays no attention to the possibility that the
bookseller and publisher William Young might have been the editor.
From all we know of this gentleman's musical career — he appears
neither in the newspapers nor elsewhere except in the vestry minutes
as psalmodist, musician or musical editor — Hildeburn was justified
in so doing.   This adds weight in favor of Hopkinson's authorship.
Still, it might be claimed that neither he nor Young compiled the
collection, but some musician interested in the welfare of the United
Congregations.

Mr. James Warrington, when exchanging a few remarks with me
on the subject, felt inclined to believe that James Bremner, the organist,
edited the book.   This would have been possible only if Bremner
resided at Philadelphia some time before its publication.

Now the first advertisement of the collection appeared in the Pa.
Gaz. on May 5, 1763, and reads :

> On Monday next will be published and sold by William Dunlap, in Market Street,
> (Price Five Shillings) a Collection of Psalm Tunes, Hymns and Anthems, with a short
> introduction for the Use of the United Churches of Christ Church and St. Peter's in Phil-
> adelphia.

As it took some time after the conception of the idea of editing
such a psalm-tune collection to compile and engrave it, Bremner, if he
was the editor, must have been in Philadelphia earlier than May, 1763.
When coming to the colonies, the foreign musicians would, as a rule,
advertise their services as music teachers, etc., very soon after their
arrival.   Bremner's name, too, is to be found in the Philadelphia
papers, but not before *December 1,* 1763.   Under this date we read in
both the Pa. Gaz. and Pa. Journal :

Mr. *Bremner* begs leave to acquaint the public that he intends to open his music school on Monday the 12th instant at Mr. Glover Hunt's, near the Coffee House in Market Street . . .

This advertisement does not state that he *re*-opened a music-school which he might have kept in 1762 or early in 1763 though not advertising the same.

Furthermore, in the vestry-minutes of Christ Church as published by Rev. Dorr, Bremner's name does not appear until 1767, when he is mentioned for the first time as organist of Christ Church. It might be said that he was in charge of the old organ of 1728 during the previous years and that there was no necessity of mentioning his name in the minutes of 1763. But in 1761

Mrs. Mary Andrews left, by will, to the minister and church wardens of Christ Church £100 towards purchasing an organ.

In 1763

A Subscription of £500 is obtained towards purchasing an organ for Christ Church. . . .

In 1765

The committee for building an organ for Christ Church, reported that the same was now ready to be put up . . .

and on January 12, 1767,

The organ in Christ Church being finished, the same was carefully examined by the governors, Mr. Bremner, the Organist, and several others who were deemed to understand such work . . .

Not once, therefore, is this organ alluded to as the "new" organ, built to replace an old one. If this alone renders it doubtful whether Christ Church possessed an organ at all in 1763 it becomes almost impossible to believe that the organ of 1728 was still in this church if we recall the remark of the editor in the dedication of his psalm-tune collection to the Rev. Peters (1763!):

It is highly probable there will be Organs erected in both our Churches before it be long, which would be but a needless Expense if the Congregations could not join their Voices with them in the singing of Psalms . . .

These lines, it seems to me, clearly prove that no organ existed in Christ Church during 1763. Consequently there was no organist.

Moreover, though, in 1763

The vestry agreed to the erecting of an organ in St. Peter's Church, providing that neither the said organ, nor the organist shall be any charge to the churches

and though this organ is mentioned under date of November 2, 1763, as "built" by Philip Feyring and "now in St. Peters," we know that in February, 1764, the subscriptions still proved insufficient "for completing the design."* Under these circumstances, Bremner can hardly have been organist at St. Peter's in 1763, especially not in May, 1763, when the Psalm-tune collection was published in the dedication of which the editor clearly states that no organ existed in St. Peter's.

But he might have been engaged before the instrument was erected, in order to teach the children psalmody, and then might have first compiled the collection of 1763 for their improvement. If this had been the case, the vestry when acknowledging the services rendered by Francis Hopkinson and William Young would not have failed to word their resolutions in a way as to show that the two gentlemen kindly *assisted* the regular psalmodist, but the tenor of the minutes does not admit of such inference.

All this may not be considered absolutely conclusive against Bremner. However, unless direct evidence is found in his favor, his authorship will remain highly improbable. On the other hand, neither chronological nor other data furnish reasonable arguments against Francis Hopkinson. On the contrary, his authorship can be rendered probable to the degree of certainty.

The title reads :

'A Collection of Psalm Tunes, with a few Anthems and Hymns. *Some of them entirely new* . . . '

It will be admitted that the words in italics signify that the entirely new tunes were written by the compiler himself. If therefore one of these can be traced to Hopkinson's pen the problem would be solved. Now, Francis Hopkinson's manuscript collection of 1759 contains on p. 179, composed by himself, the 23d Psalm. *Comparison*

---

* Philipp *Fyring*—this seems to be the correct spelling of the name—had previously, in 1762, erected an organ in St. Paul's. The Pa. Gaz. (Dec. 23, 1762) proclaimed Fyring as an organ builder to be the "best Hand at that ingenious Business on the Continent." On hearing the Organ at St. Paul's, on Christmas Day, 1762, an enthusiast signing " C. W. P." wrote a poem which begins :

" Thy Name, o Fyring thy deserving Name,
Shall shine conspicuous in the roll of fame."

The poem appeared in the Pa. Gaz. on Dec. 30, 1762, and a footnote informs us that—

" Mr. Fyring is a German by Birth, but has, for some years past, practiced the making of Musical Instruments (particularly Spinets and Harpsichords) in this City, with great Repute."

proved this manuscript piece to be identical with the 23d Psalm as contained on pl. xx of 'A collection of Psalm Tunes . . . 1763.'

If Francis Hopkinson's manuscript collection of 1759, in which he appears as composer of sacred music, were not extant, we would be able to trace at least one published psalm tune to his pen.

It was Mr. Warrington, I believe, who discovered it in

· 'The Book of Common Prayer, as revised and proposed to the Use of the Protestant Episcopal Church at a Convention of the said Church . . . Held in Philadelphia from September 27th to October 7th, 1785. Philadelphia. Printed by Hall and Sellers . . . 1786.'

The book contains as an appendix eight pages of

'Tunes. Suited to the Psalms and Hymns of the Book of Common Prayer.'

These tunes are arranged according to their metre, and on the last page we notice a

'Proper Tune for Ps. 96th by F. H. 7th Metre.'

Unquestionably Francis Hopkinson was the composer of this little piece, for when not signing his full name he was in the habit of using the initials either " F. H. Esq" or simply " F. H."

Twenty years previous a book left the press which is of by far greater importance than this psalm tune.

The New York Historical Society possesses :

'The Psalms | of | David, with | the Ten Commandments, | Creed, Lord's Prayer, etc | In Metre | Also | the Catechism, Confession of Faith, | Liturgy etc | Translated from the Dutch. | For the Use of the Reformed Protestant Dutch | Church of the City of New York. |

New York. Printed by James Parker, at the New Printing Office in Beaver-Street MDCCLXVII.'

This rare publication contains the following advertisement:

To the Reader.

The Consistory of the Reformed Protestant Dutch Church of the City of New York, having by Reason of the Declension of the Dutch Language, found it necessary to have Divine Service performed in their Church in English, have adopted the following Version of the Psalms of David, which is greatly indebted to that of Dr. Brady and Mr. Tate ; Some of the Psalms being transcribed verbatim from their Version, and others altered so as to fit them to the Music used in the Dutch Churches   .   .   .

City of New York, November 9th, 1767

By order of the Consistory,

Joannes Ritzema.

V. D. M.   P. T. Praes.

An imperfect copy of the same book, also in possession of the New York Historical Society, contains a manuscript memorandum by the late and lamented librarian William Kelby, which is of some interest in this connection :

This vol. was presented May 1817 by Egbert Benson who made an entry on the old cover that Francis Hopkinson of Phil. was the translator. This was destroyed in rebinding. Charles R. Hildeburn of Pa. has proof of the authorship of Hopkinson.

April 1881.   *W. K.*

Referring to this memorandum, the editor of the Pa. Mag. of Hist., in Vol VI, p. 124, wrote :

We are indebted to the Rev. T. W. Chambers, D. D. of New York, pastor of the Reformed Protestant Dutch Church, for the translations of the following extracts from the church records. They are the only ones in which the name of Mr. Hopkinson appears :

" New York, May 22, 1764.

"*Resolved*—That Mr. Evert Byvank be discharged from his engagement to versify the Psalms in English in the same manner as they are versified in the Low Dutch, and that the Committee with Mr. Hopkinson inquire into the best method of doing this according to the genius of the English tongue, and the versifying be done accordingly."

"New York, June 29, 1764.
"A letter was read from Mr. Francis Hopkinson dated June 11, 1764, concerning the versifying of the Psalms of David in English in the manner proposed; and the Consistory agreed to pay him for altering what has been done forty pi-toles, and for completing the whole one hundred pistoles, fifty of which shall be paid when the work on the new plan shall be half done if Hopkinson asks it; and since certain members are to pay the first mentioned 40 pistoles, the Consistory agreed to repay them out of the first printed Psalm books or out of other funds; and shall also make the necessary arrangement for paying the last named pistoles and the other needful expenses in versifying the Psalms."

Hopkinson's task was peculiar. As Mr. James Warrington, the excellent authority on psalmody, put it for me in as few words as possible:

The Metres of the Dutch Psalters are mostly ten syllables a line, four or five or six lines to a stanza.

The English Psalters are mostly in what is called Common Metre, that is alternately lines of eight and six syllables.

Hopkinson's task was to just make sufficient alterations in Tate & Brady's 'A New Version of the Psalms of David fitted to the Tunes in Churches' (First edition London 1696, frequently reprinted both in England and America) as to lengthen the lines from eight or six syllables to ten.

For instance the first two lines in Psalm I of Hopkinson reads thus:
        " How blest is he, who ne'er consents to walk
         By ill Advice, nor dares to stand and talk."
In Tate & Brady the same Psalm begins:
        " How blest is he, who ne'er consents
         By ill advice to walk."

Evidently Francis Hopkinson pleased the Consistory with his work, for he wrote in a letter to Benjamin Franklin, under date of "13 Dec. 1765":

I have finished the translation of the Psalms of David to the great satisfaction of the Dutch Congregation of New York and they have paid me £145 their currency which I intend to keep as a body reserve in case I should go to England.*

It is not likely that the Consistory should have engaged Francis Hopkinson for a work of such far-reaching importance had not his reputation as a psalmodist been well established. The fact of his pedagogic experience would not have induced the Consistory to intrust him with the versifying of the Psalms from Dutch into English. The supposition is very much more reasonable that the psalm-tune collection of 1763 attracted attention, that Hopkinson became known as its author, and that thereupon the Consistory engaged him, who was

---

* This letter is in possession of the Am. Philos. Soc. Phila. Mr. Warrington kindly permitted me to use his copy of the autograph.

familiar with the Dutch language and a poet besides, for the difficult task after Mr. Evert Byvank had proved to be a failure.

> *During the Revolution there was a very tawdry march often played by the American bands, entitled ' The Washington March.'*

Unfortunately Mr. Louis C. Elson, in whose book on ' The National Music of America and its Sources' (Boston, 1900, p 157), this information is to be found, neither reproduces the march nor refers to his authorities for the statement. Perhaps when compiling his essay he came across the following lines in George Washington Parke Custis' ' Recollections and Private Memoirs of Washington' (1860, p. 368):

> In New York . . . [in 1789] upon the president's entering the stage box with his family, the orchestra would strike up ' The President's March' (now Hail Columbia) composed by a German named " Feyles," * in '89 in contradistinction to the march of the Revolution called ' Washington's March.'
>
> The audience applauded on the entrance of the president, but the pit and gallery were so truly despotic in the early days of the republic, that so soon as ' Hail Columbia' had ceased ' Washington's March' was called for by the deafening din of a hundred voices at once, and upon its being played, three hearty cheers would rock the building to its base.

Or Mr. Elson might have relied upon 'A Monogram on our National Song' (Albany, 1869), by Rev. Elias Nason, who says on p. 33:

> The field music of the revolution consisted mainly of ' Yankee Doodle'; ' On the Road to Boston'; ' Rural Felicity '; ' My Dog and Gun'; and 'Washington's March.'†

Before submitting the article referred to, it might be of importance to quote first from Nason's Monogram the words (on p. 25):

> . . . Francis Hopkinson, Esquire, author of '*General Washington's March*,'

and then a note which the same writer seems to have communicated to the Historical Magazine in 1859. We read there (on p. 219) under the heading of 'Revolutionary Music':

> Mr. Bery. Smith of West Needham, Mass. now 93 years old, who was a fifer in the army of the Revolution informs me that the popular tunes of that period were ' The Road to Boston' and ' The President's March.' The Continental musicians hardly knew any other tunes at first, but soon learned ' Yankee Doodle,' the ' White Cockade ' etc. from hearing the British play them in the distance. . . .
>
> There is another ' President's March' sometimes called '*Washington's Quick Step,*' written in double time, whose authorship as well as that of '*Washington's Slow March*' is, I believe, unknown.   E. N.

---

* For the correct spelling of this name (Phile), and other items relating to the musical origin of ' Hail Columbia' see my ' Critical Notes . . .' on the same in Sbde. der Intern. Musik. Gesellschaft, Nov., 1901.

† Composed in G, by the Hon. *Francis Hopkinson.* See Hist. Mag. for Jan. 1859. (Nason's footnote.)

Apparently the venerable Mr. Smith's memory was not quite reliable, since he allowed the Continental troops to play a 'President's March' before a President was elected. Moreover, Mr. Smith *does not mention a 'Washington's March' as among the popular military tunes of the Revolution.*

Evidently Mr. Elias Nason gathered his information for the lines first quoted from other sources. He refers but to one of these, the January issue of the Historical Magazine, 1859. There we read:

> "... I have ... reason to believe that the 'Washington March' generally known by that title—I mean the one in key of G major, was composed by the Hon. Francis *Hopkinson*, senior, having seen it in a manuscript book of his own handwriting among others of his known compositions.   J. C."
>
> The above was published in the 'Baltimore Clipper' in 1841 by a person who well understood the subject.*

These various statements render the 'Washington's March' an interesting piece of music, at least from the standpoint of the antiquarian. In the first place, there seem to have been several tawdry marches of a similar title. In the second place, the march, being claimed as a production of Francis Hopkinson, becomes important for a monograph on his musical career. Finally, the question arises whether or not it was a revolutionary march.

The 'Recollections' of Mr. Custis would have us answer the last point in the affirmative. But, as I have pointed out in my 'Critical Notes on the origin of Hail Columbia,' we must look upon the contemporary evidence of these recollections with a good deal of scepticism. Mr. Custis was born when the War of the Revolution was drawing to its end: A. D. 1781. Consequently, what he knew of the 'Washington's March' he learned from hearsay. But evidence gained through the elastic *on dit* can not satisfy the demands of historical criticism. The historian needs facts with which to control apparently accurate information; he needs facts, not of a doubtful kind, but such as will corroborate recollections and other subjective evidence.

In our particular case, one fact only stands forth: Francis Hopkinson died in 1791.

If the 'Washington's March' was a composition of his, or if *J. C.* really saw it in Hopkinson's hand-writing, it must have been written before this year. Then we might ask if the march

---

* J. C. probably stands for Joseph Carr, who opened a "Musical Repository" in Baltimore in 1794, arriving there in 1793, from England. This date I beg to keep in mind.

can be traced in autobiographies, diaries, newspapers, magazines, musical publications and other sources, covering the period between 1776 and 1791. An absolutely exhaustive investigation of all these sources is not impossible, but it has not been tried on the narrow path which possibly would lead to the origin of said ' Washington's March.' With regard to material, which I extracted from the sources mentioned for a history of early secular music in the United States—extracts which though not absolutely exhaustive, nevertheless practically cover the ground—I might say that I have failed to find any allusion to the ' Washington's March ' before the year 1794. Nevertheless, it is possible that the march is mentioned in sources not examined by me. But even at that, it would seem strange that a march, said to have been played during the Revolution and certainly popular during the decade preceding the nineteenth century and later, should be traceable only in a very few instances, if in any.

With these remarks, I do not intend to look down upon the claimed revolutionary origin of ' The Washington's March ' as a mere myth. But we can not be too cautious in accepting reports which concern the history of our patriotic music, especially if they are full of conflicting statements. It is better to be sceptical and to leave the solution of an interesting problem to later and more fully equipped investigators rather than to surrender unconditionally to possibilities or to the desire of solving problems without the necessary evidence.

This applies strongly to Francis Hopkinson's authorship. The more so, as J. C. himself does not make a positive statement. He merely tells us his reason for *believing* that the ' Washington's March ' in G major was written by Francis Hopkinson : he saw it in a manuscript-book of his own handwriting among others of his known compositions.

We have no right to doubt J. C.'s veracity, and therefore admit that he saw a ' Washington's March ' in G major in said book. But this is no proof of Hopkinson's authorship, and emphasis should be laid upon the fact that J. C. himself did not feel justified in positively attributing the march to Hopkinson. Furthermore, between the year of Joseph Carr's arrival in the United States in 1793 and his note in the Baltimore Clipper almost fifty years had elapsed—a period long enough to invent recollections in good faith. Finally, if J. C. does not stand for Joseph Carr, but for a person belonging to a later generation, then the note bears very little acceptable evidence.

Perhaps a new investigation of the source would permit us to be more positive than he? Alas! the volume mentioned by J. C. seems to be lost, as none of Francis Hopkinson's music books extant contain a ' Washington's March.'

Consequently, if we accept J. C.'s "reason" as satisfactory, we need but examine other sources in order to find this ' Washington's March in G major' and attach, after having found it, the Hon. Francis Hopkinson's name to the tawdry piece. A very simple proceeding, it would seem, but I fear the reader will have to change his opinion before long.

The Library Company of Philadelphia possesses a volume of miscellaneous ' Marches and Battle-pieces,' mostly of American origin. In this volume I found printed on the same sheet:

' WASHINGTON'S MARCH. Philadelphia. Published and Sold at G. Willig's Musical Magazine '—

and ' WASHINGTON'S MARCH AT THE BATTLE OF TRENTON.' (See Appendix.)

George Willig published the ' Washington's March' again without date, under the following title:

' *Washington's March.* As performed at the New Theatre, Philadelphia. Publ. and sold at G. Willig's Musical Magazine.'

As will be seen in the Appendix, the march " as performed at the New Theatre" has received a setting a trifle more elaborate than when published together with the ' Washington's March at the Battle of Trenton.' From this we might infer that the version reproduced in fac-simile antedates the other.

Now Wignell & Reinagle's New Theatre was not opened until February, 1793, when a few concerts were given. It then remained closed till February, 1794, when the first theatrical performances took place. As the concert programs of 1793 do not contain the ' Washington's

March,' it is probable that the piece, as published by Willig, was performed at the new theatre not before 1794. Willig appears in the Philadelphia directories for the first time in 1796, but from the newspapers we know that he kept a musical magazine at No. 165 Market Street in March, 1795, having opened it in 1794. Therefore his publications of the ' Washington's March' may be dated 1795 or 1794, but not earlier, though the march certainly was known before this year, and though the version given in fac-simile might have been popular for years before, I failed to find any allusion to the march previous to its publication by George Willig.

If this is considered as of no importance, the situation becomes embarrassing through other observations.

Both the ' Washington's March ' and the ' Washington's March at the Battle of Trenton ' have similar titles and *both stand in the key of G major*. As if to help us to overcome our embarrassment the later march appears in a publication (issued later than 1798, as it contains ' Hail Columbia,' in fact not earlier than 1805, if we may trust the addresses given in the Philadelphia directories), without the words " at the Battle of Trenton," simply as ' Washington's March.'

I am alluding to a pamphlet of 27 pages in the possession of Yale University under the title of —

' WILLIG'S INSTRUCTIONS FOR THE GERMAN FLUTE. Philadelphia. Published and sold at G. Willig's Musical Magazine No. 171 Chestnut. Pr. 75 c.' *

---

* The same book contains on p. 23

Washington's Guard Quick March.

In the miscellaneous volume of ' Marches and Battle-pieces' we find :
' *Washington Guards March.* Composed by a member of the Washington Association. Philadelphia. Published and sold at G. Willig's Musical Magazine.'

We find there in the key of G major on p. 22 a 'Washington's March' identical with the 'Washington's March at the Battle of Trenton.'

Consequently, both marches were known under the simple title of 'Washington's March.' But which was the one *generally* known as such and believed by J. C. to have been written by Francis Hopkinson?

Very likely the one which with its earlier title seems to carry us back to the War of the Revolution. We already feel inclined to take this for granted when we notice that the revolutionary origin is destroyed by

'The Flute Preceptor or Columbian Instructor. Improv'd by R. Shaw. Philadelphia, 1802.'

Printed on the same sheet with this appears the

Washington Guards Quick-Step

In an undated publication entitled 'The Gentlemen's Amusement, a select collection of songs, duetts, dances, & marches, Properly adapted for the flute, violin, & patent flageolet. Book 4. Price 1 dol. New York. Published by W. Dubois at his Pianoforte and Music Store, 126 Broadway,' we notice on p. 23

Washington's New March   *Curphew*

Bound together with a miscellaneous collection of pieces for the Pianoforte (Gift of Charles A. Cutter. H. C. 1855 to Harv. U.) are seventy pieces in MS., some of which are to be dated later than 1830. This, however, does not apply, I believe, to a march which appears in the MS. collection under the title of

Genrl. Washington's March

Though these five 'Washington's Marches' do not affect, it seems to me, my theme, I considered it worth while to call attention to them, for obvious reasons.

In this instruction book, on p. 24, appears identical with ' Washington's March at the Battle of Trenton,' though not *notatim :*

PRESIDENT'S NEW MARCH.

History now forbids to date the ' Washington's March at the Battle
of Trenton ' *alias* ' Washington's March ' *alias* ' PRESIDENT'S New
March,' earlier than 1789, the year in which our first President was
inaugurated.

I add *alias* ' General Washington's March,' for a book in my possession called ' The Village Fifer . . . No. 1 ' (published in Exeter, N. H.,
March, 1808) contains the same piece in G major on p. 34–35, in an
arrangement for two fifes under the title of ' General Washington's
March.'

Identical with it, some unimportant alterations in the second flute
excepted, is the ' Geo. Washington's March ' as appearing on p. 61 of
Alvan Robinson, Jun.'s ' Massachusett's Collection of Martial Musick,'
the second edition of which (Exeter, 1820) is in my possession. Again
entitled ' Gen. Washington's March,' I notice the same air in Charles
Robbins' ' Drum and Fife Instructor ' (Exeter, N. H., 1812, p. 31).
Harvard University finally possesses an undated piece for the pianoforte, called

' General Washington's March.
Boston. Printed and sold by G. Graupner at his Musical Academy No. 6 Franklin
Street, Franklin Square . . .'

It is an easy arrangement of the ' Washington's March at the
Battle of Trenton,' as published by Willig.

Again concentrating our attention upon the ' Washington's March,'
as performed at the New Theatre, Philadelphia, we find it differing
from Willig's version with respect to the first bars only, on p. 25 of
Shaw's Instruction Book (1802).

Slight and equally unimportant differences will also be noticed in
a version of this ' Washington's March ' as it was printed [about 1805]
in—

' The Compleat Tutor for the Fife . . , Philadelphia. Printed for and sold by George
Willig.'

The same piece, but now under the title of '*Washington's Grand March,*' appears in

'A New and Complete Preceptor for the violin, with a collection of cotillions, marches, etc. Philadelphia. Published & sold by Klemen & Brother' on p. 29. (Yale University Library.)

The air had not ceased to be popular when we fought our second war with Great Britain. The volume of Marches and Battle-pieces in possession of the Library Company, Phila., contains:

'AMERICA AND BRITANNIA. PEACE. A New March composed by *R. Taylor* (and so arranged as to Harmonize perfectly with Washington's March, played both together. Philadelphia. Published & Sold at G. Willig's Musical Magazine.'

---

*Many years before Raynor Taylor had thus taken 'Washington's March' as a *cantus firmus,* James Hewitt, composer, leader of the New York Opera-Orchestra and music publisher, used it for a similar combination.

I am alluding to a patriotic song, very popular about 1800. The words may be found in quite a number of early newspapers and magazines. I have copied them from the Philadelphia Monthly Magazine for May, 1798, where they read as follows:

"THE NEW YORK PATRIOTIC SONG,
called
THE FEDERAL CONSTITUTION BOYS, AND LIBERTY FOREVER.

Written by Mr. Milns—Sung by Mr. Williamson, the Music adapted by Mr. *Hewitt,* from Washington's March and Yankee Doodle.

I

Poets may sing of their Helicon streams,
Their Gods and their Heroes are fabulous dreams;
They ne'er sang a line
Half so grand, so divine,
As the glorious toast,
We Columbians boast,
The *Federal Constitution* boys, and Liberty forever.

II

Adams the man of our choice guides the helm
No trumpet can harm us, no storm overwhelm;
Our sheet anchor's sure
And our bark rides secure,
So here's to the toast
We Columbians boast
The *Federal Constitution* and the *President* forever.

If all this seems to have escaped previous writers on the subject and renders our situation with respect to the ' Washington's March ' in G major, attributed to Francis Hopkinson, embarrassing enough, utmost confusion is created by the ' Complete Fifer's Museum,' of which an undated fragment is in my possession. In this torso appears on p. 20, *again in the key of G major, but entirely different from the two others,* the following

WASHINGTON'S MARCH.

etc.

III

A free Navigation, Commerce and Trade,
We'll seek for no foe, of no foe be afraid ;
Our frigates shall ride
Our defense and our pride ;
Our tars guard our coast
And huzza to our toast
The *Federal Constitution, Trade* and *Commerc*e forever.

IV

Montgomery, Warren, still live in our songs,
Like them our *young* heroes shall spurn at our wrongs.—
The world shall admire
The zeal and the fire
Which blaze in the toast
We Columbians boast
The *Federal Constitution* and its advocates forever.

V

When an enemy threats all party shall cease
We *bribe* no intruders to buy a mean peace
Columbians will scorn
Friends or foes to suborn ;
We'll ne'er stain the toast—
Which as free men we boast—
The *Federal Constitution* and *integrity* forever.

VI

Fame's trumpet shall swell in *Washington's* praise
And *Time* grant a furlough to lengthen his days ;
May health weave the thread
Of delight round his head —
No nation can boast
Such a name — such a toast —
The *Federal Constitution* Boys, and *Washington* forever."

I have not been able to find Hewitt's musical setting to this New York Patriotic Song and am therefore not in a position to decide which of the two ' Washington's Marches ' was hitched with ' Yankee Doodle.'

Raynor Taylor's 'America and Britannia' and Hewitt's New York Patriotic Song are not the only instances in which popular airs were combined in order to arouse double enthusiasm. Benjamin Carr's ' Federal Overture ' was a *pot-pourri* or *quod libet* at least as popular as 'The New York Patriotic Song, called ' The Federal Constitution Boys, and Liberty Forever.' The character of this overture may be understood from a theatrical advertisement of the Old American Company in Dunlap's Daily American Advertiser, Sept. 22, 1794 :

" Previous to the Tragedy the band will play a new Federal Overture, in which is introduced several popular airs ; Marseilles hymn [sic instead of Marseillaise] ; Ça ira ; O dear what can the matter be ; Rose Tree ; Carmagnole ; President's March ; Yankee Doodle, etc. Composed by Mr. Carr."

Three marches known under the name of ' Washington's March,' and all three in G major! Again we ask, which of the three did J. C. have in mind?　To recapitulate, before venturing an answer :

The ' Washington's March ' as originally published by Willig bears this name wherever it appears, with one unimportant exception only. The 'Washington's March at the Battle of Trenton' was known under four different names, this and ' Washington's March '; General Washington's March '; ' President's New March.' The last name proves that it was composed, at the earliest, in 1789. The third ' Washington's March ' may be dropped. Everything goes to show that the real ' Washington's March ' was a popular piece. Were the third version the one alluded to by *J. C.*, it would appear at least as often as the two others. This however is by no means the case.

It would be unscientific to positively attribute, on the basis of these investigations, one or the other of the three marches to the pen of Francis Hopkinson. If he did write a ' Washington's March' and if it was played by the Continental bands during the War of the Revolution or even later, it probably was either the ' Washington's March' or ' Washington's March at the Battle of Trenton' (*alias* 'President's New March') as published by Willig. It would be gratifying if later historians succeeded in establishing Francis Hopkinson's authorship beyond doubt for one or the other of the marches or of both. However, one possibility remains which I am not in a position to investigate at present. I faintly remember having heard this or a very similar march played by one of the German regimental bands. Should ' Washington's March ' after all not be of American but of European origin, and should it have been called ' Washington's March' in the United States merely because it was a favorite of the great general?

During the War of the Revolution many musicians left the United States for want of employment, but some remained in the country of their adoption, either hoping for a speedy return of peace, prosperity, and therewith renewed musical activity, or entering the army. Among the latter was Francis Mentges, known to all Philadelphians as the dancing-master Mr. Francis, and who won such distinction on the battle-field as to be promoted to the rank of colonel. Among the former seems to have been the organist and composer James Bremner, for " he died on the banks of the Schuylkill, Sept. 1780." This death notice is to be found in a footnote to the following dirge :

IN MEMORY OF MR. JAMES BREMNER.

Sing to his shade a solemn strain,
Let music's notes complain;
Let echo tell from shore to shore,
The swain of Schuylkill is no more.

Air.

From Scotia's land he came
And brought the pleasing art
To raise the sacred flame
That warms a feeling heart.

The magic powr's of sound,
Obey at his command,
And spread sweet influence round,
Wak'd by his skilful hand.

Oh! sanctify the ground,
The ground where he is laid;
Plant roses all around,
Nor let those roses fade.

Let none his tomb pass by,
Without a gen'rous tear,
Or sigh — and let that sigh,
Be like himself sincere.

These lines were written by Francis Hopkinson, for they appear in his 'Miscellaneous Essays' in Vol III, p. 184. The dirge may not be considered as of poetic value, but it is touching, and its sincerity proves the admiration and friendship in which the pupil held the master.

The dirge made a deep impression upon contemporaries of our poet-composer. This we know from a poem 'To the Memory of Francis Hopkinson, esqr.' published in the American Museum, Phila., in 1791 (App. p. 39) and "ascribed to John Swanwick, Esq." who thus recalls his impressions of

The elegant dirge . . . composed and set to music by Judge Hopkinson:

Notes such as once he pour'd at Bremner's urn
Lays such as those he offered at his shrine —
But ah, what muse can make a just return
For lays so mournful, or a note so fine.

It is to be regretted that Hopkinson's composition seems to be among those which are no longer extant.

About the time of Bremner's death originated in the United States the short-lived enthusiasm for everything French, which Watson has so delightfully described in his 'Annals of Philadelphia.'

The allies paid one another all possible compliments in order to fasten the ties between the young republic and the monarchy of His Most Christian Majesty, ties which withstood the test of time and the contest between " Federalists " and "Anti-Federalists " until the insolence of the hot-blooded French Republicans nearly forced us, in 1798, to declare war against a nation to which we owed so much. But about 1780 good-will, friendship and gratitude only were the key-notes in our relations with France. Balls, concerts, dinners, receptions and the like in rapid succession gave expression to these sentiments. One of the most elaborate affairs of the kind was

'THE TEMPLE OF MINERVA, a Musical Entertainment performed in
    Nov. 1781, by a Band of Gentlemen and Ladies, at the hotel of
    the Minister of France in Philadelphia.'

This is the title of a libretto as printed in the Columbian Magazine, Phila., for April, 1787, p. 391–392. The Freeman's Journal printed on December 19, 1781, the following account of the festivities:

Philadelphia, December 19.
On Tuesday evening of the 11th inst. his Excellency the Minister of France, who embraces every opportunity to manifest his respect to the worthies of America and politeness to its inhabitants, entertained his Excellency General Washington, and his lady, the lady of General Greene and a very polite circle of gentlemen and ladies with an elegant Concert, in which the following *Oratorio* composed and set to music by a gentleman whose taste in the polite arts is well known, was introduced, and afforded the most sensible pleasure: the *Temple of Minerva*, An Oratorial Entertainment . . .

Neither this report nor the Columbian Magazine mention the poet-composer. However, the reprint of the libretto is signed *"H."* This initial and the fact that ' The Temple of Minerva ' was composed and set to music by a gentleman whose taste in the polite arts was well known, furnished clues. In his role of detective the historian has frequently to reckon with possibilities, and such a possibility was, on the basis of these two items, that none but Francis Hopkinson wrote the " oratorio."

The examination of his published writings proved in vain, since they do not contain ' The Temple of Minerva.' Already had I despaired of proving Hopkinson's authorship, of which I was convinced, when luck came to my assistance.

Mrs. Florence Scovel Shinn, of New York City, a great-great granddaughter of Francis Hopkinson, had kindly given me access to her family-papers. Among these are, in the beautiful original binding

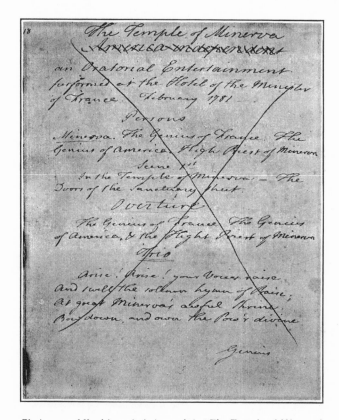

First page of Hopkinson's Autograph to ' The Temple of Minerva.'

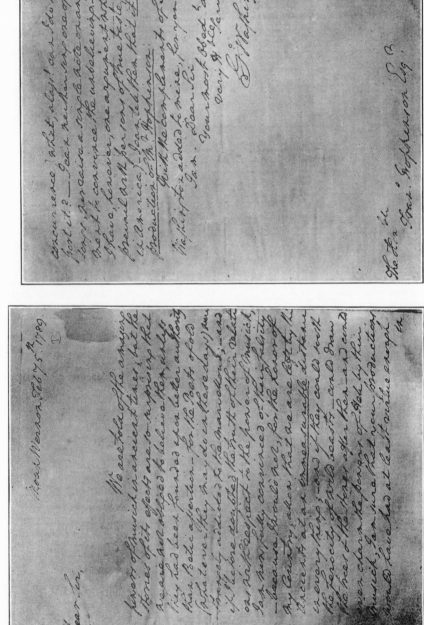

Part of Letter from George Washington to Francis Hopkinson

and in Hopkinson's manuscript, two volumes of his collected poems and prose writings. I examined these venerable volumes carefully and they showed that I had been on the right trail. It was one of those rare moments of pure joy and satisfaction, which let a historian forget months of monotonous research, when I discovered on p. 18–22 of the second volume a fragment of

'THE TEMPLE OF MINERVA.

America independent, an Oratorial Entertainment performed at the Hotel of the Minister of France. February 1781.'

The five pages appeared with cross-marks. We have no way of ascertaining Hopkinson's reason for this. But evidently, when after his death, his 'Miscellaneous Essays and Occasional Writings' were edited in the form prepared by him for publication, it was this circumstance which led to the exclusion of 'The Temple of Minerva.'

The fragmentary condition of the libretto can not have been the reason for so doing, since *the libretto reappears, perfect and without cross-marks, on unnumbered pages of the same manuscript volume* under this title:

'THE TEMPLE OF MINERVA. An Oratorial Entertainment performed in Nov. 1781 by a Company of Gentlemen and Ladies in the Hotel of the Minister of France in Presence of his Excellency General Washington and his Lady.'

The tenor of this title, especially the alteration of the date from " February 1781 " as in the fragment into " Nov (?) 1781," clearly indicate that the author himself contributed the piece to the Columbian Magazine for April, 1787, where it stands over his initial, and it would have been easy enough for the editor of the 'Miscellaneous Essays' to copy it from there even if he had overlooked it on the unnumbered pages of the manuscript volume.*

The music, unfortunately, seems not to be extant, but, as was the case with the 'Commencement Odes,' the libretto allows us to form a correct idea concerning the plan of the music. The libretto follows here as printed in the Columbian Magazine :

THE TEMPLE OF MINERVA.

A Musical Entertainment,

Performed in Nov. 1781, by a Band of Gentlemen and Ladies at the hotel of the Minister of France, in Philadelphia.

---

* Both dates represent slips of memory. 'The Temple of Minerva' was performed, as we know from the Freeman's Journal, in *Dec.* 1781.

Persons.   *Minerva, the Genius of France.*   *The Genius of America.*   *The High Priest*
of Minerva.

Scene I.   In the Temple of Minerva.   The doors of the Sanctuary shut.

Overture.

The Genius of France, the Genius of America and the High Priest of Minerva.

Trio.

Arise! arise! your voices raise,
And swell the solemn hymn of praise;
At great *Minerva's* awful shrine
Bow down, and own the pow'r divine.

Genius of America.

Oh, wise Minerva! Hear my pray'r,
And tell great Jove's decree:
Celestial goddess! Now declare
What fate has fix'd for me.
My warlike sons — the sons of fame,
In deeds of virtue bold,
Amongst the nations nobly claim
An honor'd place to hold

Say, will high *Jove* their labours crown,
And grant their arms success;
From this exalted throne look down
And my orisons bless?

Genius of France.

Wise *Minerva !* Grant her pray'r,
Make her valiant sons thy care;
To th' immortal breath of fame,
Give, oh give, her honor'd name.
O'er her councils, still preside,
In the field her armies guide:
Thus directed, she shall be
Great and glorious, wise and free.

Duetto.

Great *Minerva !* Hear our pray'r
What the fates ordain, declare.
Thus before thy throne we bow —
Hear, oh Goddess, hear us now !
Humble off'rings thus we bring,
With united voices sing;
Let our favor'd songs ascend —
Thou hast e'er been Virtue's friend.

High Priest.

With solemn rites approach the shrine,
And humble homage pay ;
Fit off'rings to the pow'r divine,
Upon her altar lay.

From the censer clouds ascending,
Hearts and voices sweetly blending,
Shall to *Minerva* grateful prove,
And call down blessings from above.

Trio.

From those radiant blest abodes,
Where thou sitt'st enthron'd with Gods
Oh! descend! thy temple grace,
With thy glories fill the place.
Hear, oh goddess! Hear our pray'r,
Make Columbia's cause thy care;
Blest and patroniz'd by thee
Great and pow'rful shall she be.

Scene II. The Doors of the Sanctuary are open.

High Priest.

Adore the great daughter of *Jove!*
Behold, how resplendent with light,
On a cloud, she descends from above,
All glories reveal'd to the sight,
Your songs have her favour obtain'd,
She comes to reply to your pray'r,
And now, what the fates have ordain'd.

Minerva.

In a golden balance weigh'd,
Have I seen *Columbia's* fate,
All her griefs shall be repaid
By a future happy state.
She with *France* in friendship join'd,
Shall opposing pow'rs defy;
Thus united, thus combin'd
Heav'n will bless the sacred tie.
Freedom on her happy shore
Shall her banners wide display;
Commerce shall her richest store
Through her numerous tides convey.
Jove declares his high command
Fate confirms the great decree;
*If our sons united stand
Great and prosp'rous shall she be.*

She, like the glorious sun,
Her splendid course shall run,
And future days
Columbia's praise
Shall spread from east to west.
The gods decree
That she shall be
A nation great confest.

Genius of America.

Let earth's inhabitants Heavn's pleasure know,
And fame her loud uplifted trumpet blow ;
Let the celestial nine, in tuneful choirs
Touch their immortal harps with golden wires.

Chorus.

Great Minerva, pow'r divine,
Praise, exalted praise be thine ;
Thus thy name in songs we bless,
Thus in songs thy pow'r confess.
Great Minerva, pow'r divine,
Praise, exalted praise, be thine.

From the friendly shores of France,
See the martial troops advance,
With Columbia's sons unite,
And share the dangers of the fight,
Equal heroes of the day,
Equal honors to them pay.

Now the dreadful conflict's o'er,
Now the cannons cease to roar,
Spread the joyful tidings round,
He comes, he comes, with conquest crown'd.
Hail Columbia's godlike son !
Hail the glorious *Washington !*

Fill the golden trump of fame,
Through the world his work proclaim ;
Let rocks, and hills, and vales, resound —
He comes, he comes, with conquest crown'd.
Hail Columbia's godlike son !
Hail the glorious *Washington.* *

                                              H.

It seems as if ' The Temple of Minerva,' called an " Oratorio " in
the newspaper report and by Hopkinson both an " Oratorial Entertainment " and a " Musical Entertainment," was really an operatic
entertainment in two scenes. Though planned on very much smaller
lines, it would belong to those mythological-allegorical-political operas,
so fashionable at the European courts during the seventeenth and eighteenth centuries, and which Hermann Kretschmar happily christened
" Hof und Staats Opern."

If Andrew Barton's ' The Disappointment, or, the Force of Credulity '
(1767) was the first comic ballad opera produced by a native American,†

---

* It is obvious that his father's ' Temple of Minerva ' still lingered in Joseph Hopkinson's memory
when he, in 1798, wrote ' Hail Columbia.'

† I do not overlook James Ralph's ' The Fashionable Lady or Harlequin's Opera ' (London, 1730), but
it is not certain whether or not Ralph really was a Pennsylvanian by birth. Compare my essay on
' Early American Operas' in Sbde der I. M. G. 1905.

that is to say, a comedy interspersed with songs, Francis Hopkinson's 'The Temple of Minerva' would have to be considered as our first attempt at "grand opera." With this term I mean an operatic entertainment in which everything is sung, nothing spoken, for, though the lines given to Minerva, the Genius of France, the Genius of America, and the High Priest of Minerva are not inscribed as "Airs," there can be little doubt that they were sung either as airs or recitatives.

Small as the plan of the two scenes may be with an overture, two trios, duetto, airs resp., recitatives, chorus, it is laid out in true operatic style. How well or how badly the first American poet-composer succeeded in setting his libretto to music, will ever remain a matter of personal prejudice unless it falls to the lot of a historian more fortunate than I was to discover the score. Not until then shall we be able to decide whether Francis Hopkinson himself composed the overture, either for harpsichord or orchestra, and the rest of the music, or selected some fashionable overture suitable to his purposes, and set his words to music, partly his own, partly by other composers.*

It is not generally known that our early magazines helped to meet the vivid demand for music by frequently adding printed or engraved music to their reading matter, in form of airs, songs, choruses, marches, dances, tunes, and the like. This laudable habit of our early reviews enables me to quote a few bars of a pastoral song by Francis Hopkinson. It is to be found, engraved on a fly-leaf, in the Columbian Magazine, Phila., for August, 1789, under the title of

'THE WORDS AND MUSIC OF A NEW SONG BY F. H. ESQ.'

After a prelude of eleven bars this strain is taken up by the voice to the ever new appeal, "Give me thy heart as I give mine."

---

* Perhaps some critics will not share my opinion that 'The Temple of Minerva' was a miniature opera, but will insist that it was a miniature cantata. At any rate, it was not an oratorio. In Colonial Times, the term "oratorial" was derived from oratory, and not from oratorio, and, as a rule, a "musical entertainment meant an "opera"! Especially immediately after the war, when operas were given under all kinds of educational and other harmless titles in order to avoid collision with the laws against the performance of plays and similar entertainments.

The adjective "new" was inserted probably in contradistinction to a collection of songs, issued in the previous year.   Being the first effort of its kind in the United States, this collection possesses unrivalled importance for the history of music in America.   If it escaped the attention of the historians, one or two possibly excepted, this fact might be due to the extreme rarity of the publication.   Personally I know but of two copies, the one at the Boston Public Library, the other in possession of Mr. Oliver Hopkinson, the grandson of Francis.

I am alluding to the undated :

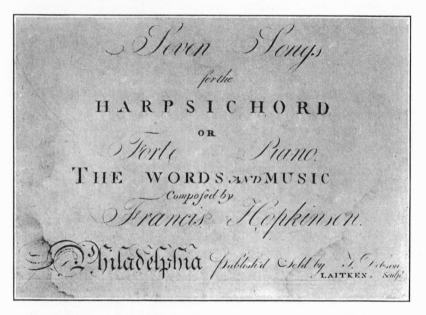

The title-page (obl. 4°) is followed on the first page of the second leaf by the printed dedication to George Washington. Beginning with the second page of the third leaf, follow neatly engraved on eleven pages Song I to Song VIII.

The contradiction between the title and the contents is apparent. A " N. B." on an unnumbered twelfth page which contains, printed, the words of the eight songs, explains it thus :

N. B.   This Eighth Song was added after the Title Page was engraved.

The songs were published in 1788, as appears from an advertisement in the Federal Gazette, Phila., Sat., Nov. 29, 1788.   It reads:

This day is Published, and to be sold by Thomas Dobson, at the Stone House, in Second street, between Chestnut and Market streets,

A Set of Eight Songs
The Words and Music composed by the Honorable Francis Hopkinson.

These songs are composed in an easy, familiar style, intended for young Practioners on the Harpsichord or Forte Piano, and is the first Work of this kind attempted in the United States. Price 7s 6. November 29.

In the following numbers the Federal Gazette printed "for the entertainment of the readers" the words of Songs VI, VII, and VIII. Single poems of the set soon appeared in various other periodicals. The entire set makes part of Francis Hopkinson's 'Miscellaneous Essays and Occasional Writings,' in Vol. III, pp. 185–192.

The object and nature of the publication becomes evident from the interesting dedication :

TO HIS EXCELLENCY
GEORGE WASHINGTON, ESQUIRE.

SIR,

I Embrace, with heartfelt satisfaction, every opportunity that offers of recognizing the personal Friendship that hath so long subsisted between us. The present Occasion allows me to do this in a manner most flattering to my Vanity; and I have accordingly taken advantage of it, by presenting this Work to your Patronage, and honouring it with your Name.

It cannot be thought an unwarrantable anticipation to look up to you as seated in the most distinguished situation that a grateful People can offer. The universally avowed Wish of America, and the Nearness of the Period in which that Wish will be accomplished, sufficiently justify such an Anticipation; from which rises a confident Hope, that the same Wisdom and Virtue which has so successfully conducted the Arms of the United States in Time of Invasion, War and Tumult, will prove also the successful Patron of Arts and Sciences in Times of national Peace and Prosperity; and that the Glory of America will rise Conspicuous under a Government designated by the *Will*, and an Administration founded in the *Hearts* of THE PEOPLE.

With respect to this little Work, which I now have the honour to present to your notice, I can only say, that it is such as a Lover, not a Master, of the Arts can furnish. I am neither a profess'd Poet, nor a profess'd Musician; and yet venture to appear in those characters united ; for which, I confess, the censure of Temerity may justly be brought against me.

If these Songs should not be so fortunate as to please the young Performers for whom they are intended, they will at least not occasion much Trouble in learning to perform them ; and this will, I hope, be some Alleviation of their Disappointment.

However small the Reputation may be that I shall derive from this Work, I cannot I believe, be refused the Credit of being the first Native of the United States who has produced a Musical Composition. If this attempt should not be too severely treated, others may be encouraged to venture on a path, yet untrodden in America, and the Arts in succession will take root and flourish amongst us.

I hope for your favourable Acceptance of this Mark of my Affection and Respect, and have the Honour to be

Your Excellency's most obedient, and Most humble Servant,

PHILADELPHIA. F. HOPKINSON.
Nov. 20th, 1788

George Washington notified his friend of a "Favourable Acceptance" with that punctuality which was so eminently characteristic of him. As the letter, now in possession of Mr. Oliver Hopkinson, seems to have remained unpublished hitherto and as it shows the peculiar smiling wit of the "General" at its best, I hope the reader will pardon me for including it in a monograph on music:

Mount Vernon Feb.y 5th 1789.

Dear Sir,

We are told of the amazing powers of Musick in ancient times, but the stories of its effects are so surprising that we are not obliged to believe them, unless they had been founded up on better authority than Poetic assertion — for the Poets of old (whatever they may do in these days) were strangely addicted to the marvellous; — and if I before *doubted* the truth of their relations with respect to the power of Musick, I am fully convinced of their falsity — because I would not, for the honor of my Country, allow that we are left by the ancients at an *unmeasurable* distance in everything;—and if they could sooth the ferocity of wild beasts—could draw the trees and the stones after them—and could even charm the powers of Hell by their Musick, I am sure that your productions would have had at least virtue enough in them (without the aid of voice or instrument) to soften the Ice of the Delaware & Potomack — and in that case you should have had an earlier acknowledgment of your favor of the 1st of December which came to hand but last Saturday.—

I readily admit the force of your distinction between "a thing *done*" and "a thing *to be done*"— and as I do not believe that you would do "a very bad thing indeed" I must even make virtue of necessity, and defend your performance, if necessary, to the last effort of my musical abilities.—*

But, my dear Sir, if you had any doubts about the reception which your work would meet with—or had the smallest reason to think that you should need any assistance to defend it—you have not acted with your usual good judgment in the choice of a Coadjutor; for, should the tide of prejudice not flow in favor of it (and so various are the tastes, opinions & whims of men, that even the sanction of Divinity does not ensure universal concurrence) what alas! can I do to support it ?—I can neither sing one of the songs, nor raise a single note on any instrument to convince the unbelieving.

But I have, however, one argument which will prevail with persons of true taste (at least in America)—I can tell them that *it is the production of Mr. Hopkinson.*

With the compliments of Mrs. Washington added to mine, for you & yours

I am—Dear Sir

Your most Obedt. and

The Honble   very Hble Servant

Frans. Hopkinson Esqr.   Go. Washington.

It would be interesting to know what the music-loving public of those days thought of Hopkinson's songs, but the musical critic had not yet made his appearance as the supposed herald of public opinion. In all probability Hopkinson met with favorable comment as well as with unfavorable. The latter I have not been able to trace, whereas

---

* Evidently Washington is alluding to a letter which accompanied Hopkinson's 'Seven Songs.' I have not been able to locate this letter.

a few encouraging lines have come down to us of which the composer certainly felt very proud. Again, it is the Jefferson correspondence where they may be found. Under date of "Philada. Dec. 21, 1788," Hopkinson wrote the following letter to Jefferson, and a very curious letter it is with its glimpses into the composer's workshop:

> I wrote to you three or four weeks ago, & I now take the Opportunity by Mr. Govr. Morris of sending you a small Package of News Papers, Pamphlets & amongst which is a Work of my own just published. I beg Miss Jefferson's Acceptance of a Copy, and wish it may be to her Taste. It is a Book of Songs which I composed, occasionally, for my Daughters, who play & sing them very well. The last Song, if play'd very slow, and sung with Expression, is forcibly pathetic — at least in my Fancy. Both Words & Music were the Work of an hour in the Heights of a Storm. But the Imagination of an Author who composes from the Heart rather than his Head, is always more heated than he can expect his Readers to be.

To these modest yet proud lines Jefferson replied under date of "Paris, March 13, 1789," in a letter that must have touched the composer deeply. It shows that his artistic intentions had been fully understood by at least one person, but it also shows how foreign to our taste and conception the lyrics of those days have become.

Jefferson to Hopkinson, Paris, Mar. 13, 1789 (Ser. I, v. 3, No. 280):

> Since my last, which was of Dec. 21 yours of Dec. 9 & 21 are received, accept my thanks for the papers and pamphlets which accompanied them, and mine and my daughter's for the book of songs. I will not tell you how much they have pleased us, nor how well the last of them merits praise for it's pathos, but relate a fact only, which is that while my elder daughter was playing it on the harpsichord, I happened to look toward the fire & saw the younger one all in tears. I asked her if she was sick? She said "no; but the tune was so mournful."

Little remains to be said. I have spoken in a previous chapter of Hopkinson's claim of having been the first native of the United States who produced a musical composition. If it is not quite clear whether he or James Lyon deserves this title, we at least can not refuse Francis Hopkinson the credit of having been our first poet-composer in general, and of songs in particular.

With respect to the 'Seven Songs' the reader might form his own opinion from the Appendix, where the seventh, in my opinion the best, has been reprinted. This much is apparent: As a composer Francis Hopkinson did not improve greatly during the thirty years which separate this song collection from his earliest efforts. His harmony is still faulty at times, and he possesses not an original musical profile. To claim the adjective of beautiful or important for these songs or his other compositions would mean to confuse the standpoint of the musical critic with that of the antiquarian. But even the critic who cares not to explain and pardon shortcomings from a historical point of view will admit that Hopkinson's songs are not without grace and that our first poet-composer obeyed the laws of musical declamation more carefully than a host of fashionable masters of that period. Artistically, of course, he resembles his contemporaries. His musical world, like theirs, was an untrue Arcadia, populated with over-sentimental shepherds and shepherdesses, or with jolly tars, veritable models of sobriety and good behavior, even when filling huge bumpers for drinking-bouts. Then again we notice in Francis Hopkinson's music the studied simplicity of that age for which treble and bass had become the pillars of the universe.

  This and much more is antiquated to-day. But why should we criticize at all our first "musical compositions"? It becomes us better to look upon these primitive efforts as upon venerable documents of the innate love of the American people for the beauties of music and as documents of the fact that among the Signers of the Declaration of Independence there was at least one who proved to be a " SUCCESSFUL PATRON OF ARTS AND SCIENCES."

THE MUSICAL CAREER

OF

JAMES LYON

PATRIOT, PREACHER, PSALMODIST

(1735-1794)

CHAPTER I.

1735–1763.

The career of James Lyon is associated with the early history of our musical life, with the beginnings of Princeton College and Presbyterianism in Nova Scotia, with the early history of Machias, Me., and with the attempted conquest of Nova Scotia during the Revolutionary War. His name or brief sketches of his life are therefore met with in numerous historical works.* Most of the writers, however, give neither place nor year of his birth. The latter is mentioned only by Mr. Williamson in his 'Bibliography of the State of Maine.' But, curious enough, after giving it correctly as 1735, he lets Lyon die, by some mysterious error, in 1801 instead of 1794.

Some writers relate to the place of birth in a general way, saying, like Greenleaf : †

Mr. Lyon was a native of New Jersey.

Mr. William B. Smith ‡ and a few others tried to locate the place of birth by calling James Lyon " a native of Princeton, N. J."

All these historians are contradicted by James Riker, Jr., in whose 'Annals of Newtown,' L. I. (1852, p. 23) we find the following passus :

Mr. Lyon who is thought to have been of Irish birth.

The contradiction becomes embarrassing, as none of the writers mention their authorities.

It will be best to destroy the Irish legend, taken up by several historians, at the beginning of my narrative.

James Lyon, the subject of this monograph, was born in 1735,

---

* For instance, (a) Alexander, Samuel Davies. Princeton College during the eighteenth century. 1872.
  (b) Porter, W. in Bangor Historical Magazine, Vol. III, No. 209-211. (This sketch is valuable.)
† Greenleaf, Jonathan. ' Sketches of the Ecclesiastical History of the State of Maine.'
‡ Compare his ' Historical Sketch ' in the ' Memorial of the Centennial Anniversary of the Settlement of Machias.' 1863.

became a Presbyterian minister, and hesitated not to declare himself in favor of the "rebels" from the outset of our great struggle for independence.

The Lyon to whom Riker alludes was indeed a native of Ireland. He, too, was surnamed James, and he, too, was a minister, but an *Episcopalian.* He had been employed as a missionary before coming to New Jersey in 1747, and he removed during the same year to Setauket, L. I., as successor to Rev. Isaac Brown. He married on February 7, 1753.* Furthermore, General Wooster wrote to Governor Trumbull from Oyster Ponds, under date of August 14, 1775, that Colonel Willart sent him

> The Reverend James Lyon, a Church of England clergyman . . . This Parson Lyon is the mainspring of all the tories on that part of Long Island.†

It is self-evident that the two Reverends by the name of James Lyon can not be identical. But whence the confusion? A caprice of chronology will have it that about the year 1785 both were employed as ministers on Long Island, James Lyon the Presbyterian in Newtown,‡ James Lyon the Episcopalian in Brookhaven,§ separated by some fifty miles only.

Fortunately, family traditions exist which enable us to follow the right path toward the place of birth of our Rev. James Lyon.

Mr. Geo. M. Lyon, of Marshfield, Me., a great-grandson of Parson Lyon, gives the following clue: ‖

> . . . Among my father's papers was one written in this way : The Rev. James Lyon was the son of Zopher Lyon of E. New Jersey. Born July 1st, 1735. . .

This tradition is corroborated and supplemented by a second one. Miss Caroline Smith, of Machias, Me., possessed a note-book ¶

> in which she herself has copied items of interest she wished to preserve. Those relating to the Parson [scil. Lyon] Mr. Edward Payson rec'd from Mrs. Amelia Mellus, the daughter of Parson Lyon. Mr. P. married Mrs. Mellus daughter Amelia, and Mr. Payson wrote them from Mrs. Mellus dictation.

---

* Compare Benj. F. Thompson's ' History of Long Island.' See Ed 1843.

† Compare Force's ' American Archives.' Fourth Series, Vol. III.

‡ Compare Riker.   § Compare Thompson.

‖ The late Mr. Stuart Wade, formerly of the New York Public Library, had the kindness to write to Mr. Geo. M. Lyon, asking in my name for information concerning his ancestor. Mr. Lyon's interesting answer dated Marshfield, Oct. 15, 1900, is now in my possession.

¶ I owe this information to the kindness of Mrs. Mary O'Brien Brown, of Machias, Me., who took the trouble of copying from the said note-book all items which might interest me.

These notes begin with the statement that

JAMES LYON, SON OF ZOPHER LYON OF NEWARK EAST NEW JERSEY, WAS BORN AT THE SAID NEWARK, JULY 1st, 1735.

If family traditions would invariably have evidential strength the two data quoted might satisfy the demands of critical history. But it is a well-known fact that family traditions can not always be relied upon without corresponding official records. In our case, the necessary *tertium comparationis*, if I am allowed to apply this term to historical research, naturally would be found in the Church Records of Newark. But

It is much to be regretted that the records of the church, extending from the year 1696 to the time of the Revolutionary War, were destroyed when the British troops had possession of the town in 1776, and those which remain date back only to August 1781.*

Nevertheless, we are enabled to strengthen the family tradition by several official documents if the clue is traced in a somewhat different direction.

The 'Essex Inventories' for 1745 to 1752 are extant, and all the Lyon wills mention but one Zophar Lyon who possibly can have been the father of James.†

He was "Yeoman of the Town of Newark" and died in 1744, when his widow, Mary Lyon, became administratrix. He left no will, and

A true Inventory of all and Singular the Goods, Chattels and Credits of Zophar Lyon

was prized by "Nathaniel Johnson, Esqr. and Isaac Lyon of said Newark, Yeoman" to the amount of £157. 15. 07. In the several documents no children are mentioned, in particular not a James Lyon, but Isaac Lyon furnishes the link between the Yeoman Zophar and our James. In a letter of guardianship ‡

Isaac Lyon and John Crane, both of the County of Essex

were appointed on July 18, 1750,

Guardian of the Body and Estate of James Lyon above fourteen years of age until he shall be of the age of twenty-one.

Consequently this James Lyon was born in 1735. The year corresponds exactly with the one given by the family tradition as birth year of James Lyon of Newark, N. J. As furthermore the identity of

---

* Compare Stearn's 'First Church Newark.' Preface, p. VII.

† Extensive copies of the pertinent documents preserved in the State House at Trenton, N. J., have been made for me by Miss Anna M. North of Trenton.

‡ Liber E, folio 500.

the two Isaac Lyons mentioned is more than probable, we no longer have the right to doubt the correctness of the tradition. It therefore may be taken for granted that JAMES LYON, the subject of this monograph, WAS BORN IN NEWARK, N. J., ON JULY 1ST, 1735, AS SON OF THE YEOMAN ZOPHAR LYON, WHO DIED 1744, AND HIS WIFE MARY.*

Of James Lyon's childhood and early youth nothing is known. Our knowledge of his life begins with the years during which he was a student at Princeton.

The first item of interest is an "original ode," which appeared in the New American Magazine (Woodbridge, N. J.) for September, 1759, under the title of "Louisburg Taken," and introduced by a note which is signed "Al . . . s" (alumnus). The poet asks his readers to

impute any impropriety in the Performance, or Incorrectness in Measure, to the Unskillfulness of a Lyre, touch'd by inexperienced Youth.

The Ode fills two pages, bears the signature "Nassovian" under date of "E. Jersey, Aug. 1759" and has been attributed to the pen of James Lyon.† I know not on what authority, but the possibility of his authorship can not be denied, as James Lyon became an *A. B.* of the New Jersey College in the same year.‡ This implies that he can not have entered college later than fall 1757, for one of the additional regulations respecting the terms of first admission into college reads:

Every student shall be obliged to reside in College at least two years before his first graduation.§

But it is not impossible that James Lyon moved with the college from Newark, where it had been since the end of 1747, to Princeton during the autumn of 1756.‖

The Commencement at which James Lyon received his first degree took place on September 26, 1759. An account of the "Exercises"

---

* We read in the 'New Jersey Archives,' Vol. XX, p. 579:

"Ezekiel Younglove of Reddistown, married Mary Lyon, May 16, 1746, and on presenting his child Dorcas for baptism, in the Morristown Church, Sept. 27, 1747, renewed his covenant as a member of the church." Was this perhaps the widow Mary Lyon?

† Compare New Jersey Archives, Vol. XX, 383. My attention was called to this Ode by Mr. Victor Paltsits of the N. Y. P. L.

‡ See Catalogus Collegii Neo-Caesariensis Princetoniae, 1747–1886, p. 40.

§ Compare John Maclean's 'History of the College of New Jersey,' p. 211.

‖ It had been opened end of May, 1747, in Elizabethtown; it was removed after the death of the first president, Dickenson (Oct. 7, 1747), "to Newark, the place of Mr. Burr," the second president. The first Commencement took place at Newark on the 9th of November, 1748. (Maclean, pp. 114, 127.) It is now readily understood why some writers named Princeton the birth-place of James Lyon. By the way, his name is not even mentioned in Maclean's work.

was communicated on the following day to the New York Mercury and was printed in this paper on October 1st.

It is of special interest, being the first unmistakable account of Lyon's musical career:

Nassau Hall, Sept. 27. 1759.

Yesterday the annual Commencement was held here . . . The Rev. Mr. Samuel Davies, lately elected President of the college of New Jersey, delivered a Latin Oration, to the universal Applause of all his learned and numerous Auditors.

The young Gentlemen (about 25 in number) who were admitted to the usual Degrees in the Arts, performed the accustomed exercises with uncommon Facility and Correctness. The whole Ceremony concluded with the following ODE, set to Music by Mr. James Lyon, one of the students.

> Cheerful, fearless and at ease
> On the downing lap of Peace,
> In the gentle Muses Seat,
> Unmov'd at War's tremendous Roar
> That Consternation spreads from Shore to Shore
> O'er solid Continents, and Falling Waves,
> From haughty Monarchs down to Slaves
> Low cringing at their Feet
> Far from Terror's loud Alarms,
> Peaceful Nassau ! in thee we sing—
> We sing great George upon the Throne
> And Amherst brave in Arms,
>   Amherst brave in Arms,
> While BERNHARD, in their milder Charms
> Makes the royal Virtues known.

CHOR.   *We sing Great George, etc. etc*

> The sword of the *Lord* and of *Amherst* from far,
> Gleaming tremendous, determines the War,
> At th' approaching Vengeance struck
> Gallic Slaves, tho' long enur'd
> To face the wide-destroying Sword
> At a proud Tyrant's Word
> Now disorder'd and broke,
> Despairing, confounded,
> With Terror's surrounded
> By AMHERST'S Name subdu'd
> By dread of Vengeance close pursu'd,
> Vengeance due to sacred British Blood,
> The useless Sword they drop.
> Nor dare for safety hope,
> But in swift flight,
> Beneath the Shade of Guilt-concealing Night.
> *We sing Great George upon the Throne,*
> *And Amherst, brave in Arms;*
> *While BERNHARD, in their milder Charms,*
> *Make the royal Virtues known.*
> Happy, happy, happy, still
> Safe from all the Alarms of ill
> While George the Friend of Man, adores [sic] the Throne,
> And Amherst shines in Arms ;
> While Bernhard makes the royal Virtues known,
> In all their milder charms.
>   Happy, etc. etc.

Strange irony of fate, the same man who set these lines to music which glorify Amherst's victory over the French in Canada was destined to draw plans, some sixteen years later, for driving the British out of Nova Scotia!

It will have been noticed that the report mentions one Ode only, giving the name of the composer but not of the poet. This is of some importance. Maclean (on p. 217 of his work quoted) writes of two

> Odes, one on Science and the other on Peace, composed by President Davies, and sung at the close of the morning and evening exercises.

Evidently the modern historian and the contemporary reporter contradict each other. Maclean, I believe, confused the performance of 1759 with one of the following year. The report which was forwarded from "Princeton (Nassau Hall), September 25, 1760," to the Pennsylvania Journal and printed in this paper on October 2, proves my statement:

> Yesterday the anniversary Commencement of the College of New Jersey was held here . . . The Singing an Ode on Science, composed by the President of the College, concluded the Forenoon Exercise . . . The Singing an Ode on Peace, composed also by the President of the College, concluded the whole [scil. "The Entertainments of the Afternoon"] to the universal Pleasure and Satisfaction of a numerous Auditory.*

One way for partly reconciling the statements of our authorities remains. The Ode which Lyon set to music for the Commencement of 1759 was indeed an Ode on Peace. Perhaps it was identical with the Ode on Peace of 1760. The Ode might have met with the approval of the audience to such a degree in 1759 that it was repeated at the Commencement of the following year. In this case we might infer that the Ode on Science, too, was set to music by James Lyon, though the composer is not mentioned in the contemporary report.

Upon inquiry I learned from the librarian of Princeton University that the music of neither ode is extant among the treasures of the institution. This is very much to be regretted. No matter how crude and amateurish the musical setting of the Ode of 1759 might have been, its historical importance is great, by far greater than that of the bombastic poem.

It is a very early, if not the earliest, specimen of American Commencement-odes; as such a very early monument of secular music in our country and consequently a strong weapon against the prevalent

---

* It should be kept in mind that the term "composed" was applied frequently to the *poets* of odes. It has this meaning of course, and not of "set to music" in the above quotation. I have used the term, as applying to musical authors only, throughout the monograph.

but incorrect theory that secular music had no stronghold in the colonies previous to the end of the eighteenth century.*

Not alone this, I have shown in the monograph on the musical career of Francis Hopkinson that with this ode of 1759 by James Lyon on record we are obliged to challenge Hopkinson's claim of having been the first native of the United States to write a musical composition. Though arguments may be brought forward for tracing additional music to the ' Masque of Alfred the Great' as performed in the College of Philadelphia during January, 1757, to Hopkinson's pen, the earliest composition of his *extant* and on record, a pastoral song, can not be dated earlier than 1759. Indeed, a peculiar coincidence, that the two first secular American compositions of which we know at present, should both have been written in the same year!

Lyon seems to have removed to Philadelphia after his graduation. Without doubt he lived there in May, 1760. We read:

> Subscriptions are taken in by . . . James Lyon in Philadelphia

in the Proposals for printing by subscription his psalm-tune collection ' Urania,' of which more will be said in the next chapter. These proposals appeared first in the Pa. Journal on May 15, and are dated " Philadelphia, May 8, 1760."

Lyon's reasons for moving to Philadelphia are unknown. One of them might have been the desire to improve his knowledge of music. How long he remained there is equally a matter of conjecture. But we have some evidence that he can not have left Philadelphia until late in 1760. The conclusion is to be drawn from an advertisement which appeared in the Pa. Journal, October 23:

> Notice is hereby given that the Singing-School, lately Kept in the Rooms over Mr. William's School in Second street, will again be opened on Monday Evening, the 3d of November next, at the same Place; where the ART OF PSALMODY will be taught, as usual, in the best Manner, on Monday and Friday Evenings, from Six to Eight. And that, if any Number of Ladies and Gentlemen incline to make up an exclusive Set, to Sing on two other Nights they may be gratified by making Application in time.
>
> N. B. Some of the first sheets of that Collection of Tunes, mentioned sometime ago in this Paper, will be published by the time above mentioned, so that those who will like them as they come from the Press may be Supplied.

---

* I am not here writing a monograph on the musical life in our colleges, and therefore beg pardon for not entering more fully into the interesting theme. But it will be of value to state briefly that the active part which our colleges took in the development of our musical life during Colonial Times has sadly been overlooked by historians. Is it not significant that very few Commencements were held without the orations, forensic disputes, etc., being interspersed—frequently five or six times—by music, "vocal and instrumental "? Is it not a peculiar coincidence that three of our earliest composers,—not to mention others,—Francis Hopkinson, James Lyon, and Andrew Law—were college graduates?

The collection mentioned certainly was Lyon's (entitled later on 'Urania') since no other collection was advertised during 1760 and the N. B. renders it probable that Lyon was personally connected with the Singing-School.

Now the following advertisement had been printed in the Pa. Journal, December 6, 1759:

> VOCAL MUSIC taught in it's various Parts, after the best Manner, in the School House behind the Rev'd Dr. Jenny's near the Church, where due Attendance will be given every Monday, Wednesday, and Friday Evening from 5 to 8 o'clock. The second and fourth Wednesday of every Month will be public. No Scholar will be received after next Monday. Any Gentlemen or Ladies may likewise be taught at their Houses.

If these two Singing-Schools were identical, then we have some reason to suppose that James Lyon took his residence at Philadelphia either early in 1760 or shortly after his graduation in 1759. In the latter case he, himself, may have been the founder of the school.

It is again a matter of conjecture whether or not he remained long enough to witness the performance of one of his Anthems at the Commencement on May 23, 1761, but it is highly probable.

A few days later, on May 28, the following interesting report was printed in the Pa. Gaz.:

> Philadelphia, May 28.
> On Saturday last the public COMMENCEMENT was held in the College of this City, before a vast Concourse of People of all Ranks. Besides the usual Exercises (which gave great satisfaction to the Audience) there was performed in the Forenoon an elegant *Anthem* composed by James LYON, A. M.* of New Jersey College, and in the Afternoon an *Ode*, sacred to the Memory of our late gracious Sovereign George II. written and set to Music in a very grand and masterly Taste by Francis Hopkinson, Esq. A. M. of the College of this City.†
> A Sett of Ladies and Gentlemen, in order to do Honour to the Entertainment of the Day, were kindly pleased to perform a Part both of the Anthem and Ode, accompanied by the Organ, which made the Music a very compleat and agreeable Entertainment to all present.

Lyon had probably left Philadelphia when the publication of 'Urania' was advertised in the Pa. Journal for June 3, 1762. He took his second degree at Princeton on September 29 and though ". . . for the second degree . . . we have no means of ascertaining . . ." the regulations respecting the terms of residence in College‡ it is but natural to believe that he prepared himself for the examination at Princeton.

---

* This, of course, is a mistake, for we know that James Lyon took his second degree in 1762.

† The Ode was published in the same year as 'An Exercise . . .' See the monograph on Francis Hopkinson.

‡ Compare Maclean, p. 211.

The Commencement exercises were described in the New York Mercury, October 11, 1762, and more fully in the Pa. Gaz. on October 21. From the latter account, dated " Princeton, Sept. 30, 1762 " I quote some important lines :

Yesterday the Trustees of the College of New Jersey with his Excellency the Governor, attended the Commencement . . .

The following Gentlemen were admitted to the Honours of Masters of Arts, James Caldwell, Jabez Campfield, John Carmichael, John Huntington, *James Lyon.* . . .

Also the Reverend Mr. Charles Beatty, and Mr. Jonathan Parsons, received the honorary Degree of Masters of Arts. In Behalf of the last mentioned Candidates was agreeably delivered an English Oration by James Lyon . . .

The whole concluded with . . . Music, which, with the whole Performance of the Day, afforded universal Satisfaction to a polite and crowded Auditory.

Thus the reporter briefly describes an entertainment which is of great importance for the history of our early Commencement-exercises.

The music alluded to was printed anonymously in the same year by William Bradford of Philadelphia under the title of:

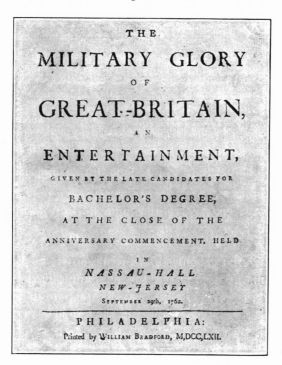

THE

MILITARY GLORY

O F

GREAT-BRITAIN,

A N

ENTERTAINMENT,

GIVEN BY THE LATE CANDIDATES FOR

BACHELOR'S DEGREE,

AT THE CLOSE OF THE

ANNIVERSARY COMMENCEMENT, HELD

I N

NASSAU-HALL

NEW-JERSEY

SEPTEMBER 29th, 1762.

PHILADELPHIA:

Printed by WILLIAM BRADFORD, M,DCC,LXII.

The libretto of this school-drama occupies (in 12mo) sixteen pages, and the music, engraved on folded leaves, consists of four different choruses, the fifth being identical with the third and· all being written in three parts.

Five "Speakers" glorify the deeds of Wolfe, Amherst, and Albemarle, proclaiming their victories over "Haughty Lewis" and uttering the prophecy that "Gallia's Sons shall vaunt no more." The fifth speaker

closes the whole with a solemn Wish for the continued Prosperity of the British Nation.

> Long may a *George* the regal Scepter sway;
> And scatter Blessings with a liberal Hand,
> Around the peaceful Globe; but dire Dismay
> On all who dare his injur'd Arms withstand.

The dialogues and monologues are interspersed with choruses and preceded by an introductory chorus with orchestral accompaniment entitled: 'Britannia's Glory.' As this piece is given here in facsimile the reader has an opportunity to form his own idea of the character and value of the music to the 'Military Glory.'*

Now those Odes of 1759 [correctly 1760]

one on Science and the other on Peace, composed [scil. written] by President Davies and sung at the close of the morning and evening service . . . were many years later

---

* Copies of this work are in the New Public Library, Pa. Hist. Soc., Library of Congress.

confounded with a poetic dialogue, recited with choral songs, at the commencement of 1762.

Maclean, in whose work quoted we find this information on p. 217, apparently had ' The Military Glory ' in mind. But certainly President Davies can not have written the libretto, as the Entertainment took place " at least eighteen months after his death."

Would it cause surprise if future investigations should succeed in claiming the musical authorship of 'The Military Glory' (and perhaps the poetical, too) for our James Lyon, who, we remember, took his second degree at this very commencement, who was admired by the Princetonians as a " great master of music," and who had composed the music to one of the Commencement-odes of 1759?

Indeed, all pertinent circumstances render it highly probable that he was connected in some way or the other with ' The Military Glory.' By far more doubtful is his part in the musical controversy which took place at Philadelphia in 1763.

In April of this year a curious book left William Dunlap's press. Its contents appear from the title :

' THE LAWFULNESS, EXCELLENCY AND ADVANTAGE OF INSTRUMENTAL MUSICK in the Public Worship of God, Urg'd and Enforc'd from Scripture and the Examples of the far greater Part of Christians in all Ages. Address'd to all (particularly the Presbyterians and Baptists) who have hitherto been taught to look upon the Use of Instrumental Musick in the Worship of God as Unlawful.   BY A PRESBYTERIAN.

> Musick has Charms to smooth the Savage Breast
> To soften Rocks, and bend the Knotted Oak.
>> *Congreve.*

Philadelphia: Printed and sold by William Dunlap at the Newest Printing Office in Market Street. 1763.' (8vo, 38 pp. Pa. H. S.)

The pamphlet was so eagerly bought that Dunlap issued a second edition on June 16 of the same year, remarking in his advertisement in the Pa. Gaz. for the same day:

The Kind Reception the Public have been pleased to give this little Performance (which is calculated to promote the Good of Religious Society in general) has induced us to give it a second Edition, the first being all disposed of in a very short Time after Publication.

But ' The Lawfulness' met also, it seems, with polemical opposition, as its publication was followed by a satirical piece, printed by Andrew Stuart in the same year.*

---

* Sabin in Vol. VI of his Bibliotheca Americana has confused the second edition of ' the Lawfulness . . .' with this publication by Stuart. My narrative is based upon advertisements in the Pa. Gaz. April 28; May 5; June 2 and 16, 1763.

I have not seen a copy of this pamphlet, but I found in the Pa. Gaz. June 2, the following advertisement:

> For one Groat may be had (just published by Andrew Stuart at the Bible-in-Heart, in Second Street) A CUDGEL to drive the Devil out of every Christian Place of Worship. Being a second Edition [with necessary Improvements, which now render the sense entirely plain] of the Lawfulness, Excellency and advantage of Instrumental MUSIC in the public Worship of GOD, but chiefly of ORGANS.
>> Old Orpheus play'd so well he mov'd Old Nick.
>> JOE MILLER.

This pamphlet, like 'The Lawfulness,' seems to have been anonymous. To ascertain the authors is quite a puzzle. To have written 'A Cudgel' would look very much like one of the merry literary pranks of Francis Hopkinson had he not been in favor of instrumental music in the public worship of God. That he was not the author of 'The Lawfulness' is evident since he was an Episcopalian and not a Presbyterian.

Perhaps John Todd, A. M., wrote 'A Cudgel,' for together with this pamphlet and on the said day was advertised as:

> Also just published by said Steuart (Price Nine pence) the PROPRIETY NECESSITY AND USE OF EVANGELICAL PSALMS IN CHRISTIAN WORSHIP. Delivered at a Meeting of the Presbytery at Hanover, in Virginia, October 6, 1762.
>> By John *Todd*, A. M.

Of course, my last remarks are very hypothetical and it is merely a suggestion if I point to James Lyon, Presbyterian and psalmodist, as the possible author of 'The Lawfulness.'

It is here not the place to discuss James Lyon's erratic but uncommonly interesting clerical and political career. However, the following cursory remarks might prove of value:

Some weeks after James Lyon took his second degree he was licensed by the Synod of New Brunswick to preach the Gospel. His ordination took place in 1764. In the following year we find him in Nova Scotia, having been sent there by the Presbytery upon the urgent request of the members of the denomination for a minister. He left the Province, where he had labored in Halifax, Onslow and other places, in 1771, unable to support himself and his family in the thinly settled and very poor district.

During the same or the following year he accepted a call to the new settlement of Machias, Me. With brief intermissions (in 1773 and about 1783–1785) he preached the gospel there to the satisfaction of his flock until his death, which occurred on December 25, 1794.

When the Revolutionary War broke out James Lyon immediately sided with the Colonies and energetically worked for their cause. He went so far as to make (very sensible) suggestions to Congress. Furthermore a long letter of his, written in 1775 and addressed to George Washington, is extant in which he outlined plans and asked for permission to conquer Nova Scotia, basing his demand on his knowledge of the country and of the people. It was fortunate for the British, as the Canadian historian John J. Bulmer admits, that his offer was not accepted, though Washington, in a polite reply, did not deny the feasibility of the plan.

Of Lyon's literary works a 'Charge' and a torso of his 'Saints Daily Assistant' are on record and extant in print.

---

*These brief notes are based upon material which I have collected for a biography of Lyon in collaboration with Mr. Victor H. Paltsits of the New York Public Library.

CHAPTER II.

The Bibliographical History of 'Urania.'

James Lyon probably did not compile his Psalm-tune Collection, which he afterwards entitled ' Urania,' during his residence at Philadelphia. He might have completed the work there, but must have conceived the idea of it and carried it out while at Princeton. A compilation like ' Urania ' calls for a laborious preparation. It can not have been the work of two or three months, however crude and superficial the effort may appear to modern critics. Even if he, previously to 1759, had mastered the rudiments of music, either autodidactically or with some psalmodist, unknown to us, so far as to be able to write an Ode with ease and fluency, the compilation of ' Urania,' with a theoretical introduction and 198 pages of music, required more time than elapsed between the composition of the Ode and the advertisement of his ' Proposals.'

We might argue that Lyon conceived the bold idea

of improving and spreading the Art of Psalmody in its Perfection, thro' our American Colonies *

about 1758, at the age of twenty-two. Perhaps the whole collection grew out of his studies in psalmody combined with his own compositorial exercises, beginning with the harmonization of psalm-tunes and gradually developing into more elaborate and free settings of anthems and hymns after the fashions of the day.

Certainly the collection was ready for the printer when appeared in the Pa. Journal and Pa. Gazette, both for May 22, 1760:

> Proposals For Printing by Subscription. A Choice Collection of
> PSALM TUNES AND ANTHEMS,
> from the best Authors, with some entirely New, and a Number of Dr. Watts'
> and Mr. Addison's Hymns set to Music:
> To which will be prefixed the plainest and most useful rules of Psalmody.
> By James Lyon, A. B.

* See the ' Proposals.'

Conditions.

That the whole Book be neatly engraved on Copper Plate, bound in the common form of Music-Books and contain about 210 Pages.

That every Person, at the Time of Subscribing, pay one Dollar and the Remainder (which shall not exceed One Dollar more) when the Book is delivered. If there are just 400 Subscribers the Sum above-mentioned will be the price of each Book; but if more, the Price will be proportionately less. As soon as 400 are subscribed for, the Tunes shall be Engraved with all possible Dispatch. But if that Number of Subscribers cannot be found, by the 1st of August, 1760 (after which Time no Subscriptions will be taken) the money shall be all returned to the Subscribers by the Gentlemen with whom they Subscribed.

Subscriptions are taken in by William Bradford and James Lyon in Philadelphia, by Mr. Samuel Nivins in Newcastle; by Mr. Henry Longhead in Oxford Township, Chester County; and by Mr. Jonathan Baldwin, in Prince-Town, New Jersey.

N. B. As this is the first Attempt of the kind to spread the ART OF PSALMODY, in its Perfection, thro' our American Colonies, and as the whole Collection will be better fitted to the Use of Churches and private Families than any ever published in America, 'tis humbly expected the Work will meet with proper Encouragement.

Philadelphia, May 8, 1760.

As will be seen, Lyon changed his mind with respect to the minimum number of subscribers to his "limited edition," and when less than two hundred subscriptions had been received he inserted the following advertisement in the Pa. Journal for July 24, 1760 (and in the Pa. Gaz. for August 14):

Those Gentlemen who have subscribed, or intend to subscribe for that valuable Collection of Psalm-Tunes, Hymns and Anthems, whose Proposals were published some time ago in this Paper, are desired to take Notice that the Engraver and Printer have both begun to engrave and print the said Tunes, and are determined to compleat them as soon as possible.

We recall from the N. B. of the advertisement in the Pa. Journal for October 23, 1760, that

" Some of the first sheets " were to be " published . . . by the 3d of November,"

but the earliest advertisement, of which I know, relating to the *publication of the entire work*, with its striking and symbolic title ' Urania,' appeared in the Pa. Journal for *June 3, 1762*.

It reads :

Just published, and to be sold by Messrs. Rivington, Bradford and Isaac Snowden in Philadelphia

URANIA, or a choice Collection of Psalm-Tunes, Anthems and Hymns from the most approved Authors, with some entirely new; in two, three and four Parts, the whole adapted to the Use of Churches and Private Families; to which are prefixed the plainest and most necessary Rules of Psalmody. By *James Lyon* A. B.

N. B. Those Subscribers who have not yet received their Books are desired to apply to Mr. Isaac Snowden.

The tenor of this N. B. and the date of the advertisement combined render it probable that the collection was not *published* before 1762. The title-page itself, as the fac-simile clearly proves, alludes with nothing to the date of publication,

Hen. Dawkins Fec. 1761

being but the usual signature of the engraver.

The only item which weakens my theory appears in the copy of 'Urania' in possession of the New York Public Library (Lenox Building). This copy evidently belonged to Miss H. Chambers, one of the original subscribers.* An ink memorandum on the first page of the dedication reads:

Hetty Chambers . . . 1761 †

This memorandum, beyond reasonable doubt, goes to show that 'Urania' was delivered to Hetty Chambers in 1761, but the fact that the book was first advertised as late as June, 1762, must be taken into consideration. The simplest solution of the problem might be this: Some of the subscribers received their copies in 1761, others in 1762, and 'Urania' *appeared on the book market for non-subscribers by June, 1762.*

Hood, when describing the book, wrote: ‡

. . . Report says that it ruined the publisher.

This *on dit* has been repeated by others,§ especially by F. L. Ritter,

---

* Compare Subscribers' Names.

† On the same page appears, stamped, the name Hetty Johnston. Apparently Miss Hetty Chambers became a Mrs. Johnston.

‡ ' History of Music in New England.' 1846. pp. 159-160.

§ Hildeburn, Sabin, Williamson.

who concluded his criticism of 'Urania' by underscoring Hood's remark :

> . . . It is not to be wondered at that the Lyon's collection was a failure.*

But the Lyon's collection was *not* a failure. On the contrary, it was a success. 'Urania' must have met with public approval, for a new edition was thus advertised in the Pa. Journal on November 26, 1767:

> Just published, and to be sold by Isaac Snowden, Philadelphia. Garrat Noel, book-seller in New York, and Joseph Mershon, in Princeton: A new and neat Edition of *'Urania'* . . By James Lyon, A.M. Price ten Shillings. Great allowance made to those that take a number and pay cash.

That this really was a new edition appears from the significant change of A. B. into A. M. A new edition generally does not indicate a failure, and very much less so a later *new* edition. Evidently a such was published in 1773 at New York.

I found the following advertisement in the New York Gazetteer for December 16, 1773 :

> To be sold by Noel & Hazard . . .
> A new Edition of Lyon's Urania, the best collection of psalm-tunes, hymns, and anthems extant, on thick paper, is just published. Price 12 s.†

The copies of 'Urania' extant which I was able to locate and to examine are in the possession of the

		Abbreviated
1. New York Public Library	One	N. Y. P. L.
2. New York Historical Society	One	N. Y. H. S.
3. Pennsylvania Historical Society	Two	Pa. H. S. I
4.　　"　　　　　"　　　　"		Pa. H. S. II
5. Yale University	Two	Y. U. I
6.　　"　　　　"		Y. U. II
7. Massachusetts Historical Society	Two	Mass. H. S. I
8.　　"　　　　"　　　"		Mass. H. S. II
9. Library of Congress	One	L. C.
10. Mr. James Warrington of Phila.	Two	Warr. I
11.　　"　　　　"　　　"		Warr. II
12. Judge Samuel W. Pennypacker of Phila.	One	P.
13. My own copy	One	S.

---

* 'Music in America.' 1895. p. 43.
　† Williamson (in 'Bibliography of Maine') and Sabin (in 'Bibliotheca Americana') both mention an edition of 1763, without giving their authorities. This year is probably a misprint. The edition of 1767 is correctly mentioned by Hildeburn and Warrington.

The collation of the individual copies is briefly as follows :

N. Y. P. L.—engraved t. p. (v. bl.), as reproduced in fac-simile; 2 pages
of dedication, printed; 1 page of Index, printed (v. bl.); 3 pages
of "Subscribers Names," printed (p. 4. bl.); p. i–xii of theoretical
instructions, engraved; p. 1–190 of engraved music; lacks pages
191–198; ink mem. on first page of dedication. "Hetty Chambers,
1761." (See my footnote on p. 136.)

N. Y. H. S.—contents like in N. Y. P. L., but contains not the "Subscribers Names"; none of the music is missing; ink mem., "Leon-
ard Chester's Book."

Y. U. i—has 198 pages of music; shows neither a dedication nor "Subscribers Names"; otherwise contents like in N. Y. P. L.

Y. U. ii—wants title page and the outer half of each of the seven or
eight leaves at beginning and end; contains neither dedication nor
"Subscribers Names"; otherwise contents like in N. Y. P. L.; 198
pages of music.

Mass. H. S. i—no "Subscribers Names"; 198 pages of music; otherwise contents like in N. Y. P. L.

Mass. H. S. ii—very defective; begins with p. i–xii; then p. 3–180;
193–194.

L. C.—contents like in N. Y. P. L.; 198 pages of music (best copy
I have seen); ink mem. on t. p., " Ebenr. Hazard "; prefixed to
' Urania ' in Hazard's hand, " a collection of tunes," etc.

Pa. H. S. i—lacks pages 197–198; otherwise contents like in N. Y. P. L.

Pa. H. S. ii (very imperfect) and P. (seemingly perfect) show such
evident signs of intermarriage that a collation would be useless.

Warr. i—has not the " Subscribers Names"; otherwise contents like
N. Y. P. L.; 198 pages of music.

Warr. ᵢᵢ—lacks index; has neither dedication nor "Subscribers Names"; contents otherwise like in N. Y. P. L.; 198 pages of music; ink mem., "Mary Thane's the Gift | Book | of Capt. Wright | Now Majr. Wright | 176 [?]." *

S.—lacks dedication, index, and "Subscribers Names."

As far as individual collation goes, all copies would seem to be alike, differing only in regard to their more or less perfect condition. But a comparative collation of the copies reveals differences of interest and of importance for the bibliographical history of ' Urania.' †

To begin with, we notice distinct differences in the headings of the dedication.

N. Y. P. L. shows:

T O

The Clergy of every Denomination

in *America.*

So do Pa. H. S. ᵢ; N. Y. H. S.; and L. C.

---

* I learned either upon inquiry or personal examination that the following institutions do not possess ' Urania ': Princeton University; New Jersey Historical Society; Boston Public Library; Newberry Library, Chicago; Harvard University; Library Company of Philadelphia; Brown University; Rhode Island Historical Society; American Antiquarian Society, Worcester, Mass.; Maryland Historical Society; Virginia Historical Society; South Carolina Historical Society; Charleston Library Association; British Museum.

† Not all the results of this comparison are due to my personal observations. Mr. James Sumner Smith, Assistant Librarian of Yale University, and Mr. James Warrington of Philadelphia, having become interested in the subject through queries of mine, called my attention to some important points, which enabled me to supplement my own observations.

But Mass. H. S. ɪ has:

TO

The Clergy of every Denomination

in *America.*

and Warr. ɪ:

TO THE

CLERGY of every DENOMINATION

in AMERICA.

Then again the word "Relying," with which the text of the dedication begins, does not show the same type in all copies.

N. Y. P. L.; N. Y. H. S.; Pa. H. S. ɪ and L. C. have

RELYING

but Mass. H. S. ɪ and Warr. ɪ:

RELYING

Not less striking differences are noticeable in the indices. N. Y. P. L.; Pa. H. S.; and L. C. show:

The INDEX.

ANGELS Hymn	36	Orange	26	———	102	67	Southwell	28	O praife the Lord ⎫	154
Bath	31	Portfmouth	18	......	112	68	Standwich	6	Is there not ⎬	
Bedford	4	Pfalm 4th	40	Old	113	70	Walfal	13	an appoint. ⎭	156
		Pfalm 5	42	New	113	72	Wells's	33	ed Time	
Brunfwick	19	...... 8 *	44	Old	119	74	Westminfter	10	Let the fhrill ⎫	165
Canterbury	2	 9	45	New	119	76	Willington	34	Trumpet's * ⎭	

N. Y. H. S. has:

The INDEX.

ANGELS Hymn	36	Orange	26	Pfalm	102	67	Southwell	28	O praife the Lord ⎫	154
Bath	31	Portfmouth	18	......	112	68	Standifh	6	Is there not ⎬	
Bedford	4	Pfalm 4th	40	Old	113	70	Walfal	13	an appoint- ⎭	156
		Pfalm 5th	42	New	113	72	Wells's	33	ed Time	
Brunfwick	19	...... 8*	44	Old	119	74	Weftminfter	10	Let the fhrill ⎫	165
Canterbury	2	 9	45	New	119	76	Willington	34	Trumpet's * ⎭	

Mass. H. S. I shows:

The INDEX.

				HYMNS.
A NGELS Hymn 36	Pfalm 4th 40	New 113	72 Weftminfter	10
Bath 31	 5	Old 119	74 Willington	34 St. Matthew's 170
Bedford 4	.... 8*	New 119	76 Windfor	3 Palmy's 172
Brunfwick 19	 9	 122	78 Wirkfworth	25 Kettleby's 174
Canterbury 2	 12	 136	80 ANTHEMS.	Italian 176

Y. U. I and Warr. I have:

The I N D E X.

A NGELS Hymn 36	Orange 26	New 102	67 Southwell	28 O Praife the Lord	154
	Portfmouth 18	—— 112	68 Standwich	6 Is there not an ap	156
Bath 31	Pfalm 4th 40	Old 113	70 Walfal	13 pointed Time,	
Bedford 4	Pfalm 5 42	New 113	72 Well's	33 Let the fhrill Trum-	165
Brunfwick 19	—— 8* 44	Old 119	74 Weftminfter	10 pets,*	

Y. U. ᴵᴵ shows:

T H E   I N

ANGELS Hymn	36	Orange	-	26	New	102	-
		Portfmouth	-	18	——	112	-
Bath	- -	Pfalm 4th	-	40	Old	113	-
Bedford	- 4	== 5		42	New	113	-
Brunfwick	- 19	== 8*	-	44	Old	119	-

The differences are obvious:

1. The type varies, especially in the headings.
2. The arrangement of the columns varies.
3. The dots and lines used instead of the words " Psalm " and " New " vary.
4. Some copies have ' Standwich,' others ' Standish,' which is the correct name of the tune. (The latter appears besides in N. Y. H. S. in both Mass. H. S. ᵢ and ᵢᵢ; the former in Y. U. ᵢᵢ) *

Further significant differences are revealed by a marginal note in all the indices which reads:

*All Tunes marked with an Asterism are new.

This note applies in the indices to the following " tunes ":

Psalm 8 (p. 44); Psalm 23 (p. 50); New 95 (p. 63); to the Anthems ' The Lord Descended . . .' (p. 125); ' Let the shrill Trumpets . . .' (p. 165); and to a Hymn of Watts' (p. 194).

However, in the engraved music the starring is not fully in accord with the indices. All copies show:

On pp. 44 and 194 ✳ (a star with eight intermediate staccato marks).†

p. 63   ✳ (a star).

p. 125   ✳ (a star of sixteen lines).

But in both N. Y. P. L. and Pa. H. S. ᵢ ‡ asterisks are missing on pp. 50 and 165.

L. C. shows on p. 165 ✳, evidently intended as a cross with four intermediate staccato marks, but lacks one on p. 50, whereas N. Y. H. S.;

---

* I beg to keep in mind that differences in the name of this tune *appear only in the indices.* In the engraved music the tune is throughout called ' Standish.' Similar differences are to be noticed in the name ' Leathered.' In the music the tune is called ' Leatherhead.'

† The fact that N. Y. P. L. lacks pp. 191–198 is of no importance. Corresponding with Pa. H. S. ᵢ in every other respect, no doubt, it possessed originally the same asterism on p. 194 as Pa. U. S. ᵢ and the other copies.

‡ Pa. H. S. ᵢ has an asterism on p. 165 but apparently by hand.

Mass. ɪ and ɪɪ; Y. U. ɪ and ɪɪ; Warr. ɪ and ɪɪ, and S. all have on p. 50 ✳ a cross with four intermediate staccato marks, but on p. 165 ✳ a cross with two intermediate staccato marks, the third line evidently having been intended as staccato marks.

These differences between the individual copies are of a nature as to exclude the possibility of their belonging to one and the same edition.   The fact that the title-pages are all identical does not weaken this statement.   It will be remembered that the title-page of ' Urania,' the rules and the music are engraved, whereas the dedication, the index and the " Subscribers Names " are printed.   The engraved parts of the book, the asterisks excepted, show no differences whatever.   We notice such in the printed sections only.   For this we can easily account : When new editions of the book were wanted, the engraving would naturally remain the same, whereas the typographical parts of the book were set up anew.

However, this explanation does not aid materially in assigning the individual copies to their respective place in the bibliographical history of ' Urania.'

Fortunately the asterisks furnish an unmistakable clue.   It is self-evident that those copies in which they are wanting on both p. 50 and p. 165 must be of earlier date than those copies in which these pages are starred in accord with index.   After the book had been delivered to subscribers either Dawkins the engraver, or the author or others noticed the omissions and Dawkins corrected either one or both. As N. Y. P. L. and Pa. H. S. ɪ lack the asterisks on pp. 50 and 165 we might claim with certainty that these two copies are of earlier date than the others.   But this would not necessarily imply that they belong to the *first* edition.   Even if this could be inferred, the fact would not exclude from the first edition such copies which do not differ in the typographical parts from N. Y. P. L. and Pa. H. S. ɪ, since the mistake in starring might have been noticed when the first copies were printed, and the engraved plates, as I said before, might have been corrected before continuing the issue of the first edition.   Consequently the asterisks lead us in the direction of a relative date only and not of an absolute date.

But the original possessor of N. Y. P. L. was kind enough to undermine all controversy with respect to this copy.   We remember that she wrote on the first page of the dedication,

Hetty Chambers 1761

The most sceptical critic will admit that N. Y. P. L. at least must be attributed without further hesitation to the first edition. The same must be claimed for Pa. H. S. $_I$, being a twin-copy of N. Y. P. L.

As to the other copies we again would be compelled to enter the labyrinth of conjectures, but now with N. Y. P. L. and Pa. H. S. $_I$ for guides. The matter being entirely hypothetical, I submit the following remarks merely as my personal opinion :

To begin with L. C., it will have been noticed that the copy differs from N. Y. P. L.—the natural basis of our investigations—in one point only; it has an asterisk on p. 165. But perhaps only the omission on p. 165 was noticed at first and consequently the asterisk on this page only was added by the engraver for such subscribers as had not yet received their copies. The difference is very slight and I am therefore inclined to attribute L. C. to the first edition.

Moreover, L. C. is the only copy besides N. Y. P. L. and Pa. H. S. $_I$ which contains the "Subscribers Names." This is of some importance. Naturally the first edition would contain such; but it would have been useless to reprint them in subsequent editions. If therefore the other copies do not show a list of subscribers, it does not follow that they are imperfect. As, furthermore, none of these copies show signs of ever having contained the list, it is reasonable to argue that the "Subscribers Names" actually never made part of them. This alone would render it probable that the copies without the "Subscribers Names" do not belong to the first edition of 'Urania.'

The idea is strengthened by the fact that in all these the missing asterisks were supplied and that all these copies have the same peculiar asterisks in common on p. 165, ✳ ; and on p. 50, ✽.

With regard to Warr. $_{II}$, one important observation stands forth. The copy can not have belonged to the New York edition of 1773, since it contains the ink memorandum :

Mary Thane's the Gift Book of Capt. Wright now Majr. Wright. 176[?]

This copy belonged probably to the edition of 1767. But as if to baffle all investigation, it lacks dedication and index. Were this not the case, then a simple comparison between this copy and others would be sufficient to separate them.

Therefore, the imperfections of Warr. $_{II}$ prevent us from using it as a basis for the comparison of the remaining copies.

Now Y. U. $_I$ and Warr. $_I$ differ so strikingly from N. Y. P. L. that it becomes almost impossible to attribute them to the first edition. Y.U. $_{II}$ apparently descended from Y. U. $_I$, which is identical with Warr. $_I$.* Certainly not *vice versa*, for it deviates from N. Y. P. L. even more than Y. U. $_I$. This becomes clear if we recollect the characteristic differences between Y. U. $_I$ and Y. U. $_{II}$. The former shows:

The INDEX and Psalm 4th

Psalm 5th

——— 8

whereas Y. U. $_{II}$:

THE INDEX and Psalm 4th

=== 5

=== 8.

The question arises whether these copies belonged to the edition of 1767 or of 1773?

Turning our attention to N. Y. H. S. we notice that the copy did not descend from Y. U. $_I$ or Y. U. $_{II}$, but directly from N. Y. P. L. This is evident from the type selected for the dedication and index (only the heading differs somewhat in the latter, and we notice Psalm 102 instead of—102). Furthermore, the arrangement of the columns in the index is the same. But it is equally apparent that it does not belong to the first edition. Besides the asterisks on p. 50 and 165 one important item shows this. N. Y. P. L. has 'Standwich,' whereas N. Y. H. S. has ' Standish,' the correct name of the tune, in the index. This alteration proves that ' Urania' must have been revised, and therefore N. Y. H. S. is to be dated later than N. Y. P. L. Now Y.U. $_I$ and Warr. $_I$ show the same mistake as N. Y. P. L. It would follow, not with certainty, but with probability, that they, too, are earlier specimens of ' Urania' than N. Y. H. S. If this be admitted, then we may conclude that Y. U. $_I$ and Warr. $_I$ belong to the Philadelphia edition of 1767, whereas N. Y. H. S. to the New York edition of 1773.

Y. U. $_{II}$ might be considered merely as a copy of a supplementary issue of the edition of 1767 unless we prefer to argue that an edition must have been printed between 1767 and 1773.

Mass. H. S. $_I$ and Mass. H. S. $_{II}$ remain. Without doubt they belong both to one edition, but to which? They have nothing in common with N. Y. P. L.—except the same heading in the index,

---

*I do not overlook the fact that Y. U. $_I$ contains no dedication. But Y. U. $_I$ and Warr. $_I$ being otherwise entirely alike, I am inclined to believe that the dedication is lacking in Y. U. $_I$.

and nothing with Y. U. $_I$, Y. U. $_{II}$, Warr. $_I$ and Warr. $_{II}$ except the asterisks on p. 50 and 165; but they have in common with N. Y. H. S. one vital point: ' Standish.'

I have been able to trace only three editions of 'Urania' in the newspapers, but Mass. H. S. $_I$ and Mass. H. S. $_{II}$ render it likely that a fourth was issued (perhaps in New England) based (with revisions) either upon the Philadelphia edition of 1767, the New York edition of 1773 or directly upon the first Philadelphia edition of the collection.

CHAPTER III.

DESCRIPTION OF 'URANIA.'

A competent history of American psalmody remains to be written. The works by Hood, Gould, Ritter and others were remarkable pioneer-efforts, but to-day the information contained in them must be considered not only antiquated but superficial. Moreover, they abound in prejudice. The predominance of New England in these histories has been especially detrimental to a clear understanding of the condition of sacred music in Colonial America. Not until the development of psalmody in all the Colonies has been thoroughly investigated will it be possible to give a trustworthy critical description of the individual psalm-tune collections and kindred publications issued in America during the eighteenth century. It would be folly, should I attempt to assign Lyon's 'Urania' to its true place in the history of American psalmody on the basis of Hood, Ritter or others.

The attempt would call for a detailed examination of the denominational character of the book. This would necessitate the minute study of religious contrasts in the Colonies. Then the confluent or diffluent influences upon the development of psalmody would have to be closely investigated. And all this with the aid of a history of the individual psalm-tunes, which does not exist! I do not desire to confuse the public still more than has been done by others, and I prefer to describe 'Urania' without making it a mirror of the universe, to disclose to a certain degree the influence which both American and English publications had upon the book, to trace in turn the influence which it exercised over later psalmodists, and to refute previous criticism of Lyon's collection as far as I consider it incorrect.

The last part of my task is the easiest. Hood,* for instance, gives the following description of 'Urania' by James Lyons [sic] A. B.:

---

* 'History of Music in New England.' (Boston, 1846.)

This book was much larger than any previous work that had been published in the colonies. Report says that it ruined the publisher. . .

The arrangement of the harmony was bad, showing the editor to have been but little acquainted with musical science. In many places the harmony could scarcely have been worse. Dissonant chords are seldom used. In a few cases, the chord of the added sixth may be found at a cadence; and in a few more, the strange idea of a seventh taken at the cadence on the subdominant; but in no one instance is one found on the dominant. This work contained the first music of a fuguing style ever published in this country. Not quite one-half of the psalm-tunes were of the plain choral style, and the rest were of a light or fuguing character. The anthems were characterized by poor attempts at fugue and imitation with long runs in the melody.

This criticism reads as if ' Urania ' was a book of original compositions by James Lyon. Hood forgot that it was a choice collection from the most approved authors. Therefore not Lyon deserves the blame for " the poor attempts at fugue " and the faulty harmonizations, but those authors who were most approved of in those days both in England and America.

Then again the statement is incorrect that not quite one-half of the psalm-tunes were of the plain choral style. On the contrary, by far the most tunes are written in this style. Very few, like 'Cranley,' the 5th, 12th, 15th psalm-tunes show a " light or fuguing character " and very many appear simply *nota contra notam.* The dreaded florid style is to be found as a rule in the anthems only, and they were by English composers.

Furthermore, why is it a strange idea to employ the seventh at the cadence on the subdominant and where are Hood's " few " cases? I found none. But there are to be found several instances in which the dominant seventh is employed at the cadence, though Hood writes " in no one instance." I simply refer to pp. 4, 20, 22, 37, 58, 61.

However, it is not James Lyon who is to be held responsible for all this. If he imitated the florid English psalmodists of his age in one or two of the starred anthems which I shall prove to be original compositions of his, we must not forget that he could not escape the spirit of the time, that he lived in a country where music was still in its infancy and that he had to depend for his wisdom in musical matters upon the motherland.

If Hood was inaccurate in his statements he, at least, tried to be impartial and fair. Not so Frederick L. Ritter. He passes the following verdict upon ' Urania ' : *

* See pp. 40–43 of his ' Music in America. . . . New ed.. with additions. 1895.'

The book was compiled mostly from Tansur, Williams, Arnold and other English psalm-tune lights of that stamp. The anthems are in the style of those florid, empty, sentimental, fuguing settings, prevalent at this epoch among some of the most popular church musicians in England. . .

To several tunes which in Williams' collection are arranged for three parts, an alto part has been added in the most clumsy manner. . .

Evidently Ritter did not feel friendly inclined toward "the dawn of musical cultivation" in the Colonies. In fact, a continuous sneer pervades the thus entitled chapters of his work and renders their study disagreeable. But to sneer is not to write history. A true historian never expects more than he possibly can find after a critical and impartial consideration of general conditions. It is especially not the method of a historian to condemn *pioneers* from the standpoint of advanced countries and ages. But Lyon certainly was a pioneer. His 'Urania'

with all its imperfections . . . is to be taken as a convincing evidence of the upwards tendency of musical effort in this country.*

Moreover, Ritter's statements can not be accepted off-hand. The superficiality which he rebuked in others is only too apparent in his own writings.†

He mentions in the lines quoted, 'Williams' Collection' as having been of influence upon Lyon. On p. 46 of his history of 'Music in America' he calls it 'A. Williams' Universal Psalmody.' Some lines below, always writing of the same work, he claims, and in part correctly claims, that "Aaron Williams'" book, 'The New Universal Psalmodist,' appeared "in 1763."

Both titles are incorrect. But Ritter's inaccuracy in quoting titles is immaterial. It is the date of 1763 which throws a peculiar light upon his critical methods. If 'Williams' Collection' appeared in 1763, how can it have influenced Lyon's 'Urania,' which appeared in 1761 or, at the latest, in 1762?

The contradiction is apparent, but Ritter did not stop to reconcile the substance of his statement with chronology. He noticed, and correctly noticed, that several tunes, both in Williams' 'Universal Psalmodist' and in Lyon's 'Urania,' are identical with respect to the Treble, Tenor, and Bass. But evidently Lyon can not have added a

---

* See (Mathews' ?) 'A Hundred Years of Music in America,' p. 20.

† I again repeat that I consider his book 'Music in America' a remarkable pioneer work, but truth compels me to be severe, for Ritter has done more harm than good with his method of writing history, which was often but superficiality under the mask of omniscience combined with a tendency to sneer at music and musicians American.

counter to settings as they appear in a book which did not exist when his compilation was published. What Ritter could have said and ought to have said is that both Williams and Lyon must have borrowed material from a common source.*

Then again Ritter claims ' Urania ' to have been compiled besides from Williams, Arnold and others, from Tansur.

Of William Tansur's various works he mentions but

1. 'A Complete Melody in three parts' (instead of 'A Compleat Melody, or The Harmony of Zion') on p. 40.
2. The ' Royal Melody Complete' on p. 45.
3. ' Musical Grammar' [*recte* 'A New Musical Grammar'].

I had occasion to examine the third edition (London, 1756) of 'A

---

*The history of 'The Universal Psalmodist' is not quite clear. Mr. Warrington in his admirable ' Short Titles' does not even mention the book He does mention Williams' ' New Universal Psalmodist' with a mark to the effect that he saw the 5th ed. (1770). But he commits the strange error of dating without having seen them, a first to fourth edition of ' The New Universal Psalmodist,' like the first—1770. In so doing, I am sure he felt the improbability of five editions having been issued in the same year. Messrs. Brown and Stratton in their valuable ' British· Musical Biography' (1900) write under Williams' ' Universal Psalmodist': "London, n. d. 3rd. edition, 1765; 4th edition 1770. ' New Universal Psalmodist,' 1770."

This information, too, is not quite correct, for the Boston Public Library possesses a dated copy of the first edition. The title reads:

' The UNIVERSAL PSALMODIST, containing

' 1. A compleat Introduction to Psalmody, or the Art of Singing Psalms etc. Interspersed with many useful Scales and Examples, carefully laid down and explained in a familiar Dialogue between Master and Scholar.

' 2. A Choice and valuable Collection of Psalms and Hymn Tunes, Canons, and Anthems, many of which were never before published; also the Tunes, Anthems etc sung at the *Magdalene* and *Foundary* Chapels, and other public Places in and about London, with Words adapted to each Tune.

' The Whole composed in a new and easy Taste for two, three and four, but generally for four Voices, in the most familiar Keys and Cliffs, according to the Advice and Direction of the most eminent Masters in London. Calculated to promote and improve this most excellent Part of Social Worship, and thereby render it both useful and delightful in all Country Choirs, as well as in the Congregations, and other Religious Societies in London and Westminster.

' By A. *Williams*. Teacher of Psalmody in London.

London. Printed for Joseph Johnson, at Mead's Head, opposite the Monument. *1763.*'

The preface, directed "To all Lovers of Psalmody," is dated "London. Jan. 6. 1763. A. Williams."

Yale University possesses a copy of the "Second Edition Corrected London, 1764," with the same preface as the first edition. In both we read:

"I have been careful to have the Music as correct as possible. As to the new Tunes, which are all marked with a star in the Index, I have kept the air of every part as smooth and pleasant as the rules would admit. As for the old Tunes, where I have altered, (which is very little) I hope I have improved. Some few of the old, and many of the modern Tunes, which were before in few parts (and some of those very unfit for the voice) I have greatly altered, and added more parts for the use of musical societies whom I would ever study to oblige."

Yale University possesses also a copy of the sixth edition of the ' New Universal Psalmodist.' This copy reveals a fact hitherto apparently overlooked. A comparison between the ' Universal Psalmodist' and the ' New Universal Psalmodist' proves beyond doubt that the latter was merely a somewhat revised reprint of the ' Universal Psalmodist.' Williams therefore numbered the ' New Universal Psalmodist' as an edition of the original work.

Perhaps we might now date the editions as follows: ' Universal Psalmodist,' 1st ed., 1763; 2d, corrected, 1764; 3d, 1765; 4th, 1770 (?); 5th, as ' New Universal Psalmodist,' 1770; 6th ditto, 177-, etc.

Compleat Melody . . .'; the second of the ' Royal Melody Compleat . . .'
(London, 1760), and the third (London, 1756) of 'A New Musical
Grammar.' Neither of these works furnished sufficient musical mate-
rial for ' Urania ' to justify Ritter's " compiled mostly from *Tansur,*
Williams, Arnold . . ."

If Ritter says :

> with regards to the use of the clefs, the editor had no judgment at all. Some
> pieces in four parts employ the bass clef, and the treble clef for the soprano, alto and
> tenor; others the four different clefs for the four different voices . . .

he involuntarily showed how superficially he read Lyon's explanation of the gamut. Lyon had his good reasons for doing what he did,
and left no doubt as to his intentions. He employs the four clefs
for mixed voices only, our Soprano, Alto,
Tenor, Bass. Where the G clef is prefixed to
the Counter and Tenor

> —which is frequently the case . . . in this book

the part is " design'd for men's voices " (p. III). In this case the two
parts sound an octave lower than written. If this method shows no
judgment, then our modern way of writing for the tenor voice is equally
absurd, as both ways are identical.

A few lines below the remark quoted, Ritter copies Lyon's four directions for singing :

> 1. In learning the 8 Notes, get the assistance of some Person well acquainted with
> the Tones and Semitones.
> 2. Choose that Part which you can sing with the greatest ease, and make yourself
> Master of that first.
> 3. Sound all the high Notes as soft as possible, but low ones hard and full.
> 4. Pitch your Tune that the highest and lowest Notes may be sounded distinctly.

Ritter sarcastically adds:

> A great help that must have been to inexperienced singers!

I confess, these rules sound rather naïve, but they certainly contain
a good deal of common-sense if properly read and properly interpreted.

James Lyon dedicated ' Urania '

> To the Clergy of every Denomination in America.

The dedication reads :

Reverend Sirs,

Relying on the evident Propriety of your patronizing this Publication, permit me to lay 'Urania' at your Feet.

Should the following Collection of Tunes be so fortunate, as to merit your Approbation ; to please the Taste of the Public; to assist the private Christian in his daily Devotion ; and to improve in any Degree, an important Part of Divine Service in these Colonies, for which it was designed : I shall think myself happy in being the Editor, notwithstanding the great Expense, Labour and Anxiety, it has cost me to compleat it.

May you long continue Ornaments of your Profession : daily see abundant Fruits of your Labour in the Reformation of Mankind ; and incessantly enjoy those sublime Pleasures, which nothing but a Series of rational and virtuous Actions can create.

I am,

Reverend Gentlemen

Your most obedient,

and humble Servant,

James Lyon.

The editor's reasons for dedicating ' Urania ' to the clergy are obvious. Sacred music has always been " an important Part of Divine Service." As such, its right use or abuse has always been a matter of deep concern to those clergymen who understand the importance of sacred music, especially of psalmody, in divine service. Whenever the clergy fails to have the dignity of church music at heart, it degenerates, either through neglect of musical culture, through the introduction of secular elements which destroy the purity of sacred music, or by playing a too prominent part in the service. The history of music furnishes abundant examples for the correctness of this statement, in particular the history of psalmody in the British colonies of North America.

About 1700, the condition of psalmody had become so deplorable that many people would rather dispense with church-music than be offended by its crudities. Not until the clergy gave the subject careful and polemical consideration, does an upward tendency again become noticeable. We need but recollect Rev. C. Mather's ' The Accomplished Singer '; Rev. T. Walter's ' Grounds and Rules of Music,' endorsed by a number of progressive clergymen ; Rev. John Tuft's ' Introduction to the Art of Singing'; Rev. T. Symmes 'A Discourse concerning Prejudice,' his ' Utile Dulci ' and other treatises. It is mostly due to an intelligent clergy if American psalmody emerged from a whirlpool of crudity and prejudice. About the middle of the eighteenth century church-music had made remarkable progress in the Colonies, but much remained to be improved, and still the welfare of psalmody rested mainly in the hands of the clergy. I doubt not that a clear understanding of the situation induced James Lyon to make his appeal to the " Reverend Gentlemen."

We have no way of ascertaining whether or not the clergy was conquered by the *captatio benevolentiae* for a book which, though not absolutely the first of its kind published in America, certainly was the boldest, most conspicuous, and most carefully prepared attempt " to spread the art of psalmody " throughout the Colonies until about 1770.

Ambitious James Lyon must keenly have felt the necessity of editing a " choice collection . . . peculiarly adapted for churches and private families." This impression we gain from the "Subscribers Names."

Originally he advertised that the money would be returned unless four hundred subscriptions toward the publication were received. Evidently Lyon preferred to edit his collection with by far less subscribers, for the list contains but 141 (not 142 as Ritter counted). Some took several copies, for instance, Jonathan Baldwin, A. M. Steward of Nassau Hall in New Jersey, six books. Adding such copies, in all 58, to the 141 we see that 199 copies had been subscribed for. Of the 141 subscribers 38 appear to have been officers or students of Nassau Hall (*id est* College of New Jersey at Princeton) subscribing for 50 books. Undoubtedly the author must have been well liked and considered worthy of encouragement by his fellow-students and professors.

The fact alone that the Princetonians were so deeply interested in ' Urania ' would be ample proof, even without the evidence furnished in the previous chapter, of the compiler's connection with the College of New Jersey. This has to be mentioned because doubts have been raised as to the identity of James Lyon, A. B. of Princeton, and James Lyon, A. B., author of ' Urania.' For instance, I find in a letter which the reference librarian of Princeton University forwarded to Mr. James Warrington and of which this gentleman had the kindness to send me a copy :

In the first place we do not know if he [scil. James Lyon, class of 1759] was the editor of 'Urania ' or not.

As the "plainest and most necessary Rules of Psalmody " represent the state of theoretical knowledge of music among our psalmodists about 1760 and as they apparently were worked out by James Lyon himself, they may follow *in extenso :*

I.

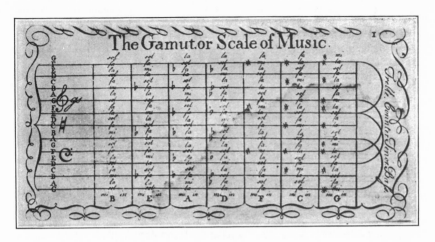

II.

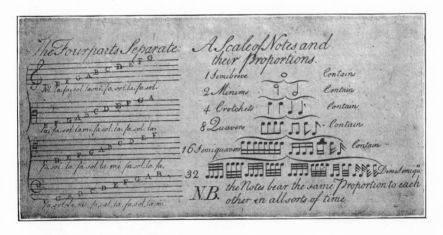

EXPLANATION OF THE GAMUT. III.

The 4 Parts of Music are distinguished from one another, by 4 Semicircles each including 5 Lines, with their Proper Cliffs and Letters. The first is the Bass or lowest Part in Music, and known by the F cliff which always stands on F. The 2d is the Tenor, with the C cliff on C. its 4th Line. The 3d is Counter with the C cliff on C, its 3d Line; And the 4th is Treble, the highest part of Music, with the G cliff on G, its 2d Line. The F. & G. cliffs in most Authors are immovable, but when they move, the Letters, which are the Names of the Lines and Spaces, always move with them, in the same order as they stand in the Gamut. The C Cliff is movable in all Authors, but the Line it stands on is always C, and must be sounded a 5th above the F cliff, and a 5th below the G cliff, except when the latter is prefix'd to a part design'd for mens Voices (which is frequently the case with the Tenor & Counter in this Book) when it is a 4th above the G. cliff, for that is now an Octave (or 8 Notes) below its usual place, and Unison (or the same sound) with the highest G in the Bass.

IV.   The four Monosyllables sol, fa, mi, fa seldom change the Order in which they stand in the Gamut, viz. from mi to mi ascending they are fa, sol, la, fa, sol, la, & descending la, sol, fa, la, sol, fa; And the two Semitones or half Notes in every Octave are invariably fix'd between mi & fa, & la & fa, throughout all the Removes of mi, except when a Flat, Sharp or Natural, is plac'd immediately before some particular Note. All Notes upon Lines and Spaces, not mark'd with either Flats or Sharps, are call'd Natural Notes, & are represented by the Monosyllables in the 2d Column of the Gamut. In all the succeeding Columns they are remov'd to other Letters by Flats & Sharps, according to the following Rules, but in such a manner, that they express those Flats & Sharps, without affecting any of the Natural Notes.

1. When neither a Flat nor Sharp is set at the Beginning of a Tune, mi is in B. But
2. If B be flat mi is in E.
3. If B, & E.be flat, mi is in A.
4. If B, E, & A be flat, mi is in D.
5. If B, E, A & D be flat, mi is in G.
6. If F be sharp, mi is in F.
7. If F and C be sharp, mi is in C.
8. If F, C & G be sharp, mi. is in G.
9. If F, C, G & D be sharp, mi is in D.

Of Time, or the Duration of Sound in Music.   V.

Time is of two kinds, viz. Common, & Triple, in one or the other of which all Movements are included. Common Time is measured by an even Number of Beats in each Bar, the first half of which must be perform'd with the Hand or Foot down, & the other with it up. Its first Mood is a very slow & grave Movement, containing one Semibreve or its Quantity, in every Bar, which ought to be sounded about 4 Seconds,

or while you may leisurely say 1. 2. 3. 4. This Mood is mark'd thus ⹂Gs𝄴⹂ The

2d Mood has a line drawn thro' the C ⹂Gs𝄵⹂ & should be sung about half as fast

again as the first. The 3d Mood is known by a C inverted ⹂Gs⹂ from which it is

called the Retortive Mood, or by a Figure of Two Gs⹂2⹂ and must be sung as

quick again as the first Mood. The last Mood worthy of Notice in this Place is

mark'd thus Gs⹂$\frac{2}{4}$⹂ & called 2 to 4 containing one Minim or two Crotchets & in a

Bar, which require nearly the same Time that ye same Notes require in the 2d Mood. In beating the 2 first of these Moods the Hand should have 4 equable Motions in every Bar, 2 down & 2 up. And in the two last Moods only 2 Motions, one down and the other up: According to the following Examples in Common Time, where d is put for down & u for up; and the Number of Beats in each

VI.   Bar shown by an equal Number of Figures, directly over them:

Triple Time is known by the following Characters  the first of which contains 3 Minims in a Bar, which ought to be sung in the Time of 2 Minims in the first Mood of Common Time.   The 2d contains 3 Crotchets in a Bar, which are sung about as quick as Crotchets, in the 2d Mood of Common Time.   The last contains 3 Quavers in a Bar, which are sung as quick as Crotchets in Retortive Time. Each Bar in Triple Time, whether quick or slow, is divided into three equal Parts, the two first of which must be perform'd with the Hand, or Foot down, & the last with it up, according to the following Examples.

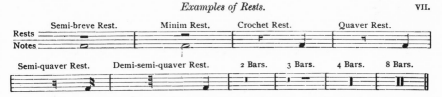

Examples of Rests.   VII.

	Semi-breve Rest.	Minim Rest.	Crochet Rest.	Quaver Rest.
Rests				
Notes				

Semi-quaver Rest.	Demi-semi-quaver Rest.	2 Bars.	3 Bars.	4 Bars.	8 Bars.

Note, A Semibreve Rest is a whole Bar in any Time whatever.

A Single Bar ═══ divides the Time according to the measure Note. A Double

Bar ═══ divides every Strain or Part of a Tune, & shows the End of the Lines in

Psalm & Hymn Tunes. A Repeat ═══ signifies that such a Part of a Tune, from the Note over or before which it is put, must be sung over again. A Hold or Pause

═══ signifies that the Note over which it is plac'd, must be sounded something

longer than its usual Time, it also denotes the End of a Tune.   A Direct ═══

is put at the End of the Lines, when broke off by the Narrowness of the Paper, to show the Place of the first Note in the succeeding Lines.   A Slur or Tye

═══ drawn over or under any Quantity of Notes signifies,

that they are all to be sung to one syllable.   Three Crotchets, with a Figure of 3

over or under them ═══ must be sung in the Time of a Minim;

& three Quavers ═══ in the time of a Crotchet etc.

VIII. *Of Flats Sharps & Naturals*

A Flat placed before any Note signifies that that Note (and all on the same Letter in that Bar, except mark'd to the Contrary) must be sung a Semitone lower than its Natural Pitch. The Sharp is of a contrary Nature, and raises a Note a Semitone higher than its Natural Sound. When Flats are set at the Beginning of a Tune, they affect all the Notes on the same Letters on which they stand, thro' the whole Movement; thus if a Flat be set on B, B must be sounded half a Note lower than its Natural Pitch, thro' the Tune, unless the Flat is removed by a Sharp or Natural. Sharps set at the Beginning of a Tune have the contrary Effect.

A Natural reduces any Note, made flat or sharp by the governing Flats or Sharps in the Beginning of a Tune to its primitive sound.

Of the Keys in Music

The Letter on which a Tune closes, is called its Key, which is known to be either flat or sharp by the third above the last Note in the Bass; if that third contains two whole Tones the Tune is on a sharp Key; but if only a Tone and Semitone, it is a flat Key.

Of Syncopation.   IX.

All Notes placed in such a Part of the Bar, that they require the Hand to be taken up or put down while they are sounding; or divided by a single Bar, as in this Example are called Notes of Syncopation   Note, they are also called driving Notes.

Of Transposition.

When a Tune happens to be on a wrong Key, either too high, or too low, it may be transpos'd or remov'd, to any other Key, by adding Flats or Sharps, or by omitting them, as Occasion requires. But great Care must be taken, that the Notes retain their old Names, & bear the same Relation to each other, as before, and that all accidental Flats and Sharps are inserted, unless Naturals will answer to the End better.

☞ The above Example shews how the same Tune may be transpos'd not only from G to C; or from C to G: But to any other of the 7 Letters.

Examples of pointed Notes.

A Dot on the right side of a Note makes it half as long again. Thus one Semibreve is equal to 3 Minims etc.

x. *Of the Graces in Music.*

The Trill or Shake is used on all descending prickt Crotchets; on the latter of two Notes on the same Line or Space; and generally before a Close. The other Graces are seldom used in plain Church Tunes, but are very popular in Hymns and Anthems. Note, the Turn may be used on a Note, that sinks a Semitone below two Notes on the same Line or Space, always beginning with the first, and also at the End of a Strain, when the last Note is grac'd, as in the following Examples

Some Directions for Singing

1. In learning the 8 Notes, get the Assistance of some Person, well acquainted with the Tones & Semitones.
2. Choose that Part which you can sing with the greatest Ease, and make yourself Master of that first.
3. Sound all high Notes as soft as possible, but low ones hard and full.
4. Pitch your Tune so that the highest and lowest Notes may be sounded distinctly.

The Eight Notes Ascending & Descending. XI.

Thirds ascending and descending.

XII.

3ds, 4ths, etc., without ye intermediate notes.

The "tunes," like the rules, are neatly engraved in 'Urania,' but unfortunately not without numerous errors.   However, unless Henry Dawkins had previous experience as a music engraver it must be admitted that he did remarkably well.

The collection contains twelve anthems, fourteen hymns, and seventy settings of psalm-tunes.   As the latter generally cover but one or two pages, more than half of the book is filled with anthems and hymns.

In detail, 'Urania' contains in accord with the Index the following tunes:

Angels Hymn	p. 36	Psalm	5	p. 42	New	122	p. 78
Bath	31	——	8*	44	——	136	80
Bedford	4	——	9	45	——	145	82
Brunswick	19	——	12	46	——	148	83
Canterbury	2	——	15	48	Old	148	84
Coleshill	11	——	23*	50	——	149	86
Cookfield	20	——	33	52	——	150	88
Cranley	38	——	40	54	Ripon		12
Crowle	7	——	43	55	Rygate		24
Dagenham	35	Old	50	56	St. Ann's		5
Darking	21	New	50	58	St. David's		8
Derby	29	——	56	60	St. Humphrey's		14
Dorchester	23	——	57	61	St. Matthew's		22
Gloucester	9	——	90	62	St. Michael's		15
Isle of Wight	16	——	95*	63	St. Peter's		30
Leathered	37	——	98	64	Southwell		28
[or Leatherhead]		Old	100	65	Standwich		6
London New	17	New	100	66	[*recte* Standish]		
Mear	1	——	102	67	Walsal		13
Morning Hymn	32	——	112	68	Wells's		33
Newcastle	27	Old	113	70	Westminster		10
Orange	26	New	113	72	Willington		34
Portsmouth	18	Old	119	74	Windsor		3
Psalm 4th	40	New	119	76	Wirksworth		25

These psalm-tunes are followed by the following *Anthems* (first words) and *Hymns:*

Preserve me, O God	p. 90	St. Matthew's	p. 170
I will bless the Lord	97	Palmy's	172
O be joyful	103	Kettelby's	174
O sing unto the Lord	111	Italian	176
O clap your Hands	118	Public Worship	178
The Lord descended *	125	Sky Lark	180
Jehovah reigns	133	Salisbury	183
I will magnify, etc.	142	Kettering	184
O give thanks unto the		Resurrection	186
Lord	157	Judgment	188
O praise the Lord	154	Whitefield's	190
Is there not an appointed		Christmas	192
Time	156	Watts's *	194
Let the shrill Trumpet's *	165	Hallelujah	196

A marginal note, of which the meaning will be explained later on, reads :

* All Tunes marked with an asterisk are new

The titles as given in the engraved music differ somewhat from those in the index. Here the anthems, for instance, appear under their first words; there with indication of the source of the words. A reference to the six starred pieces will render the difference clear. In the index we read :

<pre>
        (Psalm)   8
                  23
                  95
        Anthems   The Lord descended
                  Let the shrill Trumpet's
        Hymns   Watts's
</pre>

but in the engraved music:

<pre>
        The 8th Psalm Tune
        The 23d Psalm Tune
        The 95th Psalm Tune
        Two celebrated Verses by Sternhold &
            Hopkins set to Music
        An Anthem taken from the 150th Psalm
        The 104th Psalm by Dr. Watts.
</pre>

By far the most pieces are written for four parts. Only eight appear for three :

150th Psalms	St. Matthew's
Palm's	Kettelby's
Italian	Public Worship
Sky Lark	Hallelujah

Of two-part settings there are also eight :

An Anthem taken out of the 148th Psalm	Salisbury
Kettering	Resurrection
Judgment	Whitefield's
Christmas	Watts's 104th Psalm

A few tunes appear as written for soli and chorus. For instance, in 'Darking' and 'Dorchester,' Tenor Solo, Bass Solo, Treble Solo and Counter Solo are followed by the "Chorus." Then again we notice a few pieces in which a duet ("Treble and Bass") precedes the Chorus. The Anthem taken out of the 145th Psalm ('I will magnify Thee O Lord') shows the most elaborate form: first "Treble and Bass," then four-part chorus, a long "Bass solo," again four-part chorus, a long "Treble Solo" followed by the chorus.

The four-part settings are written for Treble, Counter, Tenor, and Bass, with the exception of 'An Anthem taken out of the 97th Psalm,' in which the Counter is replaced by a "2d Treble." The voices are carefully indicated until they disappear toward the end of the collection. Indications like "Allegro," "Adagio," "Slow," "Quick" occur but seldom. *None of the ninety-six compositions appears with a composer's name.*

As has been stated before, most of the Tunes are harmonized in plain choral style. The Anthems, however, show attempts at "imitation" (rather than at fuguing) and are too florid for our modern taste. Equally antiquated is the tendency to avoid the third at the beginning and end of the part-setting. But these and other observations are not characteristic of 'Urania' in contradistinction to other psalm-tune collections of the time, and consequently there is no necessity of dwelling upon these features of Lyon's compilation. But 'Urania' differs distinctly from most of the English collections in two respects. In the first place the psalm-tunes are given without words, and in the second, Lyon in no instance makes use of the figured bass (for organ accompaniment) or of instrumental preludes.

CHAPTER IV.

The Pedigree of 'Urania.'

The question arises, On whom did James Lyon depend for his knowledge of musical theory? As it is not known whether or not he received personal instructions from some American psalmodist, or English psalmodist emigrated to the Colonies, we are compelled to apply the comparative method in order to answer the query.

In the first place, American publications which chronology permits Lyon to have used will have to be examined. These are chiefly:

1. Editions with tunes of the ' Psalms, Hymns, and Spiritual Songs of the Old and New Testament ' (Bay Psalm Book).
2. Rev. John Tuft's ' Introduction to the Art of Singing ' [1st ed. about 1720, 11th ed. Boston, 1744].
3. Rev. T. Walter's ' Grounds and Rules of Music ' [1st ed. Boston 1721 ; 5th ed 1760].*

Of the Bay Psalm Book I have examined a copy of the ninth edition (1698).† Beginning with p. 419, it contains

the Tunes [twelve] of the *Psalms* with the Bass set under each Tune.

They are introduced by

Some few directions for ordering the Voice in setting

the tunes. These directions read :

First observe how many Notes Compass the Tune is. Next the place of your first Note; and how many Notes are above and below that ; so as you may begin the Tune of your first Note as the rest may be sung in the compass of your and the People Voices, without Squeaking above or Grumbling below."

---

* I here take occasion to point out how absolutely indispensable for the student of the history of sacred music in America are Mr. James Warrington's ' Short Titles of Books relating to or illustrating the History and Practice of Psalmody in the United States. 1620–1820. Philadelphia, 1898. Printed privately.' Being a pioneer work, the compilation is, of course, neither exhaustive nor absolutely reliable, but it is an admirable effort in the right direction.

† A copy of the twenty-third edition, Boston ; 1730, formerly ' John Edwards His Book 1736,' now in possession of his descendant Dr. Samuel Abbot Green, and which I also examined, contains on pp. 338–346 the same tunes and directions.

These naïve remarks resemble Lyon's "Directions for Singing" and possibly may have influenced him. But otherwise the "few directions" can not have been a guide to Lyon as the lines quoted are practically their essence.

The same is to be said of

> 'An Introduction to the Singing of Psalm-Tunes, in a plain & easy Method. With a Collection of Tunes in Three Parts. By the Rev. Mr. *Tufts*. The fifth Edition. Printed from Copper-Plates, neatly Engraven.
> Boston, in N. E. Printed for Samuel Gerrish, at the Lower End of Cornhill. *1726.*'

This celebrated pamphlet is of importance, not only for the history of American psalmody, but of musical notation, as Rev. Tufts employed a peculiar kind of letter notation instead of notes. For our purposes, the booklet furnishes but little material. The introduction is too short for tracing successfully a connection between Tufts and Lyon. Furthermore, two or three pages of the nine (in 16°) are given over to an explanation of the letter-notation. One passus, however, should not be overlooked, as it bears a striking resemblance to the corresponding remarks in 'Urania.'

We read on p. 3 :

> The natural place for Mi is in the line which is called B, and there you will find it in the following Tunes, provided there be no Flats or Sharps at the beginning of the 5 lines, as in *Windsor* etc. If you find a Flat mark'd thus (♭) in B, as in *London New*, then you shall find *Mi* stand in *E*. If there be a Flat in B & E, too, as in *Manchester*, there is Mi in A . . .

Of a by far more elaborate nature than Tufts' ' Introduction ' were Walter's ' Grounds and Rules of Music.' The Reverend musician gives in his pamphlet (ed. of 1746) on twenty-five pages (obl. 12°)

> Some brief and very plain Instructions for Singing by Note.

Though it is highly probable that Lyon knew Walter's 'Instructions'— the remarks on the natural place of *mi* read very much alike in both books—there are so many marked differences between the two authors that it becomes difficult to determine the extent to which the rules in ' Urania ' were shaped after Walter's ' Instructions.'

For instance, Walter employs the diamond-note throughout, whereas Lyon uses modern notes. Walter, on the first five pages, dwells upon the importance of learning to sing by note, especially in America, where this practice had sadly been neglected. Lyon has nothing to say on the subject. Then Walter devotes p. 6–21 to an explanation of fa, sol, la, mi, whereas Lyon deemed it sufficient to treat of the hexachord on one page only, and very much less confusingly than Walter. On the other hand, this author speaks of "the Length or Shortness" of the Notes in Musick "in the tuning of them" (p. 21), of Time (22–23) the "Prick of Perfection," etc., more superficially than Lyon. Then again he speaks of "the Doctrine of Concords and Discords" (24–25), of which doctrine nothing is to be found in 'Urania.' Furthermore, the examples given for "the eight notes ascending," etc. (25), do not resemble those in Lyon's collection very much. Finally, and this is the most important point, Lyon's wording of the rules distinctly differs from Walter's, Lyon appearing by far as the more musical and more modern of the two.

This last distinction is hardly less evident if we compare him with William Tansur,* who, as a composer, compiler and theoretician, exercised a powerful influence over pre-revolutionary American psalmodists.

Of Tansur's 'New Musical Grammar,' I have seen but the third edition, of which the title reads:

'A NEW MUSICAL GRAMMAR AND DICTIONARY: or, a general Introduction to the whole Art of Musick. In four Books. Teaching
I. The Rudiments of Tones, Diatonick and Semitonick; according to the Gamut.— With Rules for Tuning the Voice and Beating the Time, the Nature of Keys and Transposition; and of all other characters used in Musick.
II. . . . Directions . . . for Tuning and Playing on the Organ, Harpsichord . . .
III. The Theory of Sound, from its Natural Causes . . .
IV. The Musicians historical and technical Dictionary . . .
The Third Edition, with large Additions.
By William TANSUR, Senior, Musico Theorico. London . . . 1756.'

The scope of this work was very much wider than that of Lyon's rules in 'Urania,' the latter having in view only what Tansur teaches in the first book of his 'New Musical Grammar.' It would be easy to show that Lyon profited by this work, but I prefer to compare his collection with the latest book by Tansur which he possibly may have studied: 'The Royal Melody Compleat' (either the first ed. of 1756 or the second of 1760). Lyon knew this work. This can not be doubted, as, for instance, Lyon's "Examples of Restes" are practically

---

* Tansur, William, 1700–1783, born at Dunchurch, Warwickshire; died at St. Neots.

the same as in the ' Royal Melody Compleat,' where we find in "A new Introduction to the grounds of Musick ":

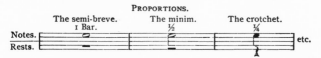

But Lyon made use of his authority in an independent way. Some parts of Tansur's Introduction, which spreads over 25 pages, he must have condensed in case he borrowed from it to any degree. Other parts he omitted as not suitable or unnecessary for his purposes, for instance, Ch. VI, § 1, "On the several Concords and Discords"; § 2, "Concerning Figures used in the Thorough Bass"; Ch. VII, " Containing some General Rules of Composition "; p. 26–31, " A New Musical Alphabet: showing the most useful Technical Terms that are generally used in Musick."

However, more important than possible condensations, or evident omissions, is the fact that Lyon's rules are clearer, more to the point, more correct, and more modern than those of his English model. Compare, for instance, the corresponding remarks in ' Urania ' with the following by Tansur, p. 2:

> The Scale is divided into Three Parts [viz. " Treble or Tenor; Treble or Counter Tenor ; Basso or Bassus."]

In fact, Lyon's entire explanation of the gamut is to be preferred to Tansur's.

Then the latter expresses himself by far less modern than Lyon when remarking on p. 6 :

> A Flat is a mark of Contraction, and causeth any Note it is set before that riseth a whole Tone, to rise but half a Tone. I mean to flat, or sink it half a Tone lower than it was before.

or, in Ch. II, instead of giving a comprehensive diagram :

> The Minim, is but half the Length of the Semibreve, having a Tail to it.
> The Crotchet, is but half the Length of the Minim, having a black Head.
> The Quaver, is but half the Length of the Crotchet, having the tail turned up.

Lyon certainly was influenced by William Tansur, but I believe to a greater extent by Tansur's rival John Arnold.* His ' Compleat Psalmodist in Four Books '—I have seen the 4th ed. 1756—contains on 24 pages " An Introduction to the Grounds of Musick," from

---

* *Arnold*, John, (1715)–1792.

which the American psalmodist borrowed freely. It is unnecessary to prove this in detail. A few references and quotations will suffice. Arnold's remarks on "Prick'd Notes" are practically the same as in 'Urania,' not less his theory "Of Time in all its Moods," and Lyon's examples for ascending and descending intervals are but a copy of Arnold's example for

> The Eight Notes, with the true Proof of every Interval in the G. Cliff.

Then again if we read on p. 6 of 'The Compleat Psalmodist'

> A single Bar is to divide the Time in Music according to the Measure Note

or

> A Direct or Guide, which is set at the End of the Lines, where they are broke off by the Narrowness of the Paper, is to Direct or Guide upon what Key the first Note of the succeeding Line is placed

we know from where James Lyon took his corresponding remarks.

If he occasionally appears more modern than William Tansur, who held a dictatorial position among English psalmodists, the same observation forces itself upon us when comparing 'Urania' with Aaron Williams' 'Universal Psalmodist' of 1763. This collection contains on forty pages in form of a dialogue between master and scholar—

> 'An Introduction to Psalmody shewing all that is necessary for the attainment of that Noble and delightful Art.'

This introduction and Lyon's rules, though different in design, length and form, resemble one another surprisingly at times. Compare, for instance, "An Example of Prick'd Notes" or "A Scale of the Notes, and their Proportions" or "Of Time in its various Moods, and how to beat them" in the 'Universal Psalmodist' with the corresponding pages in 'Urania.' This resemblance is easily explained. Evidently both psalmodists borrowed from the same sources, two of which undoubtedly were Tansur and Arnold.

But the psalmodists of the eighteenth century, as those of the nineteenth, were akin. Their theoretical ideas in particular were ruled by the same spirit of times and have the same roots. We read the explanations of one psalmodist and are not surprised to find the same ideas, often the same words and examples, in the books of others. A kind of laziness pervades these theoretical introductions. We seldom notice an effort to keep abreast of musical progress. They impress us as being relics of the sixteenth and seventeenth centuries, to which an eighteenth century label has been attached.

Circumstances forced James Lyon to breathe in this atmosphere of tombs. But it appears to me as if there was latent in his character a tendency to be more " up to date "—to use an expressive Americanism— than his forerunners. I have pointed out that his rules have not so much in conception, but in style, a more modern flavor than those of Tansur. We need but read the lengthy, pedantic, confused and conceited introduction of Williams and compare it with the inten- tionally cursory theoretical remarks of Lyon to notice that the 'Urania' of 1761 is more progressive than the 'Universal Psalmodist' of 1763. For instance, Williams writes that the

Scale is divided into three Parts . . . Treble, Tenor or Counter, Bass.

whereas Lyon bases his

" Explanation of the Gamut " upon " the 4 Parts of Musick."

This is decidedly more modern and more correct, and so are sev- eral other of his remarks.

With the criticism of Walter, Tansur, and Williams in favor of Lyon, I do not intend to exaggerate his merits. I merely endeavored to show that James Lyon used judgment when borrowing from others, and hesitated not, with apparent success, to improve upon them.

Still his ideas of musical theory remain helplessly mechanical and lead us back to a period when the lesser Buttstedts were not in the minority but in the majority. But what are we allowed to expect from James Lyon, if even the British models of our early psalmodists were still laden with the cruel burden of mi-fa, the *crux in musica,* and still trying to reconcile an antiquated system of music with exigencies grown out of " vertical " music?

This must be taken into serious consideration if a fair criticism of Lyon's theoretical explanations is to be given. Seen in this light, they do not make a bad impression, and we certainly have no right to sneer at them. In fact, some of Lyon's remarks are remarkably clear, as for instance the one that :

Time is of two kinds, viz. Common & Triple in one or the other of which all Move- ments are included.

As already stated, none of the compositions in ' Urania ' bears an author's name. This renders an investigation of the musical pedigree of Lyon's collection complicated. Only by applying the comparative method will it be possible to trace the sources of the music. The idea is simple enough, but not so its application. ' Urania' is a rare book and so are the copies extant of those collections, either English or American, from which Lyon borrowed musical settings. To increase the difficulties, where these books are obtainable, ' Urania' is some-times missing, as at Harvard University, or, *vice versa*, as at the New York Historical Society. It is hoped that these unfavorable condi-tions will partly be held responsible if a critical reader detects import-ant omissions in the following.

Of American tune collections preceding ' Urania' I have exam-ined:

> The Tunes in Rev. J. Tufts' ' Introduction to the Art of Singing . . .' (8th ed. Bos-ton, 1731);
> > in Rev. T. Walter's ' Grounds and Rules of Musick . . .' (ed. of 1746);
> The Tunes engraved by James Turner, Boston, 1752, and bound with Barnard's ' New Version of the Psalms';
> > attached on 14 p. to the 'Psalms, Hymns & Spiritual Songs . . .' Bos-ton, 1758;
> > attached to ' Brady & Tate's Psalms . . .' Boston, 1765;
> > "Engraved, Printed & Sold by Thomas Johnston, Brattlestreet, Boston. 1755."

The majority of the tunes in these collections are written for three parts and seem to have been taken from a common source, the collec-tions of 1752, 1755, and 1758 especially showing but slight differences.

Of English works I examined:

1. John *Barrow*—'A New Book of Psalmody.'—London, 1750.
2. Mathew *Wilkins*—'An Introduction to Psalmody.'—London, [1730.]
3. William *Tansur*—'A Compleat Melody, or The Harmony of Zion.'—London, 1736.
4. " " ' Heaven on Earth, or the Beauty of Holiness . . .'—London, 1738
5. The so-called ' Foundery Tunes.'—London, 1742.
6. James *Green*—'A Book of Psalmody.'—11th ed., London, 1751.
7. William *Tansur*—'The Melody of the Heart, or the Psalmodist's Pocket Com-panion.'—London, 3d ed., 1751.
8. J. *Holdroyd*—' Spiritual Man's Companion.'—5th ed., 1753.
9. 'The Divine Musical Miscellany.'—London, 1754.
10. William *Knapp*—'A Set of New Psalms and Anthems.'—6th ed., London, 1754.
11. William *Crisp*—' Divine Harmony.'—London, 1755.
12. John *Arnold*—' The Compleat Psalmodist.'—4th ed., London, 1756.
    " " ' The Leicestershire Harmony.'—London, 1767 (1st ed., 1759).
13. Rev. M. *Madan*—'A Collection of Psalms and Hymns.'—London, 1760.
15. William *Tansur*—'The Royal Melody Compleat, or New Harmony of Zion.'—2d ed., London, 1760 (1st ed., 1755).
16. William *Knapp*—' New Church Melody.'—4th ed., 1761 (1st ed., 1750).

17. C. *Ashworth*—'A Collection of Tunes.'—4th ed. enlarged, London, 1775 (1st ed., 1760).
18. Aaron *Williams*—'The Universal Psalmodist.'—2d ed. corrected, London, 1764 (1st ed., 1763).*

To these works I add 'A Compleat Book of Psalmody,' by James *Evison* (2d ed., 1751), which Mr. James Warrington had the kindness to examine for me.

I doubt very much whether 1–5; 7–8; 11; 14; and 15 had any influence upon the compilation of ' Urania.' The investigation of the other books revealed the following:

ANGELS HYMN—(compare Lyon's index)—reads exactly like in Williams 'Universal Psalmodist,' except that Lyon omitted the " trillo's" and changed one G into g in the bass.

BATH—very much like on p. 47 of Ashworth's collection.

CANTERBURY = in Arnold's 'Compleat Psalmodist,' but with interesting changes in the treble and in the harmony.

COOKFIELD = in Evison's collection.

CRANLEY = in Evison's collection.

CROWLE = in Green's ' Book of Psalmody.'

DAGENHAM = in Arnold's 'Compleat Psalmodist,' with slight changes in the second line.

---

* As the Boston Public Library, the only institution at which I found the first edition of this book, does not possess Lyon's ' Urania,' it became necessary to investigate the copy of the second edition, as extant at Yale University.

The reader is of course astonished to see a work examined which chronologically can not have influenced Lyon. My reason for so doing was that some pieces in both collections resemble one another strikingly. The fact may be explained in three ways. Either Williams knew ' Urania ' or Lyon knew ' The Universal Psalmodist' before this and his own collection were published, or, and this is by far more plausible, both compilers borrowed from the same sources and in a similar manner.

My monograph, as I have stated repeatedly, does not pretend to be exhaustive. Enough problems remain to be solved by later historians. I thought it might be of service to these if I included a comparison of ' Urania' with ' The Universal Psalmodist.' Several pieces in both collections must have come from sources common to both. If others succeeded in tracing Williams' sources, then we would know from where Lyon took the pieces alluded to.

DARKING = in Evison's collection.

DORCHESTER = in Arnold's 'Compleat Psalmodist' and in Evison's
   collection.

LEATHERED = 'Leatherhead' in Evison's collection.

NEWCASTLE = in Williams' 'Universal Psalmodist,' except that it
   appears there for three parts and with trillo. In 'Urania' a
   counter is added (in the following manner (first two lines):

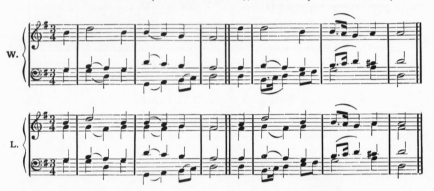

ORANGE = in Ashworth's collection.

PORTSMOUTH = 'Namur or Portsmouth' in Turner's tunes, but
   with addition of a Counter (Two first lines).

PSALM 15TH—evidently from Arnold's 'Leicestershire Harmony.'

OLD 50 = in Williams' 'Universal Psalmodist,' except that W.
   gives the piece in A minor, L. in G minor.

NEW 50 = in Williams' 'Universal Psalmodist,' but incorrectly engraved in the third bar.

PSALM 90—evidently from Arnold's 'Leicestershire Harmony.'
OLD 100 = in Green's 'Book of Psalmody,' with marked differences, however, in the treble.

NEW 100 = in Tufts' 'Introduction,' with addition of a counter.
OLD 119 = 49 Psalm Tune in Walter's 'Grounds and Rules' and Tufts' 'Introduction,' but with addition of a Counter.

OLD 148 = in Williams' 'Universal Psalmodist,' but instead of in C major in D major.

RIPON—evidently with very slight alterations from Arnold's 'Compleat Psalmodist.'

Williams' 'Universal Psalmodist' has the same piece, but (in the third and fourth line) with punctuated notes in the tune (tenor), treble, and counter. Lyon has not a single note of that kind.

RYGATE = 'Ryegate' in Evison's collection.

ST. DAVID = in Arnold's 'Complete Psalmodist.' (Lyon's treble is slightly different and the eighth bar of the counter is misprinted.)

St. Peter = in Ashworth's collection.

Southwell = in Ashworth's collection, the second bar of the counter excepted.

Standish—'Standwich' begins like 'Charleston' in Knapp's 'New Church Melody,' but deviates later on considerably.

Walsal = in Ashworth's collection, the counter excepted

Well's = in Johnson's collection, the Tune there being attributed to Holdroyd.

Westminster = in Arnold's 'Compleat Psalmodist.'

Windsor—probably from Arnold's 'Compleat Psalmodist.' The first and fourth lines are exactly alike; the second and third are slightly altered, and Lyon omitted every "trillo."

Wirksworth = in Ashworth's collection.

Anthem—'Is there not an appointed time' = in Knapp's 'New Set of Psalms' (p. 132).

Anthem—'Jehovah reigns,' in the music, p. 133, called 'An Anthem taken out of the 97th Psalm.'—This piece was a composition by William *Tuckey*. The statement might be proved in different ways, but our best authority is Andrew Law. He remarked in the "Advertisement to his 'Musical Magazine'" (4th ed. No. 1), "The Tune called 'Liverpool' composed by Mr. Tuckey of New York was published incorrectly by Mr. Lion ; and by others from him. It is now corrected, and here published by permission obtained from the heirs of Mr. Tuckey."

The Anthem 'Jehovah reigns' (Psalm 97th) in 'Urania' and the "Tune called 'Liverpool'" in the Musical Magazine are identical.*

---

* William Tuckey became a resident at New York about the year 1753. He died at Philadelphia. Till about 1773, when I lost track of him, he was one of the foremost musicians in New York city. He was organist and musical instructor of the "Free School belonging to Trinity Church," gave concerts with

ANTHEM—'I will magnify' = Anthem XIII in Arnold's 'Compleat Psalmodist,' but slightly altered in the Chorus and misprinted, as several accidentals are missing.

KETTERING = 'Kettering Tune' in the 'Divine Musical Miscellany,' but there with these words, "Sweet is the work my God
my King . . ."

RESURRECTION = 'An Hymn on the Resurrection' in the 'Divine
Musical Miscellany.'*

WHITEFIELD.—The words of this hymn, beginning "Come Thou
Almighty King," are set to (Henry Carey's ?) tune of 'God Save
the King,' an observation made first, I believe, by Mr. James
Warrington. This excellent authority, however, knows not
where the English national anthem appeared for the first time
in this disguise under the title of 'Whitefield.' But as George
Whitefield spent a great part of his life in British America,
especially in the southern and middle colonies, exercising a
most wonderful influence as pulpit orator over Methodists and
others, the paraphrase of "God save the King" possibly originated in the Colonies. That James Lyon himself was influenced by Methodism, or at least was well acquainted with
Methodist-hymns, is apparent, for the last part of 'Urania,'

good programs, and was active as composer of sacred music. He inserted in the newspapers several proposals for printing some works of his, but seems not to have met with sufficient encouragement. About
half a dozen of his compositions are scattered in the American psalm-tune collections of later years. In
one of his advertisements (N. Y. Mercury, March 11, 1771) he called himself "William Tuckey, for some
years a Professor of the Theory and Practice of Vocal Music, Vicar *Choral* of the Cathedral Church of
Bristol, and Clerk of the Parish of St. Mary Post in said City, now Resident in New York." Ritter (p. 42)
incorrectly styles him "Vicar chosen," a title which does not exist.

*The 'Divine Musical Miscellany' (London, 1754), decidedly Methodistic in its contents, is a very
curious collection. The Hymn called 'Hallelujah,' in Wesley's books appears here as 'Boston.' Furthermore, I noticed hymns entitled 'Maryland,' 'New York,' 'Philadelphia,' 'Virginia.' Should the anonymous collection be the work of an American Methodist?

dedicated to the clergy of every denomination, possesses a predominantly Methodistic character.

To these thirty-four pieces, or thirty-three, if we exclude 'Whitefield,' may be added the six 'Tunes' marked with an asterisk in 'Urania,' which were written by Lyon himself, as shall be shown, and the 'Morning Hymn,' attributed by Josiah Flagg (1764) to Lyon and not to be confused with the 'Morning Hymn' by William Tansur. Therefore, less than half of the collection has been traced to the sources from which Lyon might have compiled 'Urania.' It is not a result of which to feel proud, but I beg to remember how scattered and incomplete the working material is. Others, it is to be hoped, will meet with more success if they care to continue these comparative investigations. Possibly an examination of Woodmason's 'Psalm-Tunes' (London, 1748); Hutchinson's 'Select Set of Psalms and Hymns' (1756); 'A Choice Collection of Hymns' (Philadelphia, 1743); W. Dawson's 'The Youth's entertaining Amusement, or plain guide to Psalmody' (Philadelphia, 1754); * the various German publications of C. Saur in Germantown, Pa., and other works which I have either not seen or which are not extant, will disclose the sources of other pieces in Lyon's " choice collection."

But it will *not be sufficient to trace the tunes alone.* To know when and where the melodies first appeared will certainly prevent useless investigation of books issued prior to such dates. The *tertium comparationis* however will remain the part-setting of the tunes, as Lyon seems to have borrowed entire compositions whenever he believed them to be " peculiarly adapted " to his purposes. But not unless the original part-setting of the tunes corresponds convincingly with the setting in ' Urania,' and appears not in other collections, will it be advisable to consider the original as Lyon's source, especially not if it precedes the publication of ' Urania ' by many years, for it stands to reason that the collections issued about 1750 influenced him more than earlier ones.†

Should none of the pieces be found in any collection published prior to 1760, in the exact form as appearing in ' Urania,' then the question would arise: Did James Lyon borrow them from an unpub-

---

* Not mentioned in Warrington's 'Short Titles.'

† To avoid misunderstanding I add that Lyon probably knew such older standard compilations as, for instance, Ravenscroft's ' Whole Booke of Psalmes ' (compare 'Glo(u)cester '), but so did many other psalmodists who preceded Lyon. It therefore would be a rather delicate undertaking to point to the 17th century collections as sources of 'Urania.'

lished source, or did he himself harmonize the tunes? His remark "peculiarly adapted" might have this meaning. But as he does not mention the fact, and as the preliminary conditions for this theory are wanting, I prefer not to dwell upon the subject.

All that can be deducted from these comparative investigations may be said to consist in this: James Lyon used English publications more freely than American. In particular, he borrowed from the 'Divine Musical Miscellany' and from the collections of Arnold, Green, Knapp, Evison, but *not* from Tansur. The extent to which he copied the favorite English psalmodists of the day shows how well he had studied their works. Unless his acquaintance with English psalmody was exceptional in the Colonies, it would be of singular importance for proving the lively intercourse between Great Britain and British America even in musical matters.

CHAPTER V.

The Descendants of 'Urania' and James Lyon's Compositions.

After having investigated the influence of other publications on
'Urania,' it now becomes necessary to trace the influence of Lyon's
book upon later American collections.

Unfortunately the comparative method can no longer be applied
with satisfactory results. The reasons are obvious.

The same pieces, as contained in Lyon's "Anthem book" as it was
called, might appear in later works, but it would remain doubtful
whether the compilers took them from 'Urania' or from collections
preceding Lyon's. For instance, Simeon Jocelin in his 'Chorister's
Companion' (2d ed., 1788) takes great pains in enumerating the
"Authors." They are given for the majority of the tunes. But in
several instances we find the remark "unknown." This applies, *inter
alia*, to 'Mear,' 'Isle of Wight,' 'Angel's Hymn.' Now the settings
of these tunes are exactly like in 'Urania.' But unless James Lyon
himself harmonized the three tunes as they appear in his book or
borrowed them with alterations from sources which seem to be obscure, how are we to know whether or not Jocelin took the three
pieces from 'Urania'?

The same remark applies to Tuckey's 97th Psalm. As it became
customary with our psalmodists to solicit the assistance of psalm-tune
composers in their proposals for publication, we would not know
whether the compilers took the anthem from 'Urania,' where it appears without the author's name, or received it directly from Tuckey.
Certainly, wherever the compositions might be found not as corrected
by Andrew Law but exactly as in 'Urania,' this book would have to
be considered as the source. I fear, however, that an investigation of

the scattered literature on these lines would not produce results proportionate to the trouble taken.

To illustrate this, I examined :

Bayley's 'New Universal Psalmody' (1773) ;
Stickney's 'Gentleman and Ladies Musical Companion' (1794) ;
Jocelin's 'Chorister's Companion' (1782, 1788, 1792) ;
Read's 'American Singing Book' (1785) ;
'Worcester Collection' (Sec. ed., 1788) ;
Holyoke's 'Harmonia Americana' (1791) ;
Brownson's 'Select Harmony' (1783) ;
Benham's 'Federal Harmony' (1790) ;
Flagg's 'Collection' (1764) ;
Belcher's 'Harmony of Maine' (1794) ;

but I found Tuckey's 97th Psalm, *alias* 'Liverpool,' said by Andrew Law to have been copied from Lyon "by others," only in Stickney's book in the form in which it appears in 'Urania.' Surely a marked contrast between labor and result!

Entirely fruitless would be an investigation of the theoretical influence of 'Urania' on later publications. To be sure, now and then such an influence is apparent, for instance, in Francis Hopkinson's 'Collection of Psalm Tunes with a few Anthems and Hymns' (Phila., 1763); Josiah Flagg's 'Collection of the best Psalm-Tunes'; Simeon Jocelin's 'Chorister's Companion.' But even in these works the majority of the instructions are presented in a manner as to render it impossible to attribute this or that rule to a familiarity with 'Urania.' The fact that several editions of this book were issued and other circumstances prove that it was well known in the Colonies, but Lyon never rivalled either the favorite English psalmodists or the idolized William Billings in popularity.

It will be by far more advantageous if I restrict myself more or less to the tunes marked with an asterisk in 'Urania.' James Lyon called them "entirely new." If these six compositions appear in later works, there can be no doubt of a positive influence of 'Urania' on these collections.

THE 8TH PSALM TUNE, p. 44.

THE 23D PSALM TUNE, p. 50–51.

THE 95TH PSALM TUNE, p. 63.

TWO CELEBRATED VERSES BY STERNHOLD & HOPKINS, SET TO MUSIC, p. 125–132. (See Appendix.)

THE 104TH PSALM BY DR. WATTS, p. 194–195.

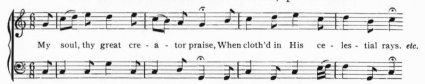

In the city of Boston appeared in 1764 Josiah Flagg's

'Collection of the best Psalm Tunes, in two, three or four parts, from the most approv'd Authors, fitted to all the measures and approv'd of by the best Masters in Boston New-England . . . Engrav'd by Paul Revere . . .'

The title-page of this collection alone would prove that 'Urania' was known to both Flagg and Revere, for its ornamental design was "borrowed" from Henry Dawkins' title-page to Lyon's book. But Paul Revere spoiled Dawkins' pretty design. For instance, where the latter has St. Cecilia throning upon clouds, Revere shows us a fruit basket.

The book contains none of Lyon's starred tunes. But we find on p. 29

MORNING HYMN.   L. M.   L—n

Certainly L—n stands for Lyon, and we find this hymn on p. 32 of 'Urania' under the title of 'The Morning Hymn.' It reappears in 'The American Harmony,' 1771, on p. 61; in John Stickney's 'Gentleman & Lady's Musical Companion,' 1779, on p. 161; and in the 'Village Harmony' (ed. of 1813) on p. 57.

In 1766, Josiah Flagg thus inserted an advertisement in the Massachusetts Gazette and Boston News Letter, October 2, which bears upon our subject :

'A COLLECTION OF ALL TANSUR'S AND A NUMBER OF OTHER ANTHEMS, from Williams, Knapp, Ashworth, and Stephenson. To which are added some Tunes from *Lion*, Smith, Ravenscroft, etc.—'
Just published and to be sold by Josiah Flagg (who teaches Psalmody on Monday and Thursday Evenings) at his House near the Old North Meeting House.

The tenor and date of this advertisement seem to imply that the collection of 1764 and this one of 1766 were not identical. It would be interesting to examine the tunes "from Lion," which of course means from "Urania," but unfortunately I know of no copy of this work extant. It is not even mentioned in Mr. James Warrington's 'Short Titles.' At any rate, the advertisement goes to show that Flagg was influenced by Lyon.

About the same time, under date of "New Haven, Sept. 19, 1766," appeared in the Connecticut Gazette, November 15, 1766, the following :

Proposals for Printing by Subscription a Book entitled the ' NEW UNIVERSAL PSALMODIST,
  or Beautiful Harmony of Zion,' containing
First, a new and correct Introduction to the Rules of Music, rudimental, practical,
  and technical
Second, a Number of the most celebrated Psalm-Tunes, collected from Arnold,
  Tansur, *Lyon*, Williams, etc. with some entirely new. By *A. Bull*, Philo-Musicae.

The proposals probably did not meet with encouragement, for
Bull's only publication on record is his ' Responsary ' (1795). This
collection, however, if I am not very much mistaken, contains none of
Lyon's starred tunes.

When Daniel Bayley published his ' New Universal Harmony or
a Compendium of Church Musick ' in 1773, he remarked in the preface, dated " Newbury Port, January 1, 1773 " :

. . . I am determined to publish two or three more Volumes in case I meet with
Encouragement in the Sale of this . . . I expect I shall be able to procure some curious
Pieces that are the Productions of *America*, by some masterly Hands, who have not yet
permitted any of their work to be made public.

Some months later he reprinted Aaron Williams' ' Universal
Psalmodist ' under the title of

'American Harmony or Universal Psalmodist . . . By A. Williams, Teacher of
  Psalmody in London.'

He wrote in the preface, dated " Newbury Port, January 5th, 1771 " :

I have added sundry Anthems and Hymn Tunes from the latest and most celebrated authors, such as I find approv'd of by musical Friends.

Among these latest and most celebrated authors seems to figure
James Lyon, for we find on p. 60 of Vol. II (1773)

'An Anthem Taken from Ps. 150th. J. Lyon.'

But the composer had already permitted it to be made public,
since it appeared, starred, in ' Urania ' on p. 165.

The same anthem is to be found in John Stickney's collection mentioned above on p. 160–161, as

'An Anthem Taken from Ps. 150th. " Let the shrill Trumpets." J. Lyon.'

Whether Stickney took the piece directly from ' Urania ' or copied it
from the 'American Harmony ' is immaterial. I am inclined to believe
that he took it directly from Lyon's collection, since his book (on p.
195) contains another composition appearing there with an asterisk,
' The 23d Psalm Tune.'

Shortly after Stickney's 'Gentleman and Lady's Musical Companion' had been published the war broke out and checked the steady progress of music in the Colonies. In the mean time, William Billings' unbalanced and eccentric but very forceful personality had appeared before the public. His music and his school soon became predominant. Still, 'Urania' was not forgotten after the war.

We find, for instance, on p. 130 of the 5th ed. of Andrew Adgate's 'Selection of Sacred Harmony' 'the 104th Psalm by Dr. Watts' as it stands starred in 'Urania' In this edition of Adgate's collection the piece is reprinted without an author's name, but in the sixth (1799) we read:

> '104th Psalm 104th. Dr. Watts. *Lyon.*'

However, more important than an occasional reprint of the tunes marked with an asterisk in 'Urania' would it be if the book was used in singing-schools and singing-societies previous to the Revolution. Unfortunately the doings of these institutions remain more or less obscure. Not even the occasional advertisements of concerts to be given by them furnish much information as regards the programs.

For this very reason it is still more remarkable that nearly a generation after the publication of James Lyon's collection we should find convincing evidence that the book was still used for concert-purposes.

In 1784 Philadelphia had an "Institution for the Encouragement of Church Music," also called "Institution for promoting the knowledge of psalmody."* Its moving spirit was Andrew *Adgate*, who, until he became a victim of the yellow fever in 1793, was one of the most prominent musicians of Philadelphia. The principal features of the institution were its monthly concerts at the University, called "Mr. Adgate's Vocal Music" or "Vocal Concert."† On June 1, 1785, the trustees agreed to declare the institution dissolved, it appearing that their funds were exhausted.‡ But Adgate drew a new and wider plan on the same day,§ and evidently met with encouragement, since he began a series of twelve concerts on October 19.|| In the mean while had been published (being chiefly designed for the use of singing-schools):

> 'INTRODUCTORY LESSONS as practiced by the Uranian Society, held at Philadelphia for promoting the Knowledge of Vocal Music.' ¶

---

* Pa. Packet, March 18, 1784.
† Pa. Packet, April 1, 1785.
‡ Pa. Gaz. June 1, 1785.
§ Pa. Gaz. Nov. 9, 1785.
|| Pa. Gaz. Oct. 19, 1785.
¶ Pa. Packet, Aug. 1785.

The name of "Uranian Society" was changed in 1786 into "Uranian Academy," * and the concerts became known as the "Uranian Concerts."† The whole institution was to be officially established under the management of twelve trustees and "at least" twenty patrons on September 3, 1787.‡

The epitheton of "Uranian" is so uncommon that we may suspect a connection between the "Uranian Academy" and James Lyon's 'Urania,' especially as both had in view to spread the art of psalmody. This supposition would seem rather vague had 'Urania' been dead and forgotten about the time that the "Uranian Academy" was founded. But this was not the case, and the book was still on the market, for Thomas Dobson advertised in 1786

> A few copies of Lyon's 'Ourania; or choice collection . . .' Price 25 s.

Furthermore, Andrew Adgate gave Lyon's music a place on the programs of the "Uranian Concerts":

> On Thursday, the 4th of May [1786], at the Reformed Church, in Race street, was performed a GRAND CONCERT of Vocal and Instrumental Music in the presence of a numerous and polite audience. The whole *Band* consisted of 230 vocal and 50 instrumental performers; which we are fully justified in pronouncing the most complete, both with respect to number and accuracy of execution, ever, on any occasion, combined in this city, and perhaps, throughout America.
>
> The first idea of this concert was suggested to the trustees of the musical institution, by the *Commemoration of Handel* in London and the *Sacred Concert* in Boston.§ It was planned in January last, and a series of preparatory measures pursued till its accomplishment . . .
>
> To the skill and attention of Mr. *Adgate*, in training and instructing the voices, and of Mr. *Juhan* in arranging and leading the instruments, may be attributed that forcible and uniform effect so manifestly produced throughout the exhibition. . . .
>
> Nearly one thousand tickets were sold; at two thirds of a dollar each, and the nett proceeds, after deducting for necessary expenses, have been delivered to the managers of the Pennsylvania Hospital, Philadelphia Dispensary, and Overseers of the Poor. . . .

The long and enthusiastic report was printed in the Pa. Packet on May 30, 1786. On May 1 the same paper published the following

> ORDER AND WORDS OF THE MUSIC.‖
> I. *Martini's Overture.*
> II. *An Anthem from the 150th Psalm.*
> "Let the shrill trumpets warlike voice,
> Make rocks and hills abound . . ."

---

* Pa. Packet, Jan. 25, 1787.   † Pa. Evening Herald, April 11, 1787.
‡ Pa. Mercury, March 30, 1787.
§ It took place on Jan. 10, 1786. Compare Mass. Gaz. Jan. 2.
‖ The Pa. Herald printed on May 3 the "order," but not the words. I considered it unnecessary to quote more than the first lines of the vocal pieces.

III. *An Anthem from the 18th Psalm, by the Rev. James Lyon.*
" The Lord descended from above
And bow'd the heaven's most high . . ."

IV. *Flute Concerto by Mr. Brown.*

V. *The Voice of Time.*
" Hark ! hark ! Time hastes away . . ."

VI. *An Anthem from the 97th Psalm, by Mr. Tuckey.*
" Jehovah reigns, let all the earth
In his just government rejoice . . ."

VII. *A Violin Concerto, by Mr. Juhan.*

VIII. *An Anthem from the 122d Psalm, by A. Williams.*
" I was glad, when they said unto me :
We will go, etc into the house of the Lord, etc . . ."

IX. *An Anthem, from the 2d of Solomon's Songs, by Mr. Billings.*
" I am the rose of Sharon, and the lily of the vallies . . ."

X. *Hallelujah Chorus from the Messiah, Handel.*
" Hallelujah—(often repeated)—. . . "

Rev. James Lyon's anthem is of course the one contained in
' Urania' on p. 125–132. The report mentions it " after Martini's
famous Overture" among

The *celebrated* anthems which were performed with a precision and effort sufficient
to enforce powers of harmony on the most untutored ears.*

The foregoing pages, I hope, have proved that ' Urania' exercised
a marked influence upon some of the early American psalmodists.
At the same time, James Lyon's marginal note in the index—

All Tunes marked with an Asterism are new

has now become clear. It undoubtedly indicates that *Lyon himself
composed the six pieces.* As three of them, the anthems ' The Lord
descended from above' and ' Let the shrill trumpets' and the 104th
psalm, were attributed to Lyon by his contemporaries, we need not
doubt his authorship, and by way of inference we may conclude that
he also wrote the remaining three starred pieces: the 8th, 23d, and
95th psalm-tunes.

As to the ' Morning Hymn,' which is not starred in ' Urania,' we
have two possibilities: Either Josiah Flagg's " L—n " signifies merely
that he took the composition from Lyon's collection or he knew that
it was by Lyon but that it was not marked with an asterisk for not
being " new." The first possibility is more convincing.

---

* Lyon's anthem and Tuckey's 97th psalm seem to have met with particular approbation, for Mr.
James Warrington possesses ' The words of Sundry Anthems. Philadelphia. Printed and sold by W.
Young . . . MDCCLXXXIX.' 'Anthem I. From the 18th Psalm. By the Rev. James Lyon. . .' 'An-
them II. From the 97th Psalm. By Mr. Tuckey.'

The question now arises whether or not it is possible to discover 'tunes' not contained in 'Urania' but nevertheless to be attributed to Lyon's pen?

We remember that Lyon entered public life with his mind bent upon the art of psalmody and its progress throughout the American Colonies. It would be a psychological mystery should his interest in music have vanished with the bold enterprise of compiling and editing 'Urania.' But the statement of one of his contemporaries proves that it did not.

When Philip Vickers FITHIAN, after leaving Princeton in 1772, became tutor at Nomini Hall in Virginia, the residence of Councillor Carter, during the years 1773 and 1774, he spent his vacations at his home in Cohansie, N. J. Here he made the acquaintance of James Lyon. We read in his delightful 'Journal and Letters' (Princeton, N. J., 1900) under date of Friday, April 22, 1774:

> Rode to the Stage early for the Papers thence I went to Mr. Hunters where I met with that great master of music, Mr. Lyon.—He sung at my request, & sings with his usual softness and accuracy—*He is about publishing a new Book of Tunes which are to be chiefly of his own Composition* — . . . I returned towards Evening but promised first to visit him again to-morrow afternoon.

For this day we find the entry:

> At home drawing off some of Mr. Lyon's Tunes, & revising my own Exercises— . . . Afternoon according to Appointment I visited Mr. Lyon at Mr. Hunters. He sings with great accuracy. I sung with him many of his Tunes & had much conversation on music, he is vastly fond of music & musical genius's. We spent the Evening with great satisfaction to me.

No doubt, Lyon's creative powers, instead of decreasing after the publication of 'Urania,' had increased considerably. The quotations from Fithian's Journal render it manifest that he had composed quite a number of "tunes" since 1761. It is therefore exceedingly to be regretted that this 'new Book of Tunes' was not published. At least, no copy of it has been found so far, nor is there any trace of the manuscript. Perhaps it was among "all the belongings" which James Lyon's second wife, "Mrs. Skillings, widow of the late Mr. Samuel Skillings," to whom he was married in 1793,* "took with her after his death."†

---

*Compare Bolton's 'Marriage Notices' . . . Salem, Mass., 1900, p. 179, copied from the Columbian Centinel for Sat. Nov. 30, 1793. The important item was communicated to me by Mr. Victor H. Paltsits of the N. Y. P. Library.

†Annotations from a letter written to me by Mrs. Mary O'Brien Brown, containing items from the family note-book.

On the other hand, it can be proved that music by James Lyon, not contained in 'Urania,' and which perhaps made part of the collection " chiefly of his own composition," was known, performed, and printed in collections by other psalmodists.

The earliest of such compositions, as far as my knowledge goes, is to be found in a work already mentioned, in Daniel Bayley's 'New Universal Harmony,' 1773. In the index appears as last of the " Hymn-Tunes, etc."

'A Marriage Hymn by James Lyon.'

The piece stands on p. 24, but here simply as 'A Marriage Hymn.' The engraving of Bayley's publication is extremely faulty, by far more so than that of 'Urania.' Lyon's 'Marriage Hymn,' too, is full of mistakes. A few bars may follow without an effort on my part to decipher all puzzles in the engraving.

Lord from Thy throne...... of flow-ing grace to choic-est bless-ings give. *etc.*

That Lyon had aroused the interest of his fellow-compilers is apparent, for he figures as the only American in the 'New Universal Harmony' among the favorite English psalmodists — Williams, Knapp, Stephenson, Arnold, and Ashworth.

Next we find him represented with compositions not contained in 'Urania' in the second edition (1788, New Haven) of Simeon Jocelin's 'Chorister's Companion.' A note informs us that—

The Tunes with this mark (*) are new, or have never before been printed.

It applies among others to a piece contained on p. 87 as ' * 17th Ps. last verse. Dr. W. L. M.' and we read in the index

' Psalm 17th. Lyon.'

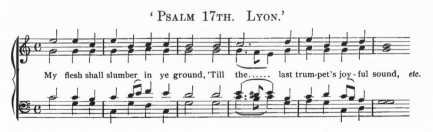

My flesh shall slumber in ye ground, 'Till the...... last trum-pet's joy-ful sound, *etc.*

Knowing how carelessly the American psalm-tune collections of this period were engraved, we are allowed to hold the compiler or the engraver and not the composer responsible for the impossible notes which offend our ears in the 17th Psalm as I have quoted it from Jocelin's 'Chorister's Companion.'

Though I possess no evidence for Lyon's authorship, I should like to call attention on behalf of its name to a tune printed by Jocelin in 1792 on p. 10 of the supplement to his 'Chorister's Companion.' This supplement contains sixteen pages. Only the first half of the tunes are given with their author's names (*Ives* and others), whereas the rest appear anonymous. Among the latter we notice a tune called 'Urania. Ps. 145th. D. W. C. M. Double.' It begins:

Long as I live I'll bless...... Thy...... name, *etc.*

As might be expected, I examined Lyon's 'Urania,' hoping to find the tune 'Urania' embodied there, but I failed. Following the 17th Psalm the reader will find a piece in the Appendix which I discovered in the fourth edition (1792) of Andrew Law's 'Rudiments of Music.' It stands on p. 11, without the name of the composer, simply as '19th Ps. 45th. D. W.' but in the index it appears as

'PSALM 19 LYON.' (See Appendix.)

If Andrew Law had but corrected and published Tuckey's 'Liverpool,' *alias* '97th Psalm' in 'Urania,' or merely used Dawkins' titlepage to Lyon's collection for one of his own books—I do not remember which, but Mr. Warrington called my attention to the fact—this would only go to prove his familiarity with 'Urania.' It would not follow that he was influenced by the book. However, the fact that he embodied a composition by Lyon in his 'Rudiments of Music' is remarkable enough. He can not have been absolutely opposed to Lyon. This observation is of importance. Andrew Law was one of the most progressive psalmodists in the United States. His influence was felt everywhere, since he established singing-schools in various sections of the Union. He was also a prolific author. Now it was Law's constant aim to raise the musical standard in the United States by introducing good European masters and by fearlessly attacking those whom he considered detrimental to progress. No more vigorous opponent of the Billings-school and its tendencies lived than he.

If therefore Andrew Law thought it proper to publish an unknown " tune " by James Lyon, there seems to have been some affinity between his own ideas of the true style of psalmody and those of Lyon. With this remark I intend to claim neither that Law's musical taste was surprisingly refined nor that the 19th Psalm by James Lyon is an elaborate composition, for, after all is said, neither of the two psalmodists can be considered well trained musicians.

The verdict must be upheld even with respect to Lyon's most important composition — this, too, unknown and not contained in ' Urania '—'*The Hymn to Friendship.*'

This piece leads us back to Andrew Adgate and the Uranian Academy. Adgate, we recollect, performed Lyon's 18th Psalm in 1786. He again appeared as exponent of Lyon's music in the following year. On April 12, 1787, the *First Uranian Concert* took place under his direction at the German Reformed Church in Philadelphia,

the object of the whole being the founding of an institution for improving such music [sacred] throughout the churches. *

It was opened with an excellent Prayer, well suited to the occasion, by the Rev. Dr. Andrews, " President of the Uranian Academy,"† and

continued about two hours. The audience and performers together, consisted of 650 persons, who will ever be considered as the original *Benefactors* and *Founders* of the "*Uranian Academy.*"

The Pennsylvania Packet published on April 9 the following :

SYLLABUS	Authors
I. Martini's celebrated Overture	
II. Jehovah Reigns : an anthem from the 97th Psalm	Tuckey
III. Te Deum laudamus	Arnold
IV. Violin Concerto	By Mr. Phile of New York
V. I heard a great voice : an anthem from Rev. xiv	Billings
VI. Vital Spark : an Anthem on Mr. Pope's Ode ' The dying Christian to his Soul '	Billings
VII. Overture in Artaxerxes	Arne
VIII. Friendship Thou charmer of the mind : From Watts' Lyric Poems	Lyon
IX. The Rose of Sharon : an Anthem from 2d of Canticles	Billings
X. Flute Concerto	By the Chevalier Du Pouceau
XI. Sunday Scriptures : an Anthem on the Nativity of Christ	Williams
XII. The Hallelujah Chorus : on the extent and duration of Christ's Government (from the Messiah)	Handel.

* Pa. Packet, April 23, 1787.
† Pa. Mercury, March 30. This gentleman had been elected (on the 23d) President ; the Rev. Dr. Henry Helmuth, Vice-President ; Mr. John Swanwick, Secretary ; and Mr. Azariah Horton, Treasurer.

A curious but interesting program, and remarkable for its well-balanced combination of European and American composers. If we compare it in this respect with our modern programs, we must confess that American music, to-day, does by no means meet with the same encouragement as in the eighteenth century. And this, notwithstanding the fact that our composers have ceased to be crude amateurs and possess, if nothing else, a skill equal to that of their European competitors !

Nowadays we are accustomed to analytical or thematic programs. Their value is open to discussion. If short and to the point like those of Mr. Henry Edward Krehbiel, or brilliantly interesting like those of Mr. Philip Hale, they certainly aid toward a just appreciation of the works performed ; if entering too deeply into technical details, as those of the Boston Symphony Orchestra used to do, they lead the attention of the audience away from a spontaneous enjoyment of the compositions toward a " literary " and inartistic. This by the way. But if my readers presume that analytical programs are an invention of the nineteenth century, they are mistaken. The syllabus quoted above is followed by " Remarks " which, in an embryonic form, are the earliest forerunners of our modern program notes. For several reasons I take pleasure in copying part of them. We read :

XII. ‘ THE HALLELUJAH CHORUS FROM THE MESSIAH.’ By HANDEL.

[*Introduced by three bars of Instrumental Music.*]

Remarks.

Hallelujah : (repeated often)

For the Lord God omnipotent reigneth :　[*here the voices unite.*]

Hallelujah (several times)

For the Lord God etc.　　　　　　　　[By the *Counter, Tenor and Bass.*]

Hallelujah (several times)

For the Lord God omnipotent reigneth :　[*1st. By the Treble ; 2d by the Tenor and Bass ; and then by the Counter and Tenor ; whilst the other parts through the whole of this passage are repeating Hal. in every variety.*]

The Kingdom of this world is become the　[*Chorus*]
　Kingdom of our Lord, and of his Christ.

And he shall reign for ever, etc.　　　[*A beautiful fugue.*]

King of Kings and Lord of Lords :　　[*By the Treble and Counter in long notes; whilst the Tenor and Bass repeat "for ever and ever Hal." in quick notes with intervals.*]

King of Kings and Lord of Lords: [*Two or three times in very low notes, by the Treble; whilst the Counter, Tenor and Bass are repeating " for ever and ever, Hal." often, in quick notes; with intervals:* The effect is wonderful.]

And he shall reign for ever and ever   [*often*]

King of Kings, and Lord of Lords: [*Several times : the harmony very full*]

And he shall reign for ever and ever, Hal. [*often : the last Hal. very slow.*]

The remarks accompanying the text of Lyon's hymn are neither so numerous nor so minute, but, naturally, they have a peculiar interest in this place.

VIII. 'FRIENDSHIP': the Words from Dr. Watts' Lyric Poems—set to Music by the Rev. James Lyon.

[the whole piece in full chorus.]

" I.

Friendship thou charmer of the mind,
Thou sweet deluding ill,
The brightest minutes mortals find
And sharpest hours we feel

Fate has divided all our shares
Of pleasure and of pain ;
In love the comforts and the cares
Are mix'd and join'd again.

} A cheerful air.

II

But whilst in floods our sorrow rolls,
And drops of joy are few,
This dear delight of mingling souls,
Serves but to swell our wo.

Oh ! why should bliss depart in haste ?
And Friendship stay to moan?
Why the fond passion cling so fast,
When every joy is gone?

} Very plaintive.

III

Yet never let our hearts divide,
Nor death dissolve the chain,
For love and joy were once allied,
And must be joined again."

} Lively.

These " remarks " have not been reprinted here merely as entertaining specimens of an early, perhaps the earliest, American analytical program. Their importance for my theme lies in a different direction, since they furnish a logical connection between Lyon's 'Friendship' and an anonymous composition which appears under the same title and to the same words on p. 17–22 of John Stickney's 'Gentleman and Lady's Musical Companion' (1774).

The "remarks" illustrating Lyon's setting and the music of this piece in Stickney correspond entirely.

Should any doubt remain as to the identity of the two settings, it certainly will disappear in face of the following facts:

The copy of 'Urania' (in its original binding) at the Library of Congress belonged to "Ebenr. Hazard," a contemporary of James Lyon. Prefixed to Lyon's book this copy, as has been stated before, contains in Hazard's hand a collection of tunes, hymns, etc.; and of this collection thirteen pages are filled with a hymn entitled:

'Friendship—Set to Music by James Lyon.'

It is identical with the piece in Stickney.

In the second place, and as still further supplementary evidence, I call attention to the fact that Elias Mann's 'Massachusetts Collection of Sacred Harmony' (Boston . . . 1807) contains on p. 170–174:

'Friendship R. Lyon.'

A comparison between this hymn and that bearing the same name in the collections of Stickney and Hazard will show all three to be identical, though Elias Mann altered the "Mood of Time," occasionally the rhythmical values, the harmony and the counterpoint,* and exchanged the tenor and treble. I would have given the hymn in the Appendix, but the piece is too full of musical impossibilities. Though Lyon's knowledge of musical grammar was poor, still I doubt

---

*That Mann surnames Lyon *R.* instead of *J.* is, of course, of no account, it being probably a misprint.

very much that the hymn, as he composed it, was such a labyrinth of blunders as published both by Stickney and Mann.

Now, Mann says in the preface :

In this collection will be found none of those wild fugues and rapid and confused movements which have so long been the disgrace of congregational psalmody, and the contempt of the judicious and tasteful amateur.

To appreciate the full significance of these words in connection with the fact that the purist Mann published 'Friendship' in 1807, we need but remember that the piece first appeared in print in 1774, more than thirty years before Mann wrote his polemical preface. During these thirty years " those wild fugues and rapid and confused movements " of William Billings' epigones had dominated in congregational psalmody. With the beginning of the nineteenth century the struggle was gradually decided in favor of men of an advanced esthetical standpoint like Elias Mann. He would not have republished a composition by James Lyon, whom we may consider the first original American psalmodist, had not Lyon's style appealed to his purist taste. This goes a good way toward showing that James Lyon's esthetic tendencies overleaped those of most of his contemporaries.

The six 'tunes' marked with an asterisk in 'Urania,' the 'Marriage Hymn,' the 17th Psalm, the 19th psalm, and 'Friendship,' represent a total of ten compositions traced to the pen of James Lyon and still extant. Their study will induce no critic to call Lyon a composer of real merit or even a musician fully conversant with musical grammar. His music, viewed from an esthetic standpoint, is in no way remarkable. He certainly gave his best in the hymn to Friendship, the minor movement of which contains a few unexpected rays of beauty. This movement and the fact that Lyon energetically occupied himself with music, when music was in its infancy in Colonial America, prove that he possessed some inborn musical talent. For nobody will compose in a musical wilderness, no matter how valueless the compositions may be, if not forced to do so by latent creative powers. Had Lyon been educated in England, Germany, or Italy, his talents would have developed to greater advantage, and his name might figure in musical dictionaries, these mausoleums of celebrity, none of which to-day mentions him.

But his importance lies not in the sphere of esthetics. It lies rather in the sphere of retrospective history. Not the absolute but the relative merits of his music attract our attention. He was a pioneer, and thereupon rests his lasting glory. Who never felt the fascination of wandering into the wilderness and following the footsteps of solitary pioneers will hardly appreciate their work. He sees the great streams of life and cares not whence they came. It is the historian who loves to explore the streams far up to their sources. The rivulets which contributed to make the musical life of the United States of to-day an ever-broadening majestic stream are widely separated and not yet sufficiently explored. I have tried to describe the contributory rivulet which had its source in James Lyon. To use the words of our pioneer psalmodist, should I be so fortunate as to merit approbation with this monograph,

I shall think myself happy . . . notwithstanding the great Expense, Labour, and Anxiety, it has cost me to compleat it.

APPENDIX

MY DAYS HAVE BEEN SO WONDROUS FREE.

Song by Francis Hopkinson, 1759 (?).

*) I suggest G sharp.

AN ANTHEM FROM THE 114th PSALM.

Francis Hopkinson, 1760.

Allegro moderato.

Vo. 1.

What aileth thee, oh thou sea that thou fleddest, And thou Jordan that thou wast driven back ? Ye

Vo. 2.

Bass.

sic.

mountains that ye skip-ped like rams, and ye lit-tle, lit-tle, lit-tle, lit-tle hills like young

lit-tle, lit-tle hills like young

sheep,

lit-tle, lit-tle hills like young sheep? Tremble thou earth, at the

sheep, And ye lit-tle, lit-tle, lit-tle, lit-tle hills like young sheep?

presence of the Lord, the God .... of Ja - cob, Trem-ble thou earth, at the

presence of the Lord, the God of Ja - cob.

At the pres-ence of the Lord,

At the presence of the Lord,

AN ANTHEM FROM THE 114th PSALM.

WASHINGTON'S MARCH.

AS PERFORMED AT THE NEW THEATRE, PHILADELPHIA, 1794 (?).

WASHINGTON'S MARCH AT THE BATTLE OF TRENTON.

Appendix.

RONDO.

(Song VII of ' Seven Songs.')

Francis Hopkinson, 1787.

gen-'rous heart dis - dains   the slave of love to be,   I scorn his ser-vile

chains, and   boast my lib - er - ty.   I scorn his ser - vile chains and boast my

lib - er - ty.   This whining   and pin-ing   and wasting with care Are

not   to my taste   be she ev - er so fair.   This whining   and pin-ing   and

RONDO.

wast-ing with care Are not to my taste be she ev - er so fair.

Shall a girls ca - pri - cious frown Sink my no - ble

spir - its down, Shall a face of white and

red Make me droop my sil - ly head, Shall I

set me down and sigh For an eye - brow

RONDO.

TWO CELEBRATED VERSES BY STERNHOLD AND HOPKINS.

James Lyon ('Urania,' 1761).

TWO CELEBRATED VERSES BY STERNHOLD AND HOPKINS.

rode.. On cher - ubs and on

cher - - u-bims, full roy - al-ly He rode, And on the wings ... of mighty

winds came fly - - - - - - - ing all a - broad, On the

wings,.... On the wings,..... on the wings ..... of might - - y winds, On

cher-ubs and on cher - u - bims, Full roy - - al - ly He rode, and on the

wings of might - y winds, came..... fly - - ing all a - broad.

19TH PSALM.

James Lyon.

My Sav - iour and...... my King,.... Thy beau - ties are di - vine, Thy

lips with bless - ings o - ver - flow And ev - 'ry grace is Thine, And ev - 'ry

grace is Thine. Now make............................ Thy glo - ry

known, Gird on Thy dreadful sword, Gird on Thy dread-ful sword; And rise in maj - es -

ty To spread the conquest of Thy sword,............ the conquest of Thy sword.

INDEX